Antecedents and
Organizational Citizenship Behavior Towards Small and
Medium-Sized Enterprises' Performance

中小型企业组织绩效的影响因素研究

——以员工的组织公民行为为中介因子

郭婉然　著

暨南大学出版社
JINAN UNIVERSITY PRESS

中国·广州

图书在版编目（CIP）数据

中小型企业组织绩效的影响因素研究：以员工的组织公民行为为中介因子 = Antecedents and Organizational Citizenship Behavior Towards Small and Medium-Sized Enterprises' Performance：英文/郭婉然著. —广州：暨南大学出版社，2022. 11
  ISBN 978 - 7 - 5668 - 3302 - 0

  Ⅰ. ①中… Ⅱ. ①郭… Ⅲ. ①中小企业—企业绩效—影响因素—研究—英文 Ⅳ. ①F276. 3

中国版本图书馆 CIP 数据核字（2021）第 248781 号

中小型企业组织绩效的影响因素研究——以员工的组织公民行为为中介因子
ZHONGXIAOXING QIYE ZUZHI JIXIAO DE YINGXIANG YINSU YANJIU——YI YUANGONG DE ZUZHI GONGMIN XINGWEI WEI ZHONGJIE YINZI
著　者：郭婉然
···

出 版 人：张晋升
责任编辑：康　蕊
责任校对：苏　洁　王燕丽
责任印制：周一丹　郑玉婷

出版发行：暨南大学出版社（511443）
电　　话：总编室（8620）37332601
　　　　　营销部（8620）37332680　37332681　37332682　37332683
传　　真：（8620）37332660（办公室）　37332684（营销部）
网　　址：http：//www. jnupress. com
排　　版：广州良弓广告有限公司
印　　刷：佛山市浩文彩色印刷有限公司
开　　本：787mm×1092mm　1/16
印　　张：17
字　　数：298 千
版　　次：2022 年 11 月第 1 版
印　　次：2022 年 11 月第 1 次
定　　价：69. 80 元

Preface

This study has examined factors influencing small and medium-sized enterprises' performance with the mediating effect of organizational citizenship behavior in Jilin Province of China. Its purpose is to motivate and improve small and medium-sized enterprises' performance. The examined motivational factors were collective distributive justice, procedural justice, interactional justice, idealized influence, inspirational motivation, intellectual stimulation and individualized consideration, surface emotion acting, deep emotion acting and true emotion acting, knowledge acquisition, knowledge distribution and knowledge interpretation. Organizational citizenship behavior was included in the framework as the mediating variable. This study uses cross-sectional survey to verify the theoretical framework. The survey data used in this empirical study were collected from 251 employees of small and medium-sized enterprises (that is, the employees of small and medium-sized enterprises in Jilin Province as the main research objects). Then, it gave the measurement of distributive justice, procedural justice, interactional justice, idealized influence, inspirational motivation, intellectual stimulation and individualized consideration, surface emotion acting, deep emotion acting and true emotion acting, knowledge acquisition, knowledge distribution and knowledge interpretation on the organizational performance and organizational citizenship behavior using principal component analysis and confirmatory factor analysis were constructs. Through testing the structural validity of each factor, the main conclusions of this study were drawn.

The findings showed that the effect of collective distributive justice, interactional justice, intellectual stimulation, inspirational motivation, individualized consideration, deep emotion acting, knowledge acquisition and knowledge interpretation had positive influence on the organizational performance of SMEs in Jilin Province of China. Additionally, distributive justice, procedural justice, interactional justice, inspirational motivation, individualized consideration, true emotion acting, surface emotion acting, deep emotion acting, knowledge acquisition, knowledge interpretation had positive influence on the organizational citizenship behavior of SMEs in Jilin Province of China. Meanwhile, distributive justice, interactional justice, inspirational motivation, individualized consideration, deep emotion acting, knowledge acquisition, knowledge interpretation and organizational performance were mediated by the organizational citizenship behavior to influence organizational performance. Practical enlightenment is to find the theory, how to provide useful information for the development of SMEs in China and make use of the identified incentives to improve their organizational performance.

List of Tables

List of Figures

Contents

Chapter Seven   Discussion, Recommendation and Conclusion / 166

Appendix: Survry Instrument / 196

Reference / 206

Chapter One   Introduction

1. 1   Research Background

In the world economic system, small and medium-sized enterprises (SMEs) promote the economic development of many countries in the world (Julian, 2019). At present, SMEs exist in large numbers and universally in developed and developing countries. SMEs have enhanced the market competitiveness, accelerated technological change, guaranteed the formation of normal and reasonable prices, and also vigorously promoted full employment and guaranteed economic growth. The economy runs smoothly and social stability is guaranteed (Kaplan & Norton, 1996; Hillman & Keim, 2001).

Since China's reform and opening up, SMEs have developed rapidly. According to the 2019 survey report of SMEs in Ministry of Industry and Information Technology of People's Republic of China, by the end of 2019, SMEs had reached more than 12 million households in China. SMEs provided 80% of urban employment posts, contributed more than 75% of enterprise technological innovation, and created about 60% of the value of final products and services equivalent to gross domestic product. Tax revenue accounts for about 50% of the total national tax revenue, which shows that SMEs have become the main force of economic growth, the driving force of increasing fiscal revenue, the main way of expanding employment scale, and the force of enhancing scientific and technological innovation (Wang, 2019).

Although SMEs in China are showing strong vitality, and their comprehensive quality (growth, competitiveness, financing, team and innovation) is constantly improving (Du, 2018). These problems seriously hindered by the factors such as the level of economic development, social culture and entrepreneurship environment in China. SMEs generally have defects and shortcomings such as low technology level, lack of related technology talents, weak competitiveness, backward management level and organizational learning is hard to be valued and carried out continuously. And the average life span of SMEs in the world is 7 – 10 years, while that of SMEs in China is only 5 – 7 years. It can be seen that there is a huge gap between the development level of SMEs in China and average level of the world (Wang, 2019).

Throughout the overall layout and form of economic development in Jilin Province, it is one of the old industrial bases in Northeast of China. SMEs have become a significant economy of economic development in Jilin Province, occupying a very significant position in the economic development of the province. With the continuous optimization of the market economy environment in Jilin Province, the number and scale of SMEs have been growing in recent years, and their contribution to the regional economy of Jilin Province has also been increasing. The economic added value of SMEs in Jilin Province has been increasing year by year, and their contribution to the GDP of the whole province has reached more than 50% since 2013. In short, the healthy development of SMEs has a positive and beneficial impact on the regional economic growth of Jilin Province. By 2017, according to the survey report of Department of Industry and Information Technology of Jilin Province, the GDP of SMEs in Jilin Province has reached 1,494. 453 billion RMB (Miao, 2019). The SMEs in Jilin Province have developed rapidly and have a good situation, but their foundation is relatively weak compared with the developed areas such as Jiangsu, Zhejiang, Guangzhou and Shenzhen (Xu, 2019). Up to 2017, SMEs' GDP of Zhejiang Province in the whole year was 5,176. 826 billion RMB according to the survey report of Department of Industry and Information Technology of Zhejiang Province. That's because Zhejiang's regional market economy is developed, and the atmosphere is active for SMEs to invest and build factories. However, as an old traditional industrial base, Jilin Province has a high proportion of state-owned enterprises, and the development of small and medium-sized enterprises is still in the growth stage (Miao, 2019). And some SMEs of Jilin Province are lack of innovative consciousness and suitable learning system, and have no effective management mechanism. These problems seriously hinder the growth of organizational performance of SMEs, which lead to decrease of organizational goal and organizational productivity and employee satisfaction and customer satisfaction (Yu, 2018).

From the above discussion it is clear that developing SMEs' performance in Jilin Province has become a challenge to many scholars and entrepreneurs. Thus, this study intends to examine factors influencing SMEs' performance in Jilin Province of China. Previous researches on SMEs' performance were linked to organizational issues (employee satisfaction, profit, organizational productivity, customer satisfaction, performance measurement system, human resource management practices, strategic planning) and national issues (economic growth, rules and policies) (Paul & Anantharaman, 2003; Hillman & Keim, 2001; Kaplan & Norton, 1996; Ruekert, Walker & Roering, 1985). This study, however, studied the performance of SMEs from the perspective of individuals or employees of SMEs. This is because of the critical role of employees in managing and implementing daily activities of SMEs (Garg & Dhar, 2017; Garg & Dhar, 2014; Balkin, 2000; Utterback, 1994; Wolfe, 1994).

The success of SMEs depends on a synergy through effective and efficient teamwork, collaboration and cooperation amongst employees (Garg & Dhar, 2017; Garg & Dhar, 2014). This scenario is termed as organizational citizenship behavior (OCB) (Podsakoff, Blume, Whiting, etc. , 2013). In other words, this study investigated SMEs' performance from the individual perspective but not from the institutional or organizational perspective. Relevant employees' values and behaviors can potentially influence organizational citizenship behavior, and in turn SMEs' performance in Jilin Province of China was proposed. This is because human resource is considered as an important valuable asset in an organization and therefore needs to be managed properly.

The organizations that operate effectively need to organize members to do the following three things: firstly, stay in the organization; secondly, be responsible for fulfilling the role requirements; thirdly, make role requirements external, innovative and proactive behavior (Katz & Kahn, 1966). Combining China's current political, economic, and cultural background with the traditional management culture of SMEs in Jilin Province, SMEs' employees in Jilin Province can complete the first and second roles, but in term of the third role, although the organizational citizenship behavior of employees is existing in small and medium-sized enterprises in Jilin Province. Most of the employees are only in order to complete their own work, and the motivation and action power are not strong to make organizational citizenship behavior (Ma, 2013). So it is very important to explore how to motivate employees in small and medium-sized enterprises from the perspective of organizational citizenship behavior. The most fundamental characteristic of human capital is that it can be encouraged, but not forced. If enterprises want employees to effectively play organizational citizenship behavior, they need to motivate existing employees through guidance, training, development and other means, and timely understand the emotional representation of employees at work, and let employees feel the fairness of the organization, which can not only save the searching cost of enterprises, but also these employees are familiar with the management system of enterprises, and can quickly apply new technologies to create more and better value in practical work (Zhou & Yao, 2008). Therefore, organizational citizenship behavior is conducive to improving employees' own work performance and promoting organizational performance (Li & Eldon, 2014). Thus, enterprise managers should pay enough attention to the organizational citizenship behavior of employees, and take relevant measures to effectively guide the organizational citizenship behavior of employees.

To achieve the above research purpose, a conceptual framework is designed. The conceptual framework consists of four constructs, namely, organizational justice (Neuhoff & Moorman, 1993), transformational leadership (Avolio & Bass, 2014), employee emotion (Diefendorff J. M. , 2005) and organizational learning (Huber, 1991). Organizational justice is a kind of sense of fairness and the corresponding behavior response, which are generated in a certain organizational environment (Neuhoff & Moorman, 1993). It consists of distributive justice, procedural justice and interactional justice (Neuhoff & Moorman, 1993). The ideal meaning of transformational leadership is that they are ethical models that work for the benefit of the team, the community, and the organization (Bass, 1988). In this study, transformational leadership behavior has four dimensions, namely, inspirational motivation, intellectual stimulation, individualized consideration and idealized influence (Avolio & Bass, 2014). Employee emotion labor is the appropriate behavior of employees to adjust their emotions according to the rules of presentation expected by the organization (Ashforth & Humphrey, 1993). It consists of surface emotion acting, deep emotion acting and true emotion acting (Diefendorff J. M. , 2005). Organizational learning is defined as the process of improving organizational activities through learning past experiences (Huber, 1991). It consists of knowledge acquisition, knowledge distribution and knowledge interpretation (Huber, 1991). It is argued that the four constructs could develop employees' organizational citizenship behavior and in turn improve SMEs' performance. Detailed explanation of the conceptual framework is offered in Chapter Two.

The intrinsic values embedded in the conceptual framework are needed to overcome barriers associated with developing employees' organizational citizenship behavior and performance of SMEs in Jilin Province of China. Thus it could be said that being equipped with positive distributive justice, procedural justice, interactional justice, idealized influence, inspirational motivation, intellectual stimulation, individualized consideration, surface emotion acting, deep emotion acting, true emotion acting, knowledge acquisition, knowledge distribution and knowledge interpretation enables employees to be highly equipped with organizational citizenship behavior in the workplace and thereafter to be contributed actively towards organizational performance of SMEs.

1.2   Problem Statement

There are also some problems in human resource management of SMEs in Jilin Province. In fact, Jilin Province ranks 24nd in the latest per capita GDP ranking of 31 provinces in China in 2018. Jilin Province is one of the provinces with relatively backward economic development (Miao, 2019). From the perspective of enterprises, the problems of internal management confusion and poor communication and coordination ability of various departments are more prominent; from the perspective of employees, employees lack team cooperation consciousness and loyalty to enterprises (Hu, 2014). Therefore, the high turnover rate and other issues are more prominent. The reasons lie in the fact that the contradiction between enterprises and employees has not been alleviated (Li, 2016).

Firstly, the principle of fairness in the employment of SMEs in Jilin Province has been questioned. The unfairness of the distribution result and the distribution procedure in the organization generally exist in the SMEs of Jilin Province, which leads to the decline of staff's sense of belonging and loyalty in Jilin Province, organizational justice has been highly concerned since it was put forward in many enterprises. If the problem of organizational justice is not handled for a long time, it will affect the effectiveness and competitiveness of the whole organization (Wang, Lu & Siu, 2015). Employees are the most important group in SMEs, good performance results of SMEs cannot be separated from employees' recognition of fair distribution, fair procedure and fair interaction in organizaitional justice (Li, 2015). So, the research choose the employees of SMEs in Jilin Province as the research object, and explore the influence mechanism of organizational justice on organizational performance.

Secondly, there is also the inefficiency of enterprise incentive mechanism, the imperfection of enterprise incentive mechanism and leadership directly affects the stability of employees in SMEs of Jilin Province (Jing, 2017). Leadership has been regarded as a powerful theoretical weapon in the organization. Leadership style can promote the performance of enterprises and make enterprises win a place in the fierce competition has been attached great importance by many leading theoretical researchers. Ribeiro, Yücel and Gomes (2018) argued that transformational leadership affects the attitudes of organizational members and enables them to strive voluntarily for the common goals of the organization so as to achieve better organizational performance. This paper studies the impact of transformational leadership on organizational performance, which has important practical significance. It can effectively motivate employees for leaders and correctly lead all employees in the organization towards organizational goals.

Thirdly, there are few studies on the emotional labor of employees in small and medium-sized enterprises in Jilin Province. The disorder of emotion labor of employees is harmful for their physical and mental health (Yu, 2013). Emotional labor is also an important part of modern service work. In routine work, employees need to provide professional and technical services to customers with full working enthusiasm and positive working attitude; in the face of customer complaints, employees need to calm the emotions of customers, even in the face of customer misunderstanding, they should manage their emotions well, in the meantime, employees should also deal with their emotion when they work with colleagues and leaders, overcome their emotional fluctuations to achieve organizational goals (Tarim, 2018). The good performance of small and medium-sized enterprises is inseparable from the emotional labor of employees. So, in this study, the SMEs' employees of Jilin Province are selected as the research object, and the three dimensions of the emotional labor are explored how to influence employees' behavior and organizational performance.

Fourthly, many SMEs in Jilin Province lack a systematic staff training and learning system. The personal and professional qualities of employees have not improved. This means that enterprises will not be progressed, which is bound to lose competitiveness (Han, 2016). Organizational learning is also closely related to organizational performance, which is considered to be an important strategic process, an important source of creating organizational competitiveness and competitive advantage, and an important determinant of organizational ability to adapt to environmental changes and achieve long-term survival and development (Majid & Mahmud, 2019). So, in this study, the SMEs' employees of Jilin Province are selected as the research object, and the three dimensions of the organizational learning is explored how to influence employee behavior and organizational performance.

Therefore, as the success of each organization relies on its employees, embedding employees in the SMEs with values to actively contribute towards that is considered necessary. This is also evident from the huge investment by public and private organizations on human capital worldwide. However, it is really hard to establish healthy working environment and rapport relationship between employees through intricately complicated lists of attitude and knowledge or through weakly defined broad terms such as leadership or influencing (Abdul, Selamat & Saad, 2013). Additionally, merely training individuals in specific skill is inadequate to guarantee that the skills will be practiced properly in the workplace (Selamat & Choudrie, 2007; Henry & Butcher, 1998). Therefore, this research is considered timely to assist SMEs of Jilin Province in improving their performance through a synergy created from organizational citizenship behavior among employees.

Organizational citizenship behavior is a kind of voluntary cooperation that can improve organizational efficiency. Employees with organizational citizenship behavior characteristics can consciously maintain the normal operation of the whole organization, effectively coordinate the activities between team members and working groups, reduce conflicts, maintain interpersonal harmony, work together to tackle core technologies, improve the production efficiency of colleagues and managers, and promote the improvement of organizational performance (Zhou & Yao, 2008).

Glomb (2011) and Zong (2010) stated that employees become passive in the workplace if they have low level of organizational citizenship behavior. This scenario is also applicable to explain the low level of participation of employees in the SMEs of Jilin Province. Although the organizational citizenship behavior of employees is objective in small and medium-sized enterprises in Jilin Province, most of the employees are in order to complete their own work, and the motivation and action power to make organizational citizenship behavior are not strong (Mang, 2013). When employees that have low level of organizational citizenship behavior towards the organization will consume a lot of time in the office in gossiping company and managers and in turn reduce their motivation to contribute towards achieving organizational goals (Turnipseed & Rassuli, 2005). The employees could also sabotage organizational operations if they have low level of citizenship behavior towards the company (Schaarschmidt, Walsh & Ivens, 2015). The absence of citizenship behavior could create a conflict between the supporters and non-supporters of management (Jin, 2013). Therefore, improving organizational citizenship behavior of SMEs in Jilin Province is important.

The findings from this research could also be used by relevant government agencies in charge of industrial development, intellectual property and human resource development in China. In this case, the involved agencies could utilize this research conceptual framework to refine and/or fine tune their policies, rules and regulations. Other government agencies could also use the conceptual framework to revise their staff training contents and programs. Being equipped with the proposed values (distributive justice, procedural justice, interactional justice, idealized influence, inspirational motivation, intellectual stimulation, individualized consideration, surface emotion acting, deep emotion acting, true emotion acting, knowledge acquisition, knowledge distribution, knowledge interpretation) could also enable organizational citizenship behavior to be established among civil servants in public organizations in China and in turn motivates them to contribute towards achieving organizational goals actively.

Other industries could also utilize this research conceptual framework to improve their soft skill development programs. By using this research conceptual framework, the companies can fine tune their training contents to ensure that employees can always be equipped with organizational citizenship behavior in the workplace and in turn contribute towards organizational development. Organizational citizenship behavior is much more needed in business enterprises as their environment is rapidly changing, which demands a high level of employees' synergy to survive. Without active teamwork, collaboration and cooperation amongst employees, it is hard to supply good products or give good service to clients at a lower cost (Boiral & Paillé, 2012).

Last but not least, this research also contributes to the academic world. This is in terms of a new conceptual framework that contains values that could develop employees' organizational citizenship behavior and in turn motivation to contribute towards achieving organizational goals actively in the workplace. As far as researcher's concerned, organizational justice, transformational leadership, employee emotion and organizational learning have never been investigated in the area of organizational citizenship behavior and organizational performance of SMEs in Jilin Province of China. Most of studies on employees' organizational citizenship behavior and organizational performance of SMEs are from the organizational perspective. This research tries to deviate from this trend by examining employees' organizational citizenship behavior and organizational performance of SMEs from the individual perspective. As human resource is the main driver for organizational success (Chen, Lin & Lien, 2010; Shahzad, Rehman, Shad, et al., 2011), investigating employees' organizational citizenship behavior and organizational performance of SMEs from individual perspective is much needed. In turn, academicians can have a new look on employees' organizational citizenship behavior and organizational performance of SMEs.

The above problematic situation encouraged the researcher to investigate the intrinsic values that could develop employees' organizational citizenship behavior and in turn ensure the success of organizational operations. This is also to ensure that financial position of the company is always strong and product or services are delivered effectively, efficiently and economically.

1.3   Research Questions

The purpose of research questions is to determine whether the suggestions made by this research can be obtained in the practical setting or vice versa. From the above discussion it can be seen that the aim of this research is to investigate organizational performance of SMEs in Jilin Province of China through individual intrinsic values and organizational citizenship behavior. Referred to this purpose, the four research questions are put forward:

(1) What is the effect of organizational justice, transformational leadership, employee emotion labor and organizational learning construct on organizational performance of SMEs in Jilin Province of China?

(2) What is the effect of organizational justice, transformational leadership, employee emotion labor and organizational learning constructs on organizational citizenship behavior of employees of SMEs in Jilin Province of China?

(3) Does organizational citizenship behavior mediate the relationship between organizational justice, transformational leadership, employee emotion labor, organizational learning and organizational performance of SMEs in Jilin Province of China?

(4) What is the effect of organizational citizenship behavior on organizational performance of SMEs in Jilin Province of China?

1.4   Research Objectives

The aim of having research objectives is to assist the researcher to answer research questions. According to the above research questions, the following research objectives were developed:

(1) To figure out the effect of organizational justice, transformational

leadership, employee emotion labor and organizational learning constructs on organizational performance of SMEs in Jilin Province of China.

(2) To figure out the effect of organizational justice, transformational leadership, employee emotion labor and organizational learning constructs on organizational citizenship behavior of employees of SMEs in Jilin Province of China.

(3) To figure out whether organizational citizenship behavior mediates the relationship between organizational justice, transformational leadership, employee emotion labor, organizational learning and organizational performance of SMEs in Jilin Province of China.

(4) To figure out the effect of organizational citizenship behavior on organizational performance of SMEs in Jilin Province of China.

1.5　Significance of the Study

Based on the problem statement, this research expands past studies on academic knowledge to make up for knowledge gap. In order to make up for knowledge gap, this research expands past studies about employee emotion labor on organizational citizenship behavior, referring to organizational justice, transformational leadership and organizational learning, this research combines past studies and focuses on the relationship between organizational citizenship behavior and performance more deeply. Therefore, this research is beneficial to organizations and their management to have a better understanding and knowledge on the impacts of organizational citizenship behavior on performance. At the same time, through the analysis of the current situation of small and medium-sized enterprises in Jilin Province, this study combs the problems faced by the development of small and medium-sized enterprises in China and tries to explore the causes and find countermeasures. The research also hopes to provide theoretical references for the healthy development of SMEs in China.

As the success of each organization relies on its employees, embedding employees in the SMEs with values to actively contribute towards that is considered necessary. This is also evident from the huge investment by public and private organizations on human capital worldwide. However, it is really hard to establish healthy working environment and rapport relationship between employees through intricately complicated lists of attitude and knowledge or through weakly defined broad terms such as leadership or influencing (Abdul Wahab, Selamat & Saad, 2013). Additionally, merely train individuals in specific skill is inadequate to guarantee that the skills will be practiced properly in the workplace (Selamat & Choudrie, 2007; Henry & Butcher, 1998). Therefore, this research is considered timely to assist SMEs in improving their performance through a synergy created from organizational citizenship behavior among employees.

The findings from this research could also be used by relevant government agencies in charge of industrial development, intellectual property and human resource development in China. In this case, the involved agencies could utilize the conceptual frame of this research to refine and/or fine tune their policies, rules and regulations. Other government agencies could also use the conceptual framework to revise their staff training contents and programs. Being equipped with the proposed values (distributive justice, procedural justice, interactional justice, idealized influence, inspirational motivation, intellectual stimulation, individualized consideration, surface emotion acting, deep emotion acting, true emotion acting, knowledge acquisition, knowledge distribution, knowledge interpretation) could also enable organizational citizenship behavior to be established among civil servants in public organizations in China and in turn motivates them to contribute towards achieving organizational goals actively.

Other industries could also utilize the conceptual frame of this research to improve their soft skills development programs. By using this research conceptual framework, the companies can finetune their training contents to ensure that employees can always be equipped with organizational citizenship behaviour in the workplace and in turn contribute towards organizational development. Organizational citizenship behavior is much more needed in business enterprises as their environment is rapidly changing, which demands a high level of employees' synergy to survive. Without active teamwork, collaboration and cooperation amongst employees, it is hard to supply good products or give good service to clients at a lower cost (Yen & Niehoff, 2004).

Last but not least, this research also contributes to the academic world. This is in terms of a new conceptual framework that contains values that could develop employees' organizational citizenship behavior and in turn motivate them to contribute towards achieving organizational goals actively in the workplace. As far as the researchers concerned, organizational justice, transformational leadership, employee emotion labor and organizational learning have never been investigated in the area of organizational citizenship behavior and organizational performance of SMEs in Jilin Province of China. Most of studies on employees' organizational citizenship behavior and organizational performance of SMEs mainly focus on organization. This research tries to deviate from this trend by examining employees' organizational citizenship behavior and organizational performance of SMEs from the individual perspective. As human resource is the main driver for organizational success (Chen, Lin & Lien, 2010; Shahzad, Rehman, Shad, et al., 2011), investigating employees' organizational citizenship behavior and organizational performance of SMEs from individual perspective is much needed. In turn, academicians can have a new look on employees' organizational citizenship behavior and organizational performance of SMEs.

1.6　Scope of the Study

From the above discussion it is clear that this research intends to investigate individual intrinsic values that are capable of enabling employees to be equipped with organizational citizenship behavior and in turn develop their motivation to contribute towards achieving organizational goals actively in the companies. In turn, analysis of this research was individual. The respondents were employees who worked in the SMEs of

Jilin Province in China. Jilin Province was selected because it has a rich history and culture in China. However, its economic development is lagging behind and in turn needs new business model to prosper (Li, 2017). The SMEs' GDP of Jilin Province were less than that in some provinces (Miao, 2019). The research intended to contribute towards this through intrinsic values that could develop employees' organizational citizenship behavior and in turn to contribute towards SMEs' performance willingly.

The employees in SMEs were selected because the performance level of SMEs in China is still relatively low and lack of good planning and creative work (Jiang, 2019). The willingness to contribute towards SMEs' performance among them is too weak and as a consequence the competitive advantage of SMEs in China is still low. Thus, the employees in SMEs need to be motivated so that they can be more willing to contribute towards SMEs' performance through organizational citizenship behavior platform in the workplace.

1.7 Dissertation Outline

To assist the readers in understanding the content of this research report, the following discussion outline is adopted. There are seven chapters in this research report. Every chapter offers detailed discussion on issues that are critical to this study so that the reader can understand this research story easily. The content of each chapter is explained below:

Chapter One offers an introduction to the main problems that this research will address. The purpose and goal of this study are also described. To justify the research, an explanation on significance of study is required and a section for that aspect is also showed in this chapter.

Chapter Two offers a discussion on theoretical information surrounding the issues to be investigated in this study. The discussion provides a focus to be researched upon by this research. These arguments provide the foundation for the description and discussion to be offered and provided in Chapters Four, Five and Six.

Chapter Three highlights the proposed conceptual framework. The following is the research hypotheses on individual values that are argued to develop employees' organizational citizenship behavior and in turn to contribute towards SMEs' performance in Jilin Province of China willingly.

Chapter Four discusses the methodology adopted to validate the research conceptual framework. The reasons and justification of the adopted methods for collecting and analyzing research data are defined and described in depth.

Chapter Five describes the survey instrument development process in depth. The findings from content validity, pre-testing and pilot study are described and discussed in detail.

Chapter Six introduces the data analysis and results of the study. In particular, this chapter provides empirical results of the impact of individual values on the development of employees' organizational citizenship behavior and the willingness to contribute towards SMEs' performance in Jilin Province of China.

Chapter Seven shows the discussion, recommendation and conclusion of the study. In particular, this chapter includes a discussion of research findings based on the research objectives, theoretical and practical implications, limitations of future research, and recommendations for future research.

1.8　Summary

The aim of this chapter is to lay the foundations of the study by providing its background, research problems, research objectives, significance, scope and discussion outline. In short, the purpose of this chapter is to briefly introduce the route adopted. The next chapter will give a literature review of the research topics.

Chapter Two　Literature Reviews

2.1　Introduction

As stated in Chapter One, this research has four research questions which are as follows: ① What is the effect of organizational justice, transformational leadership, employee emotion labor and organizational learning constructs on organizational performance of SMEs in Jilin Province of China? ②What is the effect of organizational justice, transformational leadership, employee emotion labor and organizational learning constructs on organizational citizenship behavior of employees of SMEs in Jilin Province of China? ③Does organizational citizenship behavior mediate the relationship between organizational justice, transformational leadership, employee emotion labor, organizational learning and organizational performance of SMEs in Jilin Province of China? ④What is the effect of organizational citizenship behavior on organizational performance of SMEs in Jilin Province of China? In short, this research intends to examine the values that could develop employees' organizational citizenship behavior and in turn organizational performance of SMEs in Jilin Province of China. This chapter offers theoretical information for the above questions.

2.2　Development of SMEs in China

SMEs are businesses whose personnel amount fall below certain limits, different countries have different limits. The abbreviation "SME" is used in the European Union and by the international organizations such as the World Bank, the United Nations and the World Trade

Organization. The definition of SMEs used in this study is as follows: SMEs belong to small-scale enterprises; the number of recruitment and turnover is less than large and medium-sized enterprises (Dong, 2013).

On the June 29, 2002, the National People's Congress passed the *Law of the People's Republic of China on Promotion of Small and Medium-sized Enterprises* (Lin, 2006). The law was formally implemented on January 1, 2003. This law defines Chinese SMEs qualitatively as SMEs that are established in accordance with the law in the People's Republic of China, which are conducive to meeting social needs, increasing employment, conforming to the national industrial policy, the scale of production and operation belongs to all kinds of ownership and various forms of enterprises. Later, government department made several adjustments to the definition of the number of SMEs in order to meet the needs of China's economic and enterprise development.

In June 2011, the Ministry of Industry and Information Technology, the National Bureau of Statistics, the National Development and Reform Commission and the Ministry of Finance jointly promulgated a new *Standard Regulation for SMEs* (Wang, 2016). The new regulation closely combines the scale of SMEs in China at the present stage and adds micro-enterprise standards on the basis of the original SMEs. That is to say, SMEs now include medium-sized enterprise, small enterprises and micro-enterprises. *Compared to the Interim Provisions of the Standards for SMEs* issued in 2003, the new regulations for SMEs have added new industries such as real estate, leasing and business services, and information transmission industries (Bai, 2018).

According to the different characteristics of different industries, SMEs are divided according to the number of employees, sales volume and total assets. Industry differences have a great impact on the classification criteria of SMEs (Dong, 2013). Industrial enterprises usually include the production and supply of mining, manufacturing, electric power, natural gas and water. According to the standard for the classification of small and medium-sized enterprises issued by China in 2011, there are 300 to 1, 000 employees with business income of 20 million RMB or more in medium-sized enterprises, 20 to 300 employees with business income of 3 million RMB or more in small enterprises, and 20 employees or less with business income of 3 million RMB or less in micro-enterprises. However, in terms of retail, wholesale, postal, accommodation, catering, transportation, the number of employees is significantly lower than the above-mentioned industries. Among them, 100 to 300 employees and business income of 2 million RMB or more belong to medium-sized enterprises; 10 to 100 employees and operating income of 1 million RMB belong to small businesses; less than 10 employees or operating income of less than 1 million RMB belong to micro-enterprises (Yu, 2017).

Regarding the overall development of SMEs, since the founding of the People's Republic of China in 1949, in order to restore and develop the economy, private SMEs were supported by the state. In 1952 and 1949, private enterprises increased by 260,000. The output value increased by 3.698 billion RMB. These private enterprises are basically small and medium enterprises. After 1964, due to the adjustment of national policy guidelines, SMEs did not increase substantially. After 1970, due to the consideration of employment pressure, the number of small enterprises in China has recovered. After 1978, with the reform of the rural economic system, the number of SMEs began to increase substantially in the form of township enterprises. In 1995, the number of medium-sized industrial enterprises reached 10,983 and that of small industrial enterprises reached 102,332. The number of small and medium-sized enterprises accounted for 99.68% of the total number of enterprises (Wang, 2016).

From 1978 to 1994, the number of SMEs in rural areas has increased from 347,000 to 527,000, an increase of 52%. In 1995, there were 569,100 small industrial enterprises in townships and townships nationwide, 52% more than the 3.4 million in 1978, and the number reached the highest in history. After more than 30 years of development, China's small and medium-sized enterprises experienced from small to large, from weak to strong development process, economic strength and development quality are increasing. Many private enterprises have not only become leading enterprises in the domestic industry, but also have begun to emerge in the international arena, such as Vanke, Midea, Jingdong. Since 2014, the State Council has introduced a series of measures, including mass entrepreneurship and innovation, reform of the commercial system and property rights system, which have stimulated the enthusiasm of private entrepreneurs and significantly increased the number of registered small and medium-sized enterprises. According to the statistics of the State Administration for Industry and Commerce, as the end of 2016, there were 87.54 million market entities in various countries, and the number of market entities was 16.513 million, an increase of 11.6% compared to the previous year. The economic contribution brought by small and medium-sized enterprises was also great (Wang, 2016).

SMEs account for 98.9% of the total number of Chinese enterprises, accounting for 65.6%, 63.3%, 54% and 77.3% of the total industrial output, sales revenue, total profits and employees, respectively according to the survey since 2016 (Wang, 2016). Therefore, Zhang (2019) found that SMEs in China have become one of the major industrial forces in economic and social development. Qiao (2018) believed that economic development is completely related to the development of SMEs which account for about three-quarters of the added output value of China's economy and industry. Today, SMEs continue to dominate most industrial sectors, accounting for more than 70% of the total output value of the food, paper and printing industries; more than 80% of the total output value of the leather, entertainment, sportswear, plastics and metal products industries; and more than 90% of the total output value of the timber and furniture industries. In terms of expanding employment, SMEs currently account for about three-quarters of the new jobs in the country (Tang, 2019).

2.3   Development of SMEs in Jilin Province of China

In recent years, the government of Jilin Province has vigorously promoted the development of SMEs, promulgated a number of preferential tax policies for SMEs, increased credit support for SMEs, implemented the economic take off plan and the cultivation plan for thousands of growing enterprises (Sun, 2013). Through a series of major measures, the SMEs have entered a rapid development stage (Guo, 2015). The total amount and quality of SMEs have achieved historical breakthroughs and improvements in overall quality, and improvements in economic indicators have been made, which have increased the role, contribution and potential of economic and social development in Jilin Province (Li, 2017). SMEs in Jilin Province play an important role in the economy of Jilin Province and are gradually becoming the main force in the development of social productivity. SMEs in Jilin Province are mainly involved healthcare industry, trade industry, agriculture industry, restaurant and catering industry, transportation industry, education industry, building industry and manufacturing industry. SMEs in Jilin Province play an irreplaceable role in increasing GDP, promoting tax revenue and providing jobs. SMEs in Jilin Province are also indispensable partners and assistants for large enterprises (Wang, 2015).

By the end of 2018, the income of SMEs in Jilin Province reached 1.89 trillion RMB, accounting for 50.5% of GDP of Jilin Province, and the tax paid was 59.7 billion RMB, accounting for 70.2% of the local fiscal revenue of Jilin Province. The number of SMEs has reached 1,600 households and about 80,000 employees (Wang, 2018). According to these data, SMEs in Jilin Province are a vital part of Jilin's national economy. They are not only the pillar force of Jilin's economic growth but also create a large number of employment opportunities for Jilin Province and alleviate the employment pressure in Jilin Province and maintain the stable development of society.

2. 4   Challenges of SMEs in Jilin Province of China

The number and proportion of private enterprises in Jilin Province are large and significant, accounting for 97% of the total number of SMEs in the province. However, most of private enterprises in Jilin Province are family-owned enterprises. In terms of internal management mode, property right structure and operational processes cannot be regarded as a real enterprise (Wang, 2018). Some SMEs only pay attention to the technical level but ignore the management level. There is a lack of democratic atmosphere in enterprises (Dai, 2012). Some SMEs have unclear property rights, and with the development of enterprises, there are often various kinds of disputes and conflicts even lead to the fragmentation and decline of enterprises (Li, 2016).

From the above scenario it can be seen that the management system of SMEs in Jilin Province is relatively weak (Miao, 2019). Northeast of China is an important industrial place in China. It is seriously affected by planned economy and are lack of innovative consciousness. So more than half of the SMEs in Jilin Province are engaged in traditional service industries, while the production-oriented enterprises are still at the bottom of the labor-intensive industrial chain with resource processing as the main part, and they have not created and established brand awareness (Zhao, 2016). Due to lack of well-known brands, as a result, SMEs in Jilin Province do not pay attention to the application of new technologies and research of new products and have no long-term development goals (Ma, 2013). Thus, even if the overall development of SMEs in Jilin Province shows a rapid growth trend, SMEs in Jilin Province are lack of competitive advantage. The average income of the main business of households in developed areas is only about 50%, and the profit and tax are less than 30%. It can be seen that there is still a big gap between SMEs in Jilin Province with that in other provinces.

The competition of enterprises is the competition of talents. Talents are the main body of innovation and also the most valuable resources and wealth of enterprises (Qin, 2017). But the cultural and professional qualities of most employees of SMEs in Jilin Province are low, and they are lack of professional and technical knowledge and innovation consciousness, which to some extent limits the improvement of production efficiency and technological innovation level of enterprises (Guo, 2015). The main reason for the lack of talents is that most SMEs in Jilin Province are unable to give high salary and welfare to absorb talents. Besides, many SMEs in Jilin Province don't attach importance to the construction of enterprise culture. They do not have core values, ethics, personal values, and business philosophy cannot be coordinated, lacking identity of employees will eventually leads to the loss of talent (Yang, 2012).

The service and management system of SMEs in Jilin Province are not well developed (Zhao, 2016). In recent years, government has vigorously established and improved the social service system and policy framework for SMEs, but it is still hard to full the needs of SMEs in Jilin Province. Even if some national policies have very good intentions, they lack detailed implementation rules and are ineffective (Zhao, 2016). Therefore, improving the organizational performance of SMEs in the Jilin Province is very important through every aspect, which contributes to the economic development of Jilin Province.

2. 5   Defining Organizational Performance of SMEs

There are different definitions of organizational performance because of different organizational types, ways of measuring organizational performance and the influences of organizational performance. However, scholars generally agree with the view that "performance is not a concept, but a composition". Eztoini (1964) used corporate goals to define organizational performance. Due to the clear and target corporate goals, it is suitable to define organizational performance by the status of achieving goals. Organizational performance is to measure and judge the composition of the extent to which an organization achieves its goals from the perspective of organizational goals. Yuehtman and Seashore (1967) used the system resource approach to define organizational performance, which emphasized the relationship between the organization and the external environment, and often judged organizational performance by the ability to obtain competitive resources. If the organizational performance of an organization is good, it shows that the organization can adapt to the changeable and fierce external competition environment quickly and effectively, and risk resistance of organizational degree to external uncertainty and instability is relatively high.

Campbell (1977) regarded organizational performance as a structure. He believed that the theoretical model of organizational performance was the foundation, on which any form could be called organizational performance. The theoretical model relys on the emphasis on the relationship among variables, as well as the measurement of their relationship. Steers (1977) defined performance by the interaction between members of an organization and the organization or between members. Performance measurement is defined by the interaction among members of the organization. It can be seen that the internal atmosphere of the organization will affect the achievement of organizational performance.

According to Ruekert, Walker and Roering (1985), organizational performance consists of efficiency, effectiveness and adaptability. Efficiency refers to the ratio of resources input to output. Effectiveness refers to the sales growth rate and market share of products or services provided by the organization. Adaptability refers to the ability of an organization to respond to changes or threats in the external environment. Pritchard (1995) argued that early research on organizational performance mainly used productivity as a measure. Delaney (1996) held the view that organizational performance referred to the operating efficiency of an organization within a certain operating range. It is mainly reflected in the level of operation of assets, profitability, solvency and sustainable development capacity. Watlers (2001) summarized five characteristics of organizational performance, including the contribution to the realization of corporate strategic objectives; the measurement of quantity; the measurement of quality; the measurement of efficiency; the measurement of internal staff and external customer satisfaction.

Takagi (1991) proposed performance evaluation indicators based on the general project work logic model, including workload indicators, productivity indicators, output indicators, efficiency indicators, effectiveness indicators, resource indicators, service quality indicators, customer satisfaction indicators and cost-benefit indicators. Sezgin and Sankur (2004) believed that the performance evaluation of an organization should start from the goal of the organization, considering the type of the organization, and constructing an evaluation index system according to the characteristics of the organization for performance evaluation. The evaluation indicators were divided into organizational activity indicators, target indicators and result indicators. Qian (2010) evaluated organizational performance in five aspects: current profitability, growth, risk, short-term solvency and market expectation of future profitability. These five indicators were measured by total asset return rate, main business growth rate, beta value, liquidity ratio and market-net ratio.

Additionally, from the previous literatures, it was found that the classification of organizational performance can be roughly divided into three points of view: single indicators and multiple indicators, financial indicators and non-financial indicators, subjective indicators and objective indicators. Steers (1975), Lin (2001), Xie (2005), Chen (2005) and other scholars supported the classification of organizational performance indicators. They believed that there were two kinds of measurement of organizational performance: single indicators and multiple indicators. Among them, single indicators refer to the indicators of organizational achievements, such as employee satisfaction, profit, organizational stability, organizational productivity and other factors. Multiple indicators avoid the one-sidedness of single indicators to measure organizational performance, and measure organizational goals and organizational performance from multiple perspectives. Individual indicators are easy to collect, low cost and accepted by many organizations. Multiple indicators are broader and different in system and organization, so multiple indicators are more reasonable.

Matsuno (2000), Li, Zhao and Tan (2008) and other scholars supported the classification of financial indicators and non-financial indicators of organizational performance. Scholars believe that there were two kinds of measurement of organizational performance: financial indicators and non-financial indicators. Among them, financial indicators, including return on investment, interest rate, net income growth rate, asset return rate, are often used by scholars to evaluate organizational performance. Non-financial indicators include market share, brand loyalty, customer satisfaction, brand recognition, etc. Because the data sources of financial indicators are relatively simple and easy for researchers to obtain, financial indicators often appear in the study. Comparatively speaking, the cost of acquiring non-financial performance is higher, which makes the research more difficult. However, nowadays, the image of an enterprise does not only stay in its business performance, such as public relations, customer loyalty, brand crisis ability and so on. It is too one-sided to use financial indicators to measure organizational performance, which cannot fully present the operational status of the organization. Therefore, the combined definition of financial performance and non-financial performance is scientific and reasonable, considering not only various financial indicators in organizational performance, but also other non-financial indicators such as market performance.

Dess and Robinson (1984), Delaney and Huselid (1996) supported the classification of subjective and objective indicators of organizational performance. They believed that there were two kinds of measurement of organizational performance, namely, subjective indicators and objective indicators. Among them, using the relative value of the scale to evaluate the business performance of the enterprise and the competing enterprise is called the subjective index. Using absolute values such as real data to evaluate the business performance of the enterprise is called an objective index.

To sum up, organizational performance is a way or method to measure the achievement of organizational goals. Because of the different definitions, contents, processes and types of organizational goals, scholars have different definitions of organizational performance from different perspectives and ways (Upadhaya, Munir & Blount, 2014). In addition, throughout the research of scholars, most of them use survey data such as questionnaires, interviews and other research data as sample data to measure the level of organizational performance of enterprises. Because the survey data are greatly influenced by human, researchers cannot get completely objective data. Although some scholars used financial data to explain organizational performance, with the development of market economy, pure financial data cannot fully explain the quality of organizational performance. Therefore, some researchers began to pay attention to non-financial factors affecting organizational performance, so organizational performance is regarded as the effectiveness and efficiency in the process of achieving organizational goals. So, there is no doubt that organizational performance as one of the important indicators of organizational value exists.

This study used Lin (2001), Xie (2005) and Chen (2005) to define organizational performance. Because the definition is widely applicable to China's conditions. Thus, organizational performance was defined as the indicators of organizational achievements, such as employee satisfaction, profit, organizational stability and organizational life. Then the relative value of scale was used to evaluate the organizational performance of SMEs.

2. 6   Organizational Citizenship Behavior

The concept of organizational citizenship behavior (OCB) was first proposed by Barnard (1943), a representative of the School of Social Systems. When the concept was first proposed, it was defined as "the desire to cooperate with others". Katz and Kahn (1964) pointed out that an organization may be a very unstable system if its employees only show the behavior required by the rules and regulations of the organization and there are no spontaneous, pro-organizational behavior outside the organizational norms. Katz and Kahn (1978) stated that in an effective and continuous operation organization it is not enough to require employees to complete their own tasks on time according to certain work requirements but also to make contributions to the organization spontaneously and actively and show innovative and spontaneous behavior, such as making constructive suggestions, constantly self-learning and experiencing.

Bateman and Organ (1983) stated that citizenship behavior was not explicitly stated in the formal regulations, but was beneficial to the development of the organization and was required by the organization. Organ (1988) defined organizational citizenship behavior as employees' active and self-conscious behavior. There was no explicit regulation in the rules and regulations of the organization. It didn't influence the performance appraisal of employees, but it was beneficial to the individual behavior of the organization. That is to say, organizational citizenship behavior is a kind of spontaneous behavior from the bottom of employees' hearts. If employees do not have organizational citizenship behavior, the organization will not punish it. For example, for the event that damages the good image of the organization, they will take the initiative to stand up and maintain the image of the organization. Although these are not part of the work of the employees, they are good for the organization. It is difficult for managers to distinguish this situation clearly and give corresponding rewards or punishments.

Williams and Anderson (1991) defined organizational citizenship behavior as the individual behavior directly benefiting from the organization, which may indirectly affect employee performance and promote organizational development. Borman (2004) pointed out that organizational citizenship behavior is not connected to the daily work tasks that must be completed. It was an inner choice of employees and had great subjectivity. Organizational citizenship behavior can effectively promote the improvement of interpersonal relationships, strengthen cooperation, maintain organizational harmony and promote better work completion (Borman, 2004).

Zong (2010) pointed out that although organizational citizenship behavior was made by employees themselves and had nothing to do with others, it was beneficial to help others or the development of organizations. When employees feel that managers in organizations take special care of themselves, feel that they are valued, and can meet their spiritual needs, they will enhance their sense of identity with organizations, thus showing themselves more and more beneficial organizational citizenship behavior. Glomb (2011) believed that organizational citizenship behavior was a kind of response behavior of organizational members to adhere to the collectivism principle. Employees will strive to enhance their self-cooperation with team members for improving the competitiveness of the organization. Sometimes, organizational members may even give up some personal interests for the collective interests.

Smith, Organ and Near (1983) divided organizational citizenship behavior into two dimensions, namely, altruism and obedience. Altruism represents interpersonal organizational citizenship behavior and helps another members' behavior. Behavior is an employee's earnest working attitude, supporting organizational norms, and putting organizational norms themselves in an important position. Although it cannot provide direct help to any organizational members, it will indirectly support other people in the organization. Dynel (1994) classified organizational citizenship behavior into obedience (employees' compliance with organizational rules and regulations), loyalty (promoting organizational image to outsiders and defending organizational image) and participation (employees participating in organizational governance, sharing their ideas with others in the organization). Graham (1991) proposed four-dimensional model of organizational citizenship behavior, including interpersonal help, dedication, law-abiding, personal diligence and loyalty, interpersonal help is to provide work-related help to colleagues; dedication and law-abiding is to abide by the rules and work hard and other behaviors; personal diligence is that employees voluntarily spend extra working hours on tasks or voluntarily participate in new projects; loyalty is that employees actively promote groups to outsiders of the organization. Organize the image and safeguard the image of the organization.

Organ (1988) proposed a five-dimensional model based on the two-dimensional model. His research showed that organizational citizenship behavior consists of five dimensions: due diligence (employees accept and obey the organization's rules and procedures, which are beyond the organization's basic standards), altruism (i. e. helping other members' behavior), civic virtue (participating in various processes of the organization, not only to convey their ideas, but also to attend meetings and provide information to the organization as a whole), athletes' spirit (i. e. avoiding complaints and/or aggravating unpleasant situations) and politeness (i. e. mutual courtesy and consideration to prevent problems from happening). Based on this model, an evaluation scale of organizational citizenship behavior has been developed, which has been adopted by a large number of researchers.

Farh J. L. (1997) is the representative of the five-dimensional structure of organizational citizenship behavior of Chinese scholars. On the basis of in-depth study of Western scholars' theories, he proposed that organizational citizenship behavior in Chinese context is a five-dimensional structure, including identification of organizations, altruism towards colleagues, professionalism, law-abiding, maintaining interpersonal harmony, and distinction between public and private. Affection and cultural background have also been optimized and developed in organizational citizenship behavior scale. Farh J. L. (1997) developed the Chinese organizational citizenship behavior scale. The scale has 20 items, and its overall reliability coefficient is 0. 802, and its validity is good. It is also proved in the context of Chinese culture. This study used Farh J. L. 's (1997) organizational citizenship behavior scale which was considered suitable for the China's national conditions.

2. 7　The Effect of Organizational Citizenship Behavior

Citizenship specialists contended that organizational citizenship behavior assumes a job in two key issues: the impacts of organizational citizenship behavior on assessments of execution and judgment in salary increases, advancements, and the impacts of organizational citizenship behavior on authoritative execution and achievement (Podsakoff, MacKenzie & Paine, 2000). The examination on these two key issues found that organizational citizenship behavior positively affected work force choices made by administrators, just as positive impacts on administrative judgment and basic leadership (Podsakoff, 2000). For instance, higher rates of organizational citizenship behavior increased authoritative accomplishment by improving relational connections, opening up assets for increasingly gainful purposes, decreasing the requirement for assets to be simply utilized for support capacities, serving to coordinate, activities inside and crosswise over gatherings, fortifying the association's allure to potential workers, and empowering the association to adjust all the more successfully to change that happen (Kukkar & Ahuja, 2017).

Numerous investigations and meta-examinations have been directed to take a gander at the connection among organizational citizenship behavior and hierarchical execution and achievement. Podsakoff and MacKenzie (1994) and Organ (2006) took a gander at a protection office and found that the organizational citizenship behavior urban ideals and sportsmanship were both essentially identified with records of offers' execution. Podsakoff, Ahearne and MacKenzie (1997) and Organ (2006) analyzed paper plant specialists and found that helping conduct was fundamentally identified with item quality. They also found that municipal ideals and helping conduct were essentially identified with the percent of group share deals. Walz and Niehoff (2000) and Organ (2006) analyzed 30 distinct eateries and found that helping conduct was essentially identified with working proficiency, consumer loyalty, and nature of execution. Scientists found that helping conduct was likewise adversely related with squandered sustenance.

Recently, Podsakoff, Blume, Whiting, et al. (2012) found that organizational citizenship behavior was positively correlated with personal performance and customer satisfaction. Nielsen, Hrivnak and Shaw (2013) examined the relationship between organizational citizenship behavior and group-level organizational performance in a meta-analysis of existing group literature. These researchers found that there is a positive relationship between organizational citizenship behavior and organizational performance at the group level. Moreover and Nielsen (2013) found that there are similar patterns of relationships in all dimensions of organizational citizenship behavior: civic virtue, sportsmanship, altruism, responsibility, and courtesy.

Regarding the relationship between organizational citizenship behavior and management assessment, Podsakoff and colleagues (2015) found that organizational citizenship behavior accounted for 42.9% of the variance in management performance evaluation. The results also presented that in the ten studies included, altruism or help in the eight studies was significantly associated with performance evaluation; the sportsmanship was significantly correlated with performance evaluation in five of the eight studies; responsibility was significantly associated with performance assessment in all three studies; six of the eight studies included were significantly associated with performance evaluation. In short, it can be said that according to the above research, organizational citizenship behavior has a significant effect on management performance.

2.8　Factors Influencing Employees' Organizational Citizenship Behavior and Organizational Performance of SMEs

This research proposed organizational justice (distributive justice, procedural justice, interactional justice), transformational leadership (idealized influence, inspirational motivation, intellectual stimulation, individualized consideration), employee emotion labor (surface emotion acting, deep emotion acting, true emotion acting) and organizational learning (knowledge acquisition, knowledge distribution, knowledge interpretation) constructs to enable organizational citizenship behavior and organizational performance of SMEs. Subsections 2. 8. 1 till 2. 8. 4 will discuss this in detail.

2. 8. 1   Organizational Justice

Organizational justice in influencing organizational citizenship behavior and organizational performance is significant, which means that employees' perception on the organization, through a combination of internal and external factors, affects their behavior negatively or positively (Moorman R. H. , 1991). Sacher (2010) said that "organizational justice addresses the common dilemma of understanding and describing human behavior in an organization, as well as the cognitive framework of attitudes, values, norms, and expectations shared by organizational members". Javaheri (2009) stated that organizational justice influenced people's perceptions on groups or job assignments in which they work. In other words, organizational justice influences collective consciousness and interpersonal perceptions. As these two values are strongly related to organizational performance, this research decided to include organizational justice construct in its conceptual framework. Three intrinsic values were proposed under the organizational justice construct, namely, distributive justice, procedural justice and interactional justice. The definition and description of each value are handled in the following three sections.

2. 8. 1. 1   Distributive Justice

Early studies on organizational justice mostly focused on distributive justice. Distributive justice is the individual's perception of the fairness of the reward received, the evaluation of the final results of distribution according to certain criteria. It is also known as outcome justice (Moorman, 1991; Johnson, 2007; Javahery Kamel, 2009). According to Adams' equity theory (1963; 1965), the perception of distributive justice comes from the comparison of work outcomes, taking into account the input of some reference others and the concept of comparison used by employees. Most natural environments have some reasonable reference comparisons (Ronen, 1986).

Previous equity theories have focused on the possibility of internal comparisons (i. e. comparisons with others in the organization) or external comparisons (comparisons with others outside the organization). Contrary to previous proposals (e. g. Goodman, 1974), Ronen (1986) found that internal and external comparisons were important, and workers of the same level could use both methods simultaneously. Systematic or anticipated references are also possible. Such comparisons refer to implicit contracts between individuals and organizations, involving expected benefits, and entering commitments related to communication between employers and employees.

The formation of fairness sense depends more on social comparison than on expectations in general. That is to say, even if an individual gets the same level of distribution as he expected, he may still feel unfair distribution after social comparison. This phenomenon is more common in organizations. Adam (1965) focused on how to deal with the interference and unfair behavior of managers and supervisors in the allocation of organizational resources and incentives. Because of its major in outcomes, the distributive justice is primarily related to cognitive, emotional, and behavioral responses to specific outcomes. Therefore, when a particular outcome is considered unfair, it should affect people's emotions (for example, experiencing anger, happiness, pride, or guilt), cognition (e. g. cognitive distortion of input and outcomes of oneself or others) and ultimately affecting their behavior (e. g. performance or withdrawal) (Greenberg, 2004; Chalash & Spector, 2001).

Many studies have shown that distributional justice is related to the specific aspects of satisfaction (Martin & Bennett, 1996), general job satisfaction (Dailey & Kirk, 1992; McFarlin & Sweeney, 1992) and attitudes toward institutions and authorities (McFarlin & Sweeney, 1992; Taylor, 1990). Specific aspects of satisfaction are related to specific aspects of the work, such as supervision, wages, promotion opportunities, and relationships with colleagues, while general job satisfaction is the overall satisfaction of individuals with their work (Robins, 1998). Researchers often use the exchange framework (Niehoff & Moorman, 1993) and the contractual view (Folger & Konovsky, 1989) to explain the relationship between justice and organizational attitudes.

Adams (1965) stated that if individuals perceive an unfair ratio of inputs and returns, they will reduce their input. The theory provides a theoretical explanation for the impact of fairness on performance, this means that employees can maintain fairness by changing the quality and quantity of their work. Empirical studies have also found that when individuals are underpaid, they reduce performance to decrease input, and when reward is too high, they improve performance to increase investment to maintain a fair state. These studies have also validated the relationship between distributional justice and organizational performance. Some experimental studies have found that distributive leads to high performance (Konovsky, 2000).

Alexander and Ruderman (1987) measured the relationship between distribution justice and six organizational performance variables and found that distribution justice affected five of them. Ghosh D. (2017) found that distributive justice had indirect influence on the organizational performance through organizational embeddedness. Yan and Zhang (2010), Jin (2011), Pan (2013) and Liao (2018) explored the relationship among the distributive justice and organizational citizenship behavior and organizational performance based on the China cultural background. The data collected by questionnaire validated that distributive justice has a positive and significant effect on organizational performance, and distributive justice affects organizational performance through the indirect effect of organizational citizenship behavior.

Based on the above discussion, it could be said that there is a potential relationship between distributive justice, organizational citizenship behavior and organizational performance of SMEs among employees. This is because distributive justice not only represents a completely new working style but also brings new organizational performance context and improves organizational citizenship behavior. Thus, all of them were included in this research conceptual framework.

2. 8. 1. 2   Procedural Justice

Procedural justice refers to the process and procedure of event handling and decision-making, which is fair to both stakeholders and parties (Robbins, 2005). In this process, there is no unfair and unreasonable result caused by human deviation. Therefore, it is also one of the guarantees to ensure the justice of results (Robbins, 2005; Johnson, 2007). Specifically speaking, procedural justice is to ensure and achieve justice and it is a system designed for event handling process. Procedural justice requires the designer of a procedure dealing with an event, after considering and synthesizing various factors affecting the process, to formulate a set of system and legal system to ensure transparency and justice, so as to realize the protection of interests and legitimate and reasonable rights of the parties and stakeholders in the same procedure (Folger & Greenberg, 1985; Lind & Tyler, 1988).

Procedural justice achieves impartiality and rigor in the system design (Robbins, 2005). It requires that the system should be open and transparent in guiding the implementation and supervision of event handling. It requires that the parties and stakeholders should be equal in the process of event handling. Only in this way can the fair appeal of procedural justice be embodied (Robbins, 2005; Greenberg, 2004; Rahimnia & Hasanzade, 1988).

Thibaut and Walker (1975) put forward the structure of procedural justice (i. e. process control and decision-making control) in their works of legal proceedings, which led to the study of procedural justice and the comparative study of the multidimensional impacts of justice. Leventhal (1980) applied the procedural justice to the organizational context and proposed six criteria for procedural justice. The six criteria were as follows: consistency criteria is the allocation process should be consistent with different people or at different times; avoiding prejudice criteria is giving up personal interests and prejudices in the allocation process; accuracy criteria is decision that should be based on the correct information; revisable criteria is decision that should have amendable opportunities; representation criteria is an allocation process whereby it represents and reflects the interests of all relevant personnel; and ethical criteria is the distribution procedures must conform to generally acceptable ethical and ethical standards. Since then, although the research has also focused on the distributive justice, the emphasis of the research has changed to procedural justice.

The components of procedural justice identified in previous studies can be divided into two broad categories: formal procedures or interpersonal therapy (Zhou, 2005). Through formal procedures (for example, policies and procedures for performance evaluation, compensation decisions) , the root cause of justice/unfairness is the entire system or organization. The focus is on formal actions or policies that apply to all employees as well. Besides, interpersonal relationship processing focuses on the informal behavior of people who have an authoritative position on employees. This part of justice includes any interpersonal relationship that reflects the informal behavior of an authority (for example, formal procedures, ongoing behavior such as feedback and general treatment of employees).

Alexander and Ruderman (1987) measured the relationship between procedural justice and six organizational performance variables and found that it had stronger relationships with four of them. Some researchers pointed out that procedural justice has a greater impact on the evaluation of more general organizations and authorities (Greenberg, 1990; Lind & Tyler, 1988). Sweeney and McFarlin (1993) and Organ (1990) uncovered that organizational citizenship behavior was largely influenced by procedural justice.

Moorman (1991) , Farh. J. L. (1997) , Fang (2010) , Folger and Greenberg (1985) and Lind and Tyler (1988) analysed the relationship between procedural justice and organizational citizenship behavior. The result found that procedural justice has a positive correlation with organizational citizenship behavior in turn having positive effect on organizational performance. That is because implementation of procedural justice in an organization would motivate employees to have a great emotion and behavior to improve organizational performance (Kim & Maurborgne, 1991).

Based on the above discussion, it could be said that there is a potential relationship between procedural justice, organizational citizenship behavior and organizational performance of SMEs among employees. This is because procedural justice not only represents a completely new working style but also brings new organizational performance context and improves organizational citizenship behavior. Thus, all of them were included in this research conceptual framework.

2.8.1.3 Interactional Justice

Interactional justice focuses on the impacts of the process executor's attitude and manner towards employees on employees' perception of fairness in the process of implementation (Wang, Liu & Lei, 2013). Bies and Moag (1986) and Greenberg (1990) divided interactional justice into two parts: interpersonal justice and information justice. Interpersonal justice reflects the degree of politeness and respects for employees by those in power who execute procedures and determine outcomes; information justice refers to the degree to which information is transmitted to employees, explaining why certain distribution procedures are adopted and why such distribution results are achieved.

Bies (2015) stated that interactional justice is the most common one in the organizations compared to distributive justice and procedural justice because employees experience it every day. They uncovered that only a very small part of the unfair events people experience every day can be attributed to the distributive justice and procedural justice. Mikula Petri and Tanzer (1990) stated that most of the unfairness were caused by the unfair treatment in interpersonal communication compared to structural justice (distributive justice and procedural justice). Ambrose, Shminke and Mayer (2013), Loi, Yang and Diefendorff (2009) argued that interactive justice is more controllable and can be adjusted to make corporate practice more meaningful. Interactional justice has a direct effect on employees' job satisfaction and organizational trust (Pamela, 2011). It is strongly correlated with organizational effect variables such as organizational commitment, employee performance, employee turnover intention and organizational citizenship behavior (Pamela, 2011).

　　Colquitt, Conlon, Wesson, et al. (2001), Colquitt (2015) and Moorman (1991) discovered that interactional justice develops employees' organizational citizenship behavior. Melkonian, Soenen and Ambrose (2016) found that interactional justice makes employees feel the support of the organization and trust the leader. When employees feel a high level of interaction fairness, that means they get more trust, attention and respect in their interaction with leaders (Rupp & Cropanzano, 2018). These experiences can make employees feel their importance in the organization and in turn improve their positive psychology and emotions to a certain extent (Lind, Greenberg, Scott, et al., 2000; Judge, Scott & Ilies, 2006; Xu, Loi & Ngo, 2016). Yu (2007) discovered that interactional justice was positively correlated with organizational citizenship behavior in the context of Chinese culture.

　　In short, it is generally accepted that interactional justice influences Chinese people's behavior and daily activities including organizational citizenship behavior and organizational performance. Hence, according to the above arguments, it could be said that there is a potential relationship between interactional justice, organizational citizenship behavior and organizational performance among SMEs' employees in China. In turn, the elements of interactional justice, organizational citizenship behavior and organizational performance were included in this research conceptual framework.

2. 8. 2 Transformational Leadership

Transformational leadership emphasizes that leaders use personal charm to arise employees' trust and compliance with leaders. This research put forward four intrinsic factors under transformational leadership construct, namely, idealized influence, inspirational motivation, intellectual stimulation and individualized consideration (Avolio & Bass, 1988). The definition and description for each factor are showed in the following four sections.

2. 8. 2. 1 Idealized Influence

Idealized influence is defined as an action which is trustworthy, worshipped and followed by others (Avolio & Bass, 1988; Bass, 1985). It comprises leaders as models of behavior in organization, and the subordinates may acknowledge, respect and trust their leaders. These leaders always have high moral criteria and individual attractiveness, and their subordinates adored and place confidence in him. All employees approve and are in favor of the plan proposed by the leaders, with highly expecting for his accomplishment. Idealized influence can also be said to be leadership charisma whereby it comes from Greek words and refers to extraordinary talent, such as extraordinary wisdom, predictive ability. When the followers see that kind of leader, they attribute it to heroic or outstanding leadership (Zdaniuk, 2015).

Podsakoff (1990) stated that subordinates' trust in leadership as a mediating variable can better explain the influence of leadership charm on employees' performance. Bono (2004) found that leaders with imagination, rich emotions, seeking common ground while reserving differences, creativity, strong sense of responsibility and professional ethics, enthusiasm for work, decisive decision-making, and trust in others are more likely to become transformational leaders. This kind of leader acts with impulsiveness and self-awareness.

Den Hartog (1997) showed the effect of transformational leadership and team performance, and found that the idealized influence of transformational leadership makes subordinates more likely to have a sense of respect and follow-up, and thus has a more significant incentive effect on subordinates. Dvir (2002) found that transformational leadership through training can enhance their own ability and leadership charm, more conducive to the implementation of leadership in the team, thus improving team performance is also significant. Abed and Bander (2011) revealed that leadership style and organizational citizenship behavior (OCB) were statistically and significantly related to organizational performance. OCB was found to be the best predictor of organizational performance.

A survey of 785 employees by Sui and Wang (2012) showed that idealized influence of transformational leadership can increase employees' job performance and personal satisfaction. Li (2014) found that leaders mainly influence their subordinates through three perspectives: through the release and application of their own charm, they establish a self-confidence and strong spiritual pillar for their subordinates, and increase their subordinates' confidence so as to follow them heartily.

In short, it is generally accepted that idealized influence affects Chinese people's behavior and daily activities including organizational citizenship behavior and organizational performance. Hence, referred to the above arguments, it could be said that there is a potential relationship between idealized influence, organizational citizenship behavior and organizational performance among SMEs' employees in China. In turn, the elements of idealized influence, organizational citizenship behavior and organizational performance were included in this research conceptual framework

2. 8. 2. 2 Inspirational Motivation

Inspirational motivation is that leaders present high expectations for their subordinates, motivate them to join the team, and make them a part of the team to express their dreams (Avolio & Bass, 1994). Actually, to accomplish team goals, teamwork and emotional appeal are usually utilized by team leaders to condense team efforts. Consequently, the corresponding job performance becomes far better than the one that employees strive for their own benefit. Nanus (1992) emphasizes that among all leaders, the vision must have the most profound impact. He believes that the so-called visionary leadership means that leaders can describe a dependable, actual, and appealing future for employees. It stands for the orientation to all goals and may get the organization more prosperous and thrive. At the same time, many researchers have found that effective leaders are often visionary leaders (Bennis & Nanus, 2007; Sarros, Cooper & Santora, 2008).

Vision leaders often provide insightful insights and motivate members to take new actions to achieve new goals for better development of the organization (Nanus, 1992). Hence, leaders who have ideal vision are always regarded as ideal models and innovative leaders. Bass (1997) found that through the motivation on employees' self-awareness and values, transformational leadership can achieve an ideal performance. Li and Hung (2009) found that inspirational motivation of transformational leadership can enhance employees' performance. Sui (2012) surveyed 785 employees of enterprises and found that leaders with strong inspirational motivation can improve employees' job performance and personal satisfaction. Chen, Shi and Lu (2015) argued that inspirational motivation can stimulate employees' innovative behavior by enhancing their psychological empowerment.

In short, from the above discussion it could be argued that establishing inspirational motivation in the organization can enhance employees' organizational citizenship behavior and in turn help the organization to improve its performance. This is to ensure the efficient processing of the work. In a nutshell, inspirational motivation has a potential relationship with organizational citizenship behavior and organizational performance. Thus, all of them were included in this research conceptual framework.

2.8.2.3 Intellectual Stimulation

The intellectual stimulation is to encourage subordinates to innovate and challenge themselves, including instilling new ideas into subordinates, encouraging subordinates to express new ideas, and encouraging subordinates to use new methods to solve problems (Avolio & Bass, 1988; Bass, 1985). Leaders can inspire the formation of subordinates' consciousness, beliefs and values, and change them through intellectual stimulation. (Avolio & Bass, 1988; Bass, 1985).

Leithehwood (1992) believed that intellectual stimulation is characterized by the selection of new goals and innovative direction to influence employees, through investment, stimulation, enthusiasm and other ways to improve their original vision and enhance the enthusiasm of employees. Pillai (1999) argued that intellectual stimulation is to stimulate the high-level needs of members of an organization so that subordinates can prioritize the interests of the organization and promote its extraordinary performance. Yukl (2005) believed that intellectual stimulation can reshape employees' thinking to achieve organizational goals with a more confident and positive attitude. Meanwhile, leaders should also focus on appropriate empowerment and give employees a certain degree of autonomy, so as to improve the organizational structure and promote the completion of work objectives. Li (2014) found that leader's intellectual stimulation can enhance subordinate's personal ability by means of guidance, encouragement and training, and provide diversified development opportunities for subordinates through careful analysis and understanding of subordinate's ability.

Howell (2005) applied intellectual stimulation to organizational level research and found that the leaders not only can play their own charm to attract and unite followers but also can stimulate subordinates' potential in the way of goal management, and with its own professional essence. The role of divinity and professionalism in setting an example enables everyone to move forward and achieve the same goals, thus greatly enhancing organizational performance.

Kirkpatrick and Locke (1996) stated that intellectual stimulation in transformational leadership can effectively enhance the creativity of the whole organization to a certain extent and contribute to the organizational performance. Peng, Lin and Schaubroeck (2016) constructed a performance model with the performance of scientific research team as a dependent variable, and then put forward three suggestions on how to stimulate employees' intelligence, which can increase the functional conflict of the team. This kind of conflict can greatly enhance the conflict management ability of members, and ultimately enhance team performance.

Zhang and Qiao (2006) showed that there was a significantly positive correlation between intellectual stimulation of transformational leadership behavior and organizational citizenship behavior of employees. In the process, leaders helped employees developed intelligence, employees were willing to share their ideas and helped other colleagues to finish their task. Noruzy (2013) studied manufacturing industry and confirmed that intellectual stimulation by leaders positively affected organizational innovation through employee learning and knowledge management. Yasin, Nawab and Bhatti (2014) summarized and sorted out the previous research results and found that intellectual stimulation had a significant positive correlation with the improvement of organizational innovation performance. This was because through intellectual stimulation the employees became more determined and motivated for change and in turn enabled stable innovation process, mobilizing enthusiasm and improving organizational innovation ability. Chen and Shi (2015) argued that intellectual stimulation could stimulate employees' innovative behavior by enhancing their psychological empowerment.

In short, from the above discussion it could be argued that intellectual stimulation by leaders can develop employees' performance and bring organization advantages. That is because intellectual stimulation makes the employees more determined and motivated for change and in turn enabled stable innovation process, mobilizing enthusiasm and improving organizational innovation ability. In the process of intellectual development, employees are more willing to share their intelligence achievements. In a nutshell, intellectual stimulation has a potential relationship with organizational citizenship behavior and organizational performance of SMEs in China. Thus all of them were included in this research conceptual framework.

2. 8. 2. 4   Individualized Consideration

Individualized consideration means that being concerned with the personal needs, capabilities and carrying out different training and guidance to the subordinates according to the different situations and needs of the subordinates (Avolio & Bass, 1988; Bass, 1985). The individualized consideration in transformational leadership theory pays attention to human development, which is a great progress and has been widely studied and applied in modern society. Psychologist Maslow (1970) argues that human behavior is caused by their needs, which is divided into five levels: physiological needs, security needs, love and belonging needs, self-esteem needs, and self-fulfilling needs. Therefore, in the whole process of development, people need constant innovation and progress, and the individualized consideration of leadership plays a very important role.

Individualized consideration behavior in transformational leadership has a direct effect on employees' sense of organizational performance (Pereira & Gomes, 2012). Inness, Turner and Barling (2010) found that the individualized consideration of school leaders had no direct effect on students' scores, but it indirectly affected students' scores by affecting teachers' sense of organizational commitment. It could be inferred that there may be some buffer variable or intermediary variable between personalized behavior and performance. Kark (2012) found that women were more likely to show emotional care, that was, female leaders were more able to give employees humanistic and friendship concerns in addition to work than male leaders, reflecting the personalized care of transformational leadership, but from the perspective of outsiders, there was no significant difference.

Scholar Geyer (1998) studied bank employees and found that individualized consideration could improve employees' performance. In addition, in the Chinese context, individualized consideration also had an important positive effect on organizational performance (Chen, Wang & Yang, 2012). Menguc (2007) found that individualized consideration had an obviously positive influence on organizational performance. Zacher, Pearce and Rooney (2014) thought that individualized consideration had a positive effect on team performance, while individualized consideration of leadership had a significant positive predictive effect on the ability of satisfaction and development. Li (2014) found that leaders who cared about employees' life help subordinates to solve the difficulties they face, which could further strengthen the sense of mission and loyalty of team formation and make unremitting efforts for organizational goal and improved organizational performance. Mitchell (2014) confirmed that individualized consideration could improve team performance and had a positive correlation with department performance.

According to the above discussion, it could be concluded that there is a potential relationship between individualized consideration, OCB and organizational performance of SMEs among employees. This is because individualized consideration brings new organizational performance context and improves organizational citizenship behavior. Thus, all of them were included in this research conceptual framework.

2. 8. 3　Employee Emotion Labor

The third construct is employee emotion labor. Employees' emotions affect their mental health, job burnout (especially emotional exhaustion dimension), job engagement, job satisfaction and turnover intention (Hochschild, 1979). This research put forward three intrinsic factors under employee emotion construct, namely, surface emotion acting, deep emotion acting and true emotion acting. The definition and description for each factor are dealt with in the following three subsections.

2. 8. 3. 1　Surface Emotion Acting

Surface emotion acting refers to the fact that when the individual's emotional experience is inconsistent with the organizational rules, he conceals his true emotions by changing the explicit behavior (Hochschild, 1979). In this process, there are fierce conflicts in his heart, but his emotional experience has not been changed. This is a kind of disguise that only pays attention to changing the external emotional expression, which needs to consume the individual's psychological resources. In terms of demographic, young employees tend to have surface emotion acting (Hoffmann, 2016).

Several studies have found that surface emotion acting had a positive impact on employee emotional exhaustion (Magdalene, 2012; Grandey, 2012; Wagner & Barnes, 2014; Zou, 2016). Kruml and Geddes (2000) pointed out that surface emotion acting of emotional labor can lead to individual psychological discomfort, emotional unreality and job dissatisfaction. Employees who adopt surface emotion acting strategies make their behavior meet the requirements of the company's service customers by concealing and disguising their true inner thoughts, controlling and changing their external expressions and behaviors. Individuals with surface emotion acting disguise their behavior and expression more often, but their behavior and inner thoughts are contradictory. The unreality caused by this contradiction makes them more likely to feel nervous and tired when serving customers, which has a negative impact on job satisfaction (Bhave & Glomb, 2016)

When employees conduct surface emotion acting, they consume a lot of psychological resources because of the inconsistency between internal feelings and external emotional expression, resulting in emotional exhaustion and stress (Grandy, 2000). Thus, surface emotion acting had a negative impact on emotional transmission (Grandy, 2000). Under the long-term surface emotion acting, the psychological resources of employees are exhausted, the work pressure is high and the work efficiency is low, thus affecting the output of employees in the work performance (Dahling, 2010). Some scholars have found that daily surface emotion acting can cause physical health problems such as anxiety, tension and stress (Wagner & Barnes, 2014; Hu & Sun, 2016).

However, Chen and Qin (2011) found that there was no significant correlation between surface emotion acting and emotional exhaustion, depression and anxiety, and organizational performance. They believed that this conclusion was partly influenced by Chinese traditional culture. This conclusion was completely consistent with Cheung (2015). They found that surface emotion acting had no significant correlation with emotional exhaustion, depression and anxiety, and organizational performance. Zou and Yang (2017), Liu and Zhang (2014) and Cheung (2015) found that surface emotion acting positively affected organizational citizenship behavior. However, Yang (2015) found that surface emotion acting negatively affected organizational citizenship behavior.

From the above discussion it can be seen that there were inconsistent findings on the impact of surface emotion acting on organizational citizenship behavior and organizational performance. However, this study included it in the conceptual framework because of its potential in influencing employees' feeling and in turn organizational performance. Thus all of them were included in this research conceptual framework.

2. 8. 3. 2　Deep Emotion Acting

Deep emotion acting refers to a series of psychological activities, which not only change employee's explicit behavior, but also make emotional experience conform to the rules of organization when one's inner experience and organizational requirements are violated in the process of interpersonal communication and work (Hochschild, 1979). In this process, although the individual's inner conflict occurs due to their own efforts to play a positive emotional role and make the conflict reconciled. There is a gap between the emotions they feel and the rules of the organization at work. Only by actively adjusting their internal emotions can they keep healthy psychology better (Grandy, 2000; Feldma, 2006; Gosserand, 2003).

Carmeli and Josman (2006) found that emotions are closely related to emotional labor. They believed that "in positive and positive emotions, employees will exert more altruistic behavior in organizational citizenship behavior". George and Brief (1990) and Isen and Baron (1991) pointed out that employees' positive emotions stimulate more extra oral and altruistic behavior. This is because when an individual conducts deep emotion acting, his inner feelings are consistent with the external emotions, he will feel more positive emotions, which triggers more organizational citizenship behavior of the individual. The inner thoughts and external behaviors of employees in deep emotion acting are consistent, and fully meet the requirements of the company's display rules, save psychological resources, and the deep emotion acting behavior is easy to get customers (Zou, 2017). Positive feedback from households can create a sense of achievement for employees, which stimulates a positive emotional experience and then improves organizational performance (Shu, 2013).

Elfenbein (2008) pointed out that employee's deep emotion acting role playing was conducive to creating a positive interactive atmosphere in the organization and improving employee performance and customer satisfaction through emotional contagion effect. Chen (2012) and Cheung (2015) found that deep emotional acting behavior ultimately affected organizational performance through organizational citizenship behavior. Han, Moon and Yoo (2015) found that emotional labor further affected job performance by affecting employee job satisfaction. Kim and Hur (2017) found that the positive relationship between deep emotion acting and job performance was strengthened through the support of supervisors and colleagues.

According to the above discussion, it can be said that there is a potential relationship between deep emotion acting, organizational citizenship behavior and organizational performance of SMEs among employees. This is because deep emotion acting brings new organizational performance context and improve organizational citizenship behavior. Thus, all of them were included in this research conceptual framework.

2. 8. 3. 3   True Emotion Acting

Diefendorff (2003) endorsed Hochschild's (1979) division and understanding of emotional labor, and based on Hochschild's (1979) research, developed a third dimension, "true emotional acting" to describe the emotional experience and performance rules that employees feel. When they are consistent, the interaction between the employee and the customer naturally shows their true emotions, and there is no conflict between the inner emotional experience and the explicit behavior. Therefore, this strategy does not require any effort and does not consume its own psychological resources.

Huang Miner, Wu and Tang (2010) studied the role of emotional labor in traits and mental health among frontline employees in multiple service industries. They found that employees who are kind, directed by others, and pointing to things rarely use surface movements and use automatic adjustments. Emotional employees rarely perform deep movements. Hennig-Thurau and Groth (2006) found that true emotion acting changed customer sentiment, which in turn affected customer-employee relationships and customer satisfaction, and ultimately affected customer loyalty. Yang and Ma (2015) found that true emotion acting positively affected customer loyalty through customer identification.

Zapf (2002) believed that true emotion acting was more effective than surface and deep behavior. True emotion acting not only meets the organizational requirements of external emotional expression, but also can express internal emotions naturally without too much loss of individual psychological resources. Wei (2017) and Wang and Zhang (2018) discovered that true emotion acting strategies and job satisfaction were positively correlated. Salami (2007) studied service industry employees as the research objective and found that employees' true emotion acting significantly affected their organizational citizenship behavior. Wang (2014) found that true emotion acting had a positive correlation with organizational citizenship behavior among commercial bank employees. Zhang (2014) found that true emotion acting positively affected organizational performance through the intermediary role of organizational citizenship behavior.

Based on the above discussion, it can be said that there is a potential relationship between true emotion acting, organizational citizenship behavior and organizational performance of SMEs among employees. This is because true emotion acting brings new organizational performance context and improve organizational citizenship behavior. Thus, all of them were included in this research conceptual framework.

2. 8. 4   Organizational Learning

Based on previous literature, this research examined three intrinsic values under organizational learning structure, namely, knowledge acquisition, knowledge distribution and knowledge interpretation. The definition and description of each value are offered in subsections 2. 8. 4. 1 till 2. 8. 4. 3.

2. 8. 4. 1   Knowledge Acquisition

It refers to the procedure of organizing employees to acquire technology and management knowledge through various ways and means, namely the development and creation of skills, horizons and relationships (Huber, 1991). Cepeda and Vera (2007), Jiang (2009) and Zeng (2011) believed that knowledge acquisition could not only discover alternative knowledge and resources, enable organizations to maintain and enhance their competitive advantages in fierce competition, but also promote knowledge innovation and then spread to the whole enterprise, thus improving their capabilities and coping with environmental changes.

Yang (2012) believed that in the process of development, enterprises must establish a complete knowledge acquisition learning system, which is accompanied by the whole process of enterprise development, and through a series of strategic activities the organizational learning will deliver the expected benefits. Pilar Jose and Ramon (2006) found that knowledge acquisition was the ability to organize knowledge management and correct behavior based on new cognitive conditions to improve organizational performance.

Feng (2016) studied the relationship between basic practice of quality management, organizational learning and enterprise performance in

Zhejiang manufacturing enterprises and found that knowledge acquisition had an important impact on organizational performance. Zhang (2008) found that knowledge acquisition of organizational strategic had a positive impact on organizational citizenship behavior of employees, thereby improving organizational performance.

In short, from the above discussion it could be argued that knowledge acquisition can develop employees' organizational citizenship behavior and in turn improve organizational performance. This is because knowledge acquisition makes the employees more determined and motivated for change and in turn enabled stable innovation process, mobilizing enthusiasm and improving organizational innovation ability. In a nutshell, knowledge acquisition has a potential relationship with organizational citizenship behavior and organizational performance of SMEs in China. Thus all of them were included in this research conceptual framework.

2. 8. 4. 2   Knowledge Distribution

It refers to the process of organizing employees to share information from different sources and obtain new information from them, as well as the diffusion of knowledge that has been learned. Knowledge distribution is a process that explores how an organization learns, adapts and understands the relationship in the internal and external environment (Huber, 1991). Early scholars believed that knowledge distribution could change enterprise behavior (Camp & Oltra, 2016) and encourage members to share knowledge and ideas (Namada, 2017), so that when faced with problems, members could discuss and solve together (Mubeen & Ashraf, 2016), ultimately improving the ability of enterprises to take effective action (Jain & Moreno, 2015), and developing new knowledge or insights that can influence behavior to adapt the change of environment (Slater & Narver, 1995).

Yu (2004) stated that knowledge distribution is a process of continuous exchange of knowledge among individuals, groups and organizations to generate innovative behavior in order to suit the environment and achieve corporate goals. Wang (2003) argued that enterprises employees change their own thinking and behavior patterns, and promote them to adopt innovative and pioneering activities and then influence organizational performance by sharing information and creating organizational memory.

Gao (2014) believed that knowledge distribution is a process in which members share knowledge and solve problems collaboratively so as to improve the competitiveness of the organization and organizational citizenship behavior of employees. Zhang (2008) made a detailed study of 16 family businesses and found that knowledge distribution had a significant positive impact on the organizational performance.

In short, from the above discussion it could be argued that knowledge distribution can develop organizational citizenship behavior of employees and in turn improve organizational performance. This is because knowledge distribution makes the employees more determined and motivated for change and in turn enabled stable innovation process, mobilizing enthusiasm and improving organizational innovation ability. In a nutshell, knowledge distribution has a potential relationship with organizational citizenship behavior and organizational performance of SMEs in China. Thus all of them were included in this research conceptual framework.

2. 8. 4. 3   Knowledge Interpretation

Knowledge interpretation refers to organizing employees to interpret information on knowledge so that everyone can have a common understanding of information and make full use of it (Huber, 1991). For this need adapting to enterprise's changes of internal and external environment and gain competitive advantage, enterprises constantly use existing knowledge and experience to interpret knowledge at all levels of enterprises and constantly change the innovative process of enterprises' concepts and behaviors through the integration and solidification of new knowledge (Rui, 2005).

Li (2013) used the cross-level dynamic process of knowledge description, integration and transformation among individuals, teams and organizations to explain knowledge, so as to improve organizational performance. Cai and Chen (2013) stated that knowledge interpretation was an information interpreting process, aiming at acquiring new knowledge and enhancing insight to generate innovative behavior, thereby affecting organizational performance. Zou and Gao (2017) had similar views with Li, Xiang and Yang (2016) and Yang and Long (2008). They held the opinion that that knowledge interpretation was a process of processing acquired knowledge to suit the environment, meet internal and external needs and gain competitive advantage, and explained the process of achieving the unified goal.

Raystata (2010) found that knowledge interpretation affected the whole process of organizational innovation from innovation invention to dissemination to implementation, which is conducive to improving organizational performance. Stata (2018) put forward that knowledge interpretation within an organization can promote production of organizational citizenship behavior and keep the organization competitive advantage, thereby obtaining excess profits and improving organizational performance.

In short, from the above discussion it could be argued that knowledge interpretation can develop organizational citizenship behavior of employees and in turn improve organizational performance. That is because knowledge interpretation makes the employees more determined and motivated for change and in turn enabled stable innovation process, mobilizing enthusiasm and improving organizational innovation ability. In a nutshell, knowledge interpretation has a potential relationship with organizational citizenship behavior and organizational performance of SMEs in China. Thus all of them were included in this research conceptual framework.

2.9　Underpinning Theories

The theories that were used to develop the conceptual framework of this research were equity theory, incentive theory and social exchange theory. Accordingly this section discusses the underpinning theories that support the conceptual framework.

2. 9. 1   Equity Theory

The focus of equity theory is to determine whether resource allocation is fair to both partners (Adams, 1965). Equity is measured by comparing the contribution (or cost) to the benefit (or reward) of each individual. Equity theory is considered one of the theories of justice. Adams (1967) claims that employees find fairness between their output and input. A job and the results obtained from it are compared with the perceptual input and results of others. It is believed that people value fair treatment, which motivates them to maintain fairness in their colleague and organizational relationships. The fair structure of the workplace is based on the ratio of input to output. Input is the contribution of employees to the organization.

Equity is measured by comparing the contribution rate and return rate of each person in the relationship. As long as the ratio of these benefits to contributions is similar, partners do not have to obtain the same benefits (e. g. the same amount of love, care and financial security) or make the same contributions (e. g. invest the same amount of effort, time and financial resources) (Wei, 2016). Like other popular motivation theories, such as Maslow's hierarchy of needs theory and equity theory, subtle and variable individual factors can affect everyone's evaluation and perception of their partnership (Wu, 2015). According to Adams (1965), anger is caused by underpayment inequity, while guilt is caused by overpayment of equity.

The theory of fairness points out that people's enthusiasm for work is not only related to the amount of personal actual reward, but also more closely related to whether people feel fair about the distribution justice of reward. People will consciously or unconsciously compare their labor costs and their rewards with others, and make a judgment on fairness. The sense of fairness directly affects the work motivation, behavior and performance of employees. Therefore, in a sense, the motivation process is actually a process of comparing people, making a fair judgment and guiding behavior. The main content of equity theory research is the rationality and fairness of the distribution of employee's remuneration and its positive impact on employees (Sun, 2004).

In any position, employees want to be rewarded for their contribution and performance. If employees feel that their salaries are fairly distributed, company procedures are fairly implemented, and interpersonal and information exchanges are fairly obtained, they will have good behavior and performance. However, if employees feel unfair treatment, it will lead to hostility towards the company and colleagues, which may result in low performance at work (Cao, 2017). Therefore, organizational justice plays a significant role in the employees' behavior and performance.

2.9.2　Incentive Theory

Incentive theory is supported by many behavioral psychologists, the most famous of whom is B. F. Skinner. Skinner (1929) argued that a person is more likely to take actions that are positively acceptable, while he is more likely to avoid actions that are negatively acceptable (i. e. bring about negative reinforcement). Motivation theory regards stimulation as something attractive, rather than something that causes people to reduce or eradicate stimulation completely (Bao, 2005).

Motivation is a commitment or action made for greater action. In business, incentives can be to give employees additional benefits, remuneration, or job promotion in recognition of their achievements or to encourage them to work better. Additional compensation or benefits motivate employees to do more. What's more, according to this theory, non-monetary incentives, for example, job promotion, job security, achievement pride and job satisfaction are also incentives for employees (Brown, 2015).

The incentive measures to provide positive assurance to meet individual needs are called positive incentives. These incentive measures involve the principle of optimism and are designed to full the psychological needs of employees (Gerhart, 2017). And transformational leadership are great motivation for employees to get good performance. For example, a leader praises a new employee for doing well and care employees' psychological need. Other positive incentives include recognition, job promotion, extra allowances, trophies and medals and organizational leader guide each employee in career development planning to fully tap the potential of employees. These incentive measures have a positive impact on subordinates' organizational citizenship behavior for their companies and colleagues, and promote organizational performance improvement (Caillier, 2016).

2.9.3   Social Exchange Theory

The social exchange theory, which rose in the United States around 1960, began to spread all over the world. The founder of this theory is an American sociologist—Homans (1967). Social exchange theory mainly emphasizes the influence of psychological factors on behavior, and is also regarded as behaviorist social psychology theory. This theory regards all social activities as a kind of exchange relationship. It was regarded as the most influential conceptual paradigm to a comprehensive understanding towards organizational behavior. In other words, social exchange is not specified obligation for individuals who enjoy the discretion.

Human resource is the most valuable resource of an enterprise. Leaders of every enterprise expect to stimulate the potential of human resources in the enterprise. Therefore, one of the scholars' strong academic interests is to reveal the social exchange process in the organization, in order to stimulate the personal potential of employees (Emerson, 1976). Social exchange theory is one of the main theoretical bases to explain and predict employees' work attitude and behavior. In the field of organizational behavior research, there are two kinds of social exchange relationship: organization and employee exchange as well as manager and employee exchange (Cropanzano & Mitchell, 2005).

Organization-employee exchange: the employees in the enterprise feel that the enterprise recognizes the individual's work and the enterprise cares about the employees, and enterprise is like to invest more resources in the employees to help them develop and solve the difficulties in work and life. The employees will have the belief and psychology of repay (Ma, 2006). Manager-employee exchange: in addition to the formal obligations and rights of both parties, managers should invest personal resources, such as emotional resources and information resources, help employees to solve work doubts, provide emotional support to employees under pressure, by this way, subordinates will have the psychology of giving back and repay for managers through actual actions. The above two types of social exchange affect employees' work attitude and behavior. Social exchange theory is very effective to explain employees' loyalty to the enterprise. Some studies have shown that when the organization makes positive and beneficial actions to employees, it will promote employees' perception of fairness and trust. Fairness and trust are the key factors for the long-term maintenance and development of social exchange between employees and enterprises. Employees will work hard to repay the organization (Wayne, Shore & Liden, 1997).

The microcosm of society comes from the exchange of individual expectations for social rewards. Individuals communicate with individual groups because they can get what they need from each other. Brau (1984) also distinguishes two kinds of social remuneration: intrinsic remuneration and extrinsic remuneration. Intrinsic remuneration refers to the inner feelings of pleasure, social approval, love and gratitude obtained from social relations, and then the so-called remuneration. For example, when employees feel good emotion acting and this emotional acting meets his inner needs, the employees will have great job performance. Extrinsic remuneration refers to the remuneration of money, goods, knowledge invitations, help and obedience obtained outside social relations (Dong & Gao, 2018).

Reciprocity is a typical form of social exchange, and most of management research focuses on the explanation of reciprocity in this field. Researchers believe that reciprocity is a kind of income, because it leads to the sense of responsibility, gratitude and trust of individuals.

People share knowledge in order to expect future reciprocity and gain recognition from others (Wang, 2010). The empirical research results from Bock (2005) show that the expected reciprocal relationship has a significant impact on knowledge sharing attitude. People generally regard sharing knowledge with others as an effective means to expand interpersonal relationship, maintain interpersonal relationship and strengthen interpersonal relationship, and expect to obtain the benefits of knowledge sharing from these interpersonal relationships. Therefore, when employee exchange knowledge, such as knowledge distribution and interpretation, employee get more benefits and have good behavior contributing to the organizational performance (Shi, 2015).

Moreover, the fundamental principles of social exchange theory is that the relationship will grow into trust, loyalty and mutual commitment over time, as long as both partied abide by certain rules of exchange. When organization provide a fair distribution and procedural justice, in return, employees are motivated to perform behavior well and contribute to the organizational performance (Daud, Holiam & Zhang, 2014; Gilbert, De Winne & Sels, 2011; Xerri & Brunetto, 2013). There are also some scholars who use social exchange theory to explain and predict the work behavior of employees (Cropanzano & Mitchell, 2009). For example, Konovsky & Pugh (1994) took nurses as research objects to test the social exchange relationship model between situational factors and organizational citizenship behavior. The results show that procedural justice has an important impact on employees, and employees feel that procedural justice can promote organizational citizenship behavior.

Therefore, the performance of social responsibility of small and medium-sized enterprises can have a direct and positive impact on employees' perceived organizational support and organizational citizenship behavior. The performance of social responsibility of employees is the key point of corporate social responsibility management. Enterprises must implement human resource management policies with social responsibility, pay attention to the interests and development needs of employees. Therefore, when employees' emotional needs and knowledge needs are met, employees will make citizenship behavior that contributes to the organizational performance (He, 2011).

2.10 Summary

This chapter discusses theoretical information on the issues to be investigated in this research. The discussion also includes the theories used in the current study, which are equity theory, incentive theory, social exchange theory. The chapter also explains the conceptual framework and its constructs.

Chapter Three   Research Framework and Hypotheses

3. 1   Introduction

This chapter illustrates this research conceptual framework. The hypotheses on motivational factors which were argued to enable organizational citizenship behavior and in turn organizational development among SMEs in China were developed. The motivational factors were grouped under four constructs, namely, organizational justice, transformational leadership, employee emotion labor and organizational learning. Subsequently, a summary for the discussion is offered.

3. 2   Proposed Conceptual Framework

Based on the discussion in section 2. 2, 2. 3, 2. 4 and 2. 6, and equity theory, incentive theory, social exchange theory, this research conceptual framework was generated which is depicted in Figure 3. 1. The conceptual framework postulates that organizational citizenship behavior of employees and in turn organizational performance of SMEs in China were influenced by the following constructs: ① organizational justice; ②transformational leadership; ③employee emotion labor; and ④organizational learning.

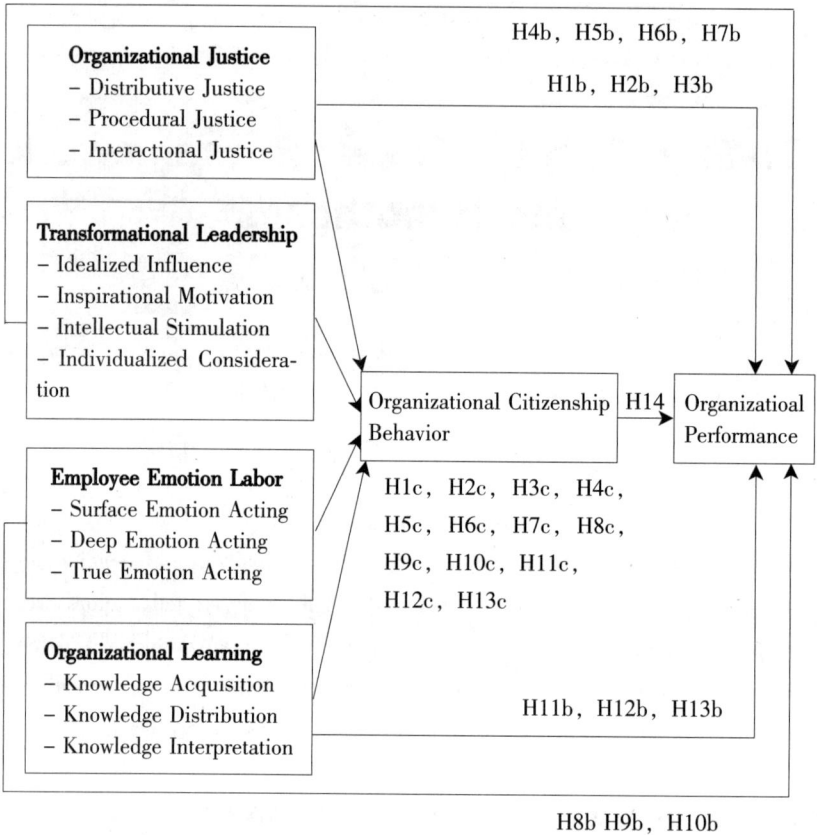

Figure 3.1 Conceptual Framework for Improving Organizational Performance of SMEs in China

Organizational justice consists of the elements of distributive justice, procedural justice and interactional justice. Transformational leadership consists of the elements of idealized influence, inspirational motivation, intellectual stimulation and individualized consideration. Employee emotion labor consists of the elements of surface emotion acting, deep emotion acting and true emotion acting. Organizational learning consists of the elements of knowledge acquisition, knowledge distribution and knowledge interpretation. All these independent variables were argued to have positive effect on employees' organizational citizenship behavior

（mediating variable） and organizational performance of SMEs in China
（dependent variable）. In addition, organizational performance of SMEs
in China was considered as the outcome of this research conceptual
framework.

3. 3　Hypotheses Development

This section discusses the hypotheses that were developed according
to the relationships that are depicted in the above conceptual framework.
The relationships were between thirteen antecedents（distributive justice,
procedural　justice, interactional　justice, idealized　influence,
inspirational　motivation, intellectual　stimulation, individualized
consideration, surface emotion acting, deep emotion acting, true emotion
acting, knowledge acquisition, knowledge distribution and knowledge
interpretation）, organizational citizenship behavior and organizational
development of SMEs in China. Organizational citizenship behavior was
functioned as the mediating variable. The description of hypotheses for
each factor are dealt with in subsection 3. 3. 1 till 3. 3. 15.

3. 3. 1　Distributive Justice

Distributive justice refers to the justice of the results and rewards
obtained by employees（Niehoff & Moorman, 1993）. Because of its
focus on results, distributive justice is expected to be mainly related to
cognitive, emotional and behavioral responses to specific outcomes
（Moorman, 1991; Johnson, 2007; Bahrami, 2014）. Pan（2010）,
Yan and Zhang（2010）, Jin（2011）, Liao（2018）explored the
relationship among the distributive justice and organizational citizenship
behavior and organizational performance from the perspective of China
cultural background. The results showed that distributive justice affected
organizational performance. The organizational citizenship behavior played
a mediation role. In other words, when a particular outcome is considered
fair it should affect people's emotions, cognition and ultimately their
behaviors. These behaviors can influence the organizational performance

(Greenberg, 2004; Lather & Kaur, 2015). According to the above researches, the following hypotheses were put forward:

H1a: There is a positive relationship between distributive justice and employees' organizational citizenship behavior of SMEs in Jilin Province of China.

H1b: There is a positive relationship between distributive justice and organizational performance of SMEs in Jilin Province of China.

3.3.2 Procedural Justice

Moorman (1991), Farh J. L. (1997) and Fang (2010) analyzed the relationship between procedural justice and organizational citizenship behavior. The result indicated that procedural justice had positive correlation with organizational citizenship behavior, which led to positive effect on organizational performance. This is because the implementation of procedural justice in an organization would motivate employee to have a great emotion and behavior to improve organizational performance (Kim & Maurborgne, 1996). According to the above researches, the following hypotheses were proposed:

H2a: There is a positive relationship between procedural justice and employees' organizational citizenship behavior of SMEs in Jilin Province of China.

H2b: There is a positive relationship between procedural justice and organizational performance of SMEs in Jilin Province of China.

3.3.3 Interactional Justice

Moorman (1991) also found that interactional justice positively affected employees' organizational citizenship behavior. Otto and Mamatoglu (2015) found that organizational performance was significantly affected by interactional justice. This is because interactional justice involves the source of justice and all aspects of the communication process between the recipients, such as courtesy, honesty, respect and transfer information. Thus, when organizational employees feel the interactional justice, they incline to improve organizational performance. This leads to the following hypotheses:

H3a: There is a positive relationship between interactional justice and employees' organizational citizenship behavior of SMEs in Jilin Province of China.

H3b: There is a positive relationship between interactional justice and organizational performance of SMEs in Jilin Province of China.

3.3.4 Idealized Influence

Idealized influence refers to the action of transformational leaders as role models (Avalio & Bass, 2014). If leaders show the idealized influence behavior, then in return, employees also change their behavior in work. As a result, organizational performance is improved (Blau, 1964; Ferrin, 2002; Samad, 2012). Humphrey (2012), Bycio (1995), Pillai (1999), Stockeret (2001) and Wang (2011) supported idealized influence can influence organizational citizenship behavior. Thus, idealized influence of leader is very important for employees to develop their behavior to improve organizational performance. Referring to the above researches, the following hypotheses were proposed:

H4a: There is a positive relationship between idealized influence and employees' organizational citizenship behavior of SMEs in Jilin Province of China.

H4b: There is a positive relationship between idealized influence and organizational performance of SMEs in Jilin Province of China.

3.3.5 Inspirational Motivation

Inspirational motivation is that transformational leader compels an inspiring and appealing vision to motivate employee (Lowe, 1996). Elenkov (2002), Judge and Piccolo (2004) and Walumbwa and Hartnell (2011) found direct linkage between inspirational motivation and organizational performance. Purvanova, Bono and Dzieweczynski (2006) studied a total of 988 exempt employees of a large petrochemical company and found that inspirational motivation had a significant impact on organizational citizenship behavior. Therefore, inspirational motivation of transformational leader can encourage employees to work hard for the organization. Thus, the following hypotheses were proposed:

H5a: There is a positive relationship between inspirational motivation and employees' organizational citizenship behavior of SMEs in Jilin Province of China.

H5b: There is a positive relationship between inspirational motivation and organizational performance of SMEs in Jilin Province of China.

3.3.6 Intellectual Stimulation

Intellectual stimulation encourages subordinates to innovate and challenge themselves, including instilling new ideas into subordinates, and inspiring subordinates to express new ideas and methods to solve problems in the work (Bass, 1985). Howell and Avolio (1993), Samad (2012) and Datche (2015) found that intellectual stimulation had a positive relation with organizational performance. Li (2006) and Shi (2003) also confirmed that intellectual stimulation had a significant positive effect on organizational citizenship behavior through empirical research. Positive-minded employees that are developed through intellectual stimulation by the leaders incline to actively contribute towards organizational performance. According to the above researches, the following hypotheses were proposed:

H6a: There is a positive relationship between intellectual stimulation and employees' organizational citizenship behaviour of SMEs in Jilin Province of China.

H6b: There is a positive relationship between intellectual stimulation and organizational performance of SMEs in Jilin Province of China.

3.3.7 Individualized Consideration

Zhang and Qiao (2005), Colbert (2008) and Ojokukuku (2012) uncovered that individualized consideration was positively correlated with organizational performance. Yun, Cox and Sims (2007) found that leaders' individualized consideration had a positive impact on the organizational citizenship behavior of team members. The leaders' individualized consideration promotes communication and cooperation within the team. In turn, organizational performance was improved. When the employees get the corresponding suggestions, support, guidance and consideration from the leaders they will work hard for improving the organization (Howell, 2005). According to the above researches the following hypotheses were proposed:

H7a: There is a positive relationship between individualized consideration and employees' organizational citizenship behavior of SMEs in Jilin Province of China.

H7b: There is a positive relationship between individualized consideration and organizational performance of SMEs in Jilin Province of China.

3.3.8 Surface Emotion Acting

Goodwin, Groth and Frenkel (2011) and Xu (2013) found that surface emotion acting strategies are negatively correlated with employee personal performance. The reason behind this is that the employees consume a lot of psychological resources because of the inconsistency between internal feelings and external emotional expressions when they conduct surface emotion acting, which results in emotional exhaustion and stress. Moreover, surface emotion acting had a negative impact on emotional transmission (Krial, 2016). Under the superposition of physical and mental exhaustion and negative emotions, individuals weaken their willingness to conduct organizational citizenship behavior (Grandy, 2000). Therefore, the following research hypotheses were put forward:

H8a: There is a significant relationship between surface emotion acting and employees' organizational citizenship behavior of SMEs in Jilin Province of China.

H8b: There is a significant relationship between surface emotion acting and organizational performance of SMEs in Jilin Province of China.

3.3.9   Deep Emotion Acting

Berkowitz and Connor (1996), George and Brief (1990), Isen and Baron (1991), Salami (2007), Xu (2013) found out that employee's positive emotions stimulated more out-of-role behavior and more altruistic behavior. When individuals conduct deep emotion acting, they will feel more positive because their inner feelings are consistent with the external emotional expression, which triggers more organizational citizenship behavior and is conducive to improving organizational performance. According to the above researches, the following hypotheses were proposed:

H9a: There is a positive relationship between deep emotion acting and employees' organizational citizenship behavior of SMEs in Jilin Province of China.

H9b: There is a positive relationship between deep emotion acting and organizational performance of SMEs in Jilin Province of China.

3.3.10   True Emotion Acting

Zapf (2002) believed that true emotion acting not only meets the organizational requirements of external emotional expression but also can express internal emotions naturally without too much loss of individual psychological resources. Salami (2007) and Lee and Woo (2017) found that true emotion acting had a positive correlation with commercial bank employees' organizational citizenship behavior. Zhang (2014) found that true emotion acting positively affected organizational performance through the intermediary role of organizational citizenship behavior. According to the above researches, the following research hypotheses were put forward:

H10a: There is a positive relationship between true emotion acting and employees' organizational citizenship behaviour of SMEs in Jilin Province of China.

H10b: There is a positive relationship between true emotion acting and organizational performance of SMEs in Jilin Province of China.

3.3.11 Knowledge Acquisition

One of the purposes of organizational learning research is to explore how to improve enterprise performance in the complex and changeable business environment (Calantone, 2002). A large number of empirical studies revealed the relationship between organizational learning and organizational performance (Michna, 2009; Harrim, 2008; Simon, Bulent & Robert, 2010). There are two main conclusions: one is that organizational learning directly affects organizational performance; the other is that organizational learning influences organizational performance through mediating factors. Zhang (2008) and Zuo and Li (2009) found that knowledge acquisition of organizational strategic had a positive impact on employees' organizational citizenship behavior in turn get more organizational performance. Based on the above researches, the following hypotheses were proposed:

H11a: There is a positive relationship between knowledge acquisition and employees' organizational citizenship behavior of SMEs in Jilin Province of China.

H11b: There is a positive relationship between knowledge acquisition and organizational performance of SMEs in Jilin Province of China.

3.3.12 Knowledge Distribution

Knowledge distribution is the product of organizational members' involvement in the process of sharing the experiences and knowledge in the workplace (Nevis, Dibella & Gould, 2010). The knowledge distribution is shared in a systematic way by the organizational members. Darroch and McNaughton (2002) and Tippins and Sohi (2003) found positive impact of knowledge distribution on organizational performance. Zhang (2008) found that knowledge distribution had a significant positive impact on organizational citizenship behavior and in turn improved organizational performance. Skerlavaj (2010) stated that knowledge distribution can change the behavior and cognition of organizational members, which has a positive impact on organizational performance. Based on the above researches, the following hypotheses were proposed:

H12a: There is a positive relationship between knowledge distribution and employees' organizational citizenship behavior of SMEs in Jilin Province of China.

H12b: There is a positive relationship between knowledge distribution and organizational performance of SMEs in Jilin Province of China.

3.3.13 Knowledge Interpretation

Calantone, Cavusgil and Zhao (2002), Jiang (2008), Tang, Mu and Maclachlan (2010) uncovered that knowledge interpretation had a significant positive impact on organizational performance, which is indirectly influenced by organizational citizenship behavior. This is because the employees help each other to gain experience and method in the process of knowledge interpretation, which improves organizational citizenship behavior and finally increases organizational performance (Simon, Bulent & Robert, 2010). According to the above researches, the following hypotheses were proposed:

H13a: There is a positive relationship between knowledge interpretation and employees' organizational citizenship behavior of SMEs in Jilin Province of China.

H13b: There is a positive relationship between knowledge interpretation and organizational performance of SMEs in Jilin Province of China.

3.3.14 Mediating Role of Organizational Citizenship Behavior

Organ (1997) proposed that the accumulation of organizational citizenship behavior can improve organizational performance. In particular, organizational citizenship behavior helps to create a positive team atmosphere, create a more enjoyable work environment, and enhance the organization's ability to adapt to environmental changes and create organizational social capital, thereby improving the efficiency of employees and organizational performance. Over the years, there have been many such studies, but they are most based on theoretical basis inference, and empirical research is still very few. Therefore, in this study, organizational citizenship behavior was assumed to have a potential to mediate the relationships between antecedents (distributive justice, procedural justice, interactional justice, idealized influence, intellectual stimulation, inspirational motivation, individualized consideration, true emotion acting, surface emotion acting, deep emotion acting, knowledge acquisition, knowledge distribution and knowledge interpretation) and organizational performance. This argument leads to the following hypotheses:

H1c: The relationship between distributive justice and organizational performance is mediated by organizational citizenship behavior.

H2c: The relationship between procedural justice and organizational performance is mediated by organizational citizenship behavior.

H3c: The relationship between interactional justice and organizational performance is mediated by organizational citizenship behavior.

H4c: The relationship between idealized influence and organizational performance is mediated by organizational citizenship behavior.

H5c: The relationship between inspirational motivation and organizational performance is mediated by organizational citizenship behavior.

H6c: The relationship between intellectual stimulation and organizational performance is mediated by organizational citizenship behavior.

H7c: The relationship between individualized consideration and organizational performance is mediated by organizational citizenship behavior.

H8c: The relationship between surface emotion acting and organizational performance is mediated by organizational citizenship behavior.

H9c: The relationship between deep emotion acting and

organizational performance is mediated by organizational citizenship behavior.

H10c: The relationship between true emotion acting and organizational performance is mediated by organizational citizenship behavior.

H11c: The relationship between knowledge acquisition and organizational performance is mediated by organizational citizenship behavior.

H12c: The relationship between knowledge distribution and organizational performance is mediated by organizational citizenship behavior.

H13c: The relationship between knowledge interpretation and organizational performance is mediated by organizational citizenship behavior.

3.3.15 Relationship between Organizational Citizenship Behavior and Organizational Performance

To complement the above hypotheses and in tandem with this research theoretical framework (as illustrated in Figure 3.1), the following hypothesis was proposed as the final hypothesis:

H14: There is a relationship between organizational citizenship behavior and organizational performance.

3.4 Summary

This chapter has illustrated the diagram for this research conceptual framework and the resulted research hypotheses. All of these will be the basis for the research instrument development, data analysis and results interpretation. The research methodology employed in this study is presented in the next chapter.

Chapter Four　Research Methodology

4. 1　Introduction

As mentioned in the previous chapters, this research intends to examine the factors that can be used to develop organizational citizenship behavior and in return organizational performance of SMEs in Jilin Province of China. To assist in this process, one conceptual framework is developed (as depicted in Figure 3. 1). This chapter provides the methods which were used to attain the best data type for the research. The discussion is divided into five sections, namely, overview of philosophical assumptions, research equation, operational definition and measurement of variables, data collection and data analysis. At last, a summary of the chapter is provided.

4. 2　Overview of Philosophical Assumptions

The philosophical assumption is a process of social research that not only produces research data but also understands and explains it. Indeed, the philosophical assumption is the approach and paradigms that are utilized to collect, analyze and explain the data within the research (Walsham, 1995). Orlikowski and Barudi (2002) and Hua (1986) divided the paradigms into three models which are positivist paradigm, interpretive paradigm and critical paradigm. Philosophically, the three models are different (Myers & Avison, 2002). Thus, the following paragraphs discuss the paradigms and their relevance to this study in detail.

The assumption of positivism is realism whereby the reality is assumed to exist (Guba & Lincoln, 2005). The positivist paradigm focuses on the explanation, prediction, and control. From the ontological perspective, the positivist paradigm defines reality as objective and its measurement and properties are independent from the researchers (Chua, 1986). From the epistemological perspective, positivism defines knowledge as objective and quantifiable, which emphasis is placed on quantitative methodology of collecting data and analyzing data. The researchers use systematic and quantitative method to enhance the precision of parametric description and the relationship between them (Orlikowski & Barudi, 2002; Straub, et al. , 2004). As this study investigated the factors affecting organizational citizenship behavior and in return organizational performance of SMEs in Jilin Province of China, the positivist paradigm was the most applicable research method to be adopted by the researcher. This was to enable the perception on the issues being investigated to be collected and analyzed systematically.

The second philosophical assumptions are interpretive paradigm. It emphasizes qualitative methodology of collecting data and analyzing data. The interpretive research produces meaning and it is relevant to all personal actions, which are depending on an individual's subjective experiences. Interpretive researchers develop meaning from the interviews and observations that depend on the subjective opinions of researchers and the respondents (Merriam, 1998; Trauth, 2001). The interpretive paradigm uses text, verbal and nonverbal form and the precondition that affect communication. Since this research is not intended to construct an interactive relationship between researchers and research participants, this paradigm was considered irrelevant.

Critical paradigm is transactional and the epistemology of subjectivism, that is the researchers and the participant being assumed and the investigated object is assumed to be interactively associated (Myers & Avison, 2002), whereby its purpose is critique and emancipation (Chua, 1986). The critical paradigm aims at the assessor reflection and query, which presume that the social reality is established historically (Myers & Avison, 2002), and seek to the conflict and constraints in contemporary society. Ethnographic research and case studies are commonly used data collection methods for critical paradigm researchers (Chua, 1986). Since this study focused on the factors influencing OCB within an organization and in turn organizational performance of SMEs in Jilin Province of China that has no intention to establish the theory based on detailed historical explanations using ethnographic or case study approach, critical paradigm was considered irrelevant for this study.

To recapitulate this research adopted positivist paradigm in validating the conceptual framework, collecting the empirical evidence and testing the research hypothesis, multiple regression analysis and hierarchical linear regression were adopted to explain the research questions as proposed in Chapter One.

4. 3　Research Equation

Based on the discussion in Chapter Three, this research planned to check the effect of the independent variables, namely, organizational justice (distributive justice, procedural justice, interactional justice), transformational leadership (idealized influence, inspirational motivation, intellectual stimulation, individualized consideration), employee emotion (surface emotion acting, deep emotion acting, true emotion acting) and organizational learning (knowledge acquisition, knowledge distribution, knowledge interpretation) on dependent variables (organizational performance of SMEs) with the mediating variable (organizational citizenship behavior). Research equations for these relationships were formed based on standard multiple regression analysis. The general mathematical equation in standard multiple regression analysis is as follows:

$$Y = \alpha + \beta_0 + \beta_1 X_1 + \beta_2 X_2 + \cdots + \beta_n X_n + \varepsilon$$

Where α: represents the y-intercept; Y: dependent variable; X: independent variable; β_n: Coefficient of data (Bata); ε: error.

Therefore, the research equations for this research are as follows:

$$OP = \alpha + \beta_1 DJ + \beta_2 PJ + \beta_3 IJ + \beta_4 II + \beta_5 IM + \beta_6 IS + \beta_7 IC + \beta_8 SEA + \beta_9 DEA + \beta_{10} TEA + \beta_{11} KA + \beta_{12} KD + \beta_{13} KI + \varepsilon$$

$$OCB = \alpha + \beta_1 DJ + \beta_2 PJ + \beta_3 IJ + \beta_4 II + \beta_5 IM + \beta_6 IS + \beta_7 IC + \beta_8 SEA + \beta_9 DEA + \beta_{10} TEA + \beta_{11} KA + \beta_{12} KD + \beta_{13} KI + \varepsilon$$

Where:

OP: organizational performance

OCB: organizational citizenship behavior

a: constant

β: regression coefficient

DJ: distributive justice

PJ: procedural justice

IJ: interactional justice

II: idealized influence

IM: inspirational motivation

IS: intellectual stimulation

IC: individualized consideration

SEA: surface emotion acting

DEA: deep emotion acting

TEA: true emotion acting

KA: knowledge acquisition

KD: knowledge distribution

KI: knowledge interpretation

The above equations show that thirteen independent variables (distributive justice, procedural justice, interactional justice, idealized influence, inspirational motivation, intellectual stimulation, individualized consideration, surface emotion acting, deep emotion acting, true emotion acting, knowledge acquisition, knowledge distribution, knowledge interpretation) were used to predict organizational performance of SMEs in

Jilin Province of China (dependent variable). The relative contribution of each independent variable was assessed in terms of regression coefficient (β) (Pallant, 2010).

In addition, according to the mediator model, the hierarchical regression analysis method was applied to investigate the influence of mediating variable (organizational citizenship behavior). Mediating is a hypothetical causal chain, one variable influences another variable, and in turn, influences the third variable. The intermediate variable M is a mediation variable. In general, when the independent variable has a significant influence on the mediation variable, and the independent variable has a significant influence on the dependent variable in the absence of the mediator, the mediator has a significant unique influence on the dependent variable. The effect of the independent variable on the dependent variable shrinks addition of the mediator to the model. (Mackinnon, Warsi & Dwyer, 1995). Figure 4.1 depicts the mediator model.

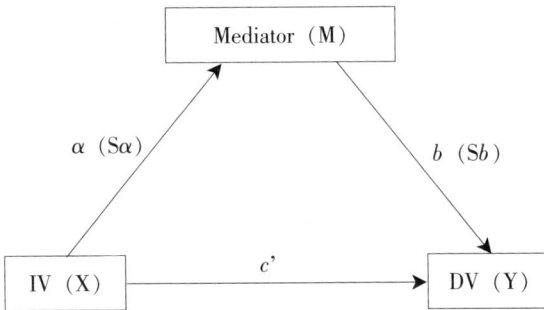

Figure 4.1 Mediator Model

Where

a, b, c' are path coefficients. α = raw (unstandardized) regression coefficient for the association between IV and mediator.

S_{α} = standard error of α

b = raw coefficient for the association between the mediator and the DV.

S_b = standard error of b

In this research the mediator variable was organizational citizenship behavior, which supposes mediate the relationships between thirteen factors of independent variables (distributive justice, procedural justice, interactional justice, idealized influence, inspirational motivation, intellectual stimulation, individualized consideration, surface emotion acting, deep emotion acting, true emotion acting, knowledge acquisition, knowledge distribution, knowledge interpretation) and organizational performance of SMEs in Jilin Province of China (dependent variable). Therefore, the research equations for the above relationship are expressed as follow:

$$X \xrightarrow{\ \alpha\ } M \xrightarrow{\ b\ } Y$$

X (independent variables): ① distributive justice; ② procedural justice; ③ interactional justice; ④ idealized influence; ⑤ inspirational motivation; ⑥ intellectual stimulation; ⑦ individualized consideration; ⑧surface emotion acting; ⑨deep emotion acting; ⑩true emotion acting; ⑪ knowledge acquisition; ⑫ knowledge distribution; and ⑬ knowledge interpretation.

M (MV): mediating variable (organizational citizenship behavior)

Y (DV): dependent variable (organizational performance of SMEs)

Hierarchical regression was used to exam the impact of employees' organizational citizenship behavior as mediating variable on the relationships between distributive justice, procedural justice, interactional justice, idealized influence, inspirational motivation, intellectual stimulation, individualized consideration, surface emotion acting, deep emotion acting, true emotion acting, knowledge acquisition, knowledge distribution, knowledge interpretation and organizational performance of SMEs in Jilin Province of China. According to the above research, this leads to the following research equation:

$$OP = \alpha + \beta_1 DJ\Delta OCB + \beta_2 PJ\Delta OCB + \beta_3 IJ\Delta OCB + \beta_4 II\Delta OCB + \beta_5 IM\Delta OCB + \beta_6 IS\Delta OCB + \beta_7 IC\Delta OCB + \beta_8 SEA\Delta OCB + \beta_9 DEA\Delta OCB + \beta_{10} TEA\Delta OCB + \beta_{11} KA\Delta OCB + \beta_{12} KD\Delta OCB + \beta_{13} KI\Delta OCB + \varepsilon$$

Where:

OP: organizational performance

OCB: organizational citizenship behavior

a: constant

β: regression coefficient

Δ = changing level

DJ: distributive justice

PJ: procedural justice

IJ: interactional justice

II: idealized influence

IM: inspirational motivation

IS: intellectual stimulation

IC: individualized consideration

SEA: surface emotion acting

DEA: deep emotion acting

TEA: true emotion acting

KA: knowledge acquisition

KD: knowledge distribution

KI: knowledge interpretation

4.4 Operational Definition and Measurement of Variables

This section discusses the operational definition and measurement of variables. As mentioned in Chapters One, Two and Three, independent variables of this research consist of thirteen motivational factors (distributive justice, procedural justice, interactional justice, idealized influence, inspirational motivation, intellectual stimulation, individualized consideration, surface emotion acting, deep emotion acting, true emotion acting, knowledge acquisition, knowledge distribution, knowledge interpretation), which were grouped under four constructs, namely, organizational justice, transformational leadership, employee emotion labor and organizational learning. The organizational performance of SMEs was the dependent variable of the research. The relationships between independent variables and dependent variable were expected to be mediated by the organizational citizenship behavior in the organizations— mediating variable. The following sections provide the operational definitional and measurement of each variable.

4.4.1　Independent Variables

As described above, the independent variables of this research are as follows: ① distributive justice; ② procedural justice; ③ interactional justice; ④idealized influence; ⑤inspirational motivation; ⑥intellectual stimulation; ⑦ individualized consideration; ⑧ surface emotion acting; ⑨deep emotion acting; ⑩true emotion acting; ⑪knowledge acquisition; ⑫ knowledge distribution; and ⑬ knowledge interpretation. Operational definitional and measurement for each independent variable is provided below.

4.4.1.1　Distributive Justice

This variable is the impartial perception of the individual's reward, it is also the evaluation of the final result of the distribution according to certain criteria. Distributive justice is employees' views on the amount of remuneration, working hours and arrangements, and the fairness of their distribution. As illustrated in Table 4.1, four items were adopted to measure this variable.

Table 4. 1   Items Constituting Distributive Justice

My work schedule is fair.

My work salary is fair compared to my job performance.

My workload is fair compared with other colleagues with the same job and duties.

The reward I receive is fair based on my contribution to the organization.

All the items were adopted from Neuhoff and Moorman (1993). The Likert seven-point scale is used in these items. The highest score (4 items × 7 points = 28 points) indicates that the respondents perceive this variable as important within an organization and lowest score (4 items × 1 point = 4 points) indicates vice versa.

4. 4. 1. 2   Procedural Justice

This variable refers to the requirement that the procedure should be open and transparent in guiding the implementation and supervision of event handling and that the parties and stakeholders should be equal in the process of event handling. As illustrated in Table 4. 2, four items were adopted to measure this variable.

Table 4. 2   Items Constituting Procedural Justice

My company's work procedure is designed in an unbiased approach.

My company can collect accurate and complete information when making job decisions.

My company's rules are applied fairly to all relevant employee.

My company provides employees with opportunities to appeal or challenge the decision.

All the items were constructed by Neuhoff and Moorman (1993). The Likert seven-point scale is used in these items. The highest score (4 items × 7 points = 28 points) indicates that the respondents perceive this variable as important within an organization and lowest score (4 items × 1 point = 4 points) indicates vice versa.

4. 4. 1. 3   Interactional Justice

This variable refers to the sense of justice of employees in the process of interaction, which includes not only the fairness of results but also a judgment respected in the process of communication and communication. As shown in Table 4. 3, four items were adopted to measure this variable.

Table 4. 3   Items Constituting Interactional Justice

My colleagues have no prejudice against me.
My colleagues treat me with kindness and respect.
My work partners are able to consider my viewpoint.
My organization provides me with timely feedback about the company decision and its implication.

All the items were adopted from Neuhoff and Moorman (1993). The Likert seven-point scale is used in these items. The highest score (4 items ×7 points = 28 points) indicates that the respondents perceive this variable as important within an organization and lowest score (4 items × 1 point = 4 points) indicates vice versa.

4. 4. 1. 4   Idealized Influence

This variable refers to behaviors that can generate trust, worship and follow from others. It comprises leaders as models of behaviour in organization, and the subordinates may acknowledge, respect and trust their leaders. These leaders always have high moral criteria and individual attractiveness, and their subordinates adored and place confidence in him. All employees approve and are favor of the plan proposed by the leaders, with highly expecting for his accomplishment. As illustrated in Table 4. 4, four items were adopted to measure this variable.

Table 4. 4　Items Constituting Idealized Influence

My leaders display a sense of power and confidence.

My leaders go beyond self-interest for the benefit for the company.

My leaders specify the importance of having a strong sense of purpose.

My leaders emphasize the importance of having a collective sense of mission.

All the items were adopted from Avolio and Bass (2014). The Likert seven-point scale is used in these items. The highest score (4 items × 7 points = 28 points) indicates that the respondents perceive this variable as important within an organization and lowest score (4 items × 1 point = 4 points) indicates vice versa.

4. 4. 1. 5　Inspirational Motivation

This factor is defined as the extent to which leaders present high expectations for their subordinates, motivate them to join the team, and make them become a part of the team to express their dreams. Actually, to accomplish team goals, teamwork and emotional appeal are usually utilized by team leaders. Consequently, the corresponding job performance becomes far better than the one that employees strive for their own benefit. As shown in Table 4. 5, four items are adopted to measure this variable.

Table 4. 5　Items Constituting Inspirational Motivation

My leaders talk optimistically about the future work task.

My leaders talk enthusiastically about what needs to be accomplished.

My leaders articulate a compelling vision of the future.

My leaders express confidence that goals will be achieved.

All the items were adopted from Avolio and Bass (2014). The Likert seven-point scale is used in these items. The highest score (4 items × 7 points = 28 points) indicates that the respondents perceive this variable as important within an organization and lowest score (4 items × 1 point =4 points) indicates vice versa.

4. 4. 1. 6　Intellectual Stimulation

This factor is thought as the way leaders encourage subordinates to improve and challenge themselves, including ingraining new thoughts into subordinates and urging subordinates to utilize new strategies to solve issues experienced in their work. Through intellectual stimulation of leaders, subordinates can stimulate and change the development of consciousness, beliefs and values. As shown in Table 4. 6, four items are used to measure this variable.

Table 4. 6　Items Constituting Intellectual Stimulation

My leaders re-examine critical assumption to question whether they are appropriate.
My leaders seek different perspectives when solving problems.
My leaders get employees to look at problems from many different angles.
My leaders suggest new ways of looking at how to complete assignments.

All the items were adopted from Avolio and Bass (2014). The Likert seven-point scale is used in these items. The highest score (4 items × 7 points = 28 points) indicates that the respondents perceive this variable as important within an organization and lowest score (4 items × 1 point = 4 points) indicates vice versa.

4. 4. 1. 7　Individualized Consideration

This variable refers to leaders looking after each subordinate, emphasizing personal needs, abilities and aspirations, listening patiently and meticulously, and carrying out different training and guidance to subordinates according to the different situations and needs of subordinates. Transformational leaders, such as coaches and consultants, help employees grow in the face of challenges. As shown in Table 4. 7, four items were used to measure this variable.

Table 4. 7 Items Constituting Individualized Consideration

My leaders spend time teaching and coaching me.
My leaders treat employees as individuals rather than just as a member of the group.
My leaders consider each individual as having different needs, abilities and aspirations from employees.
My leaders help employees to develop their strengths.

All the items were adopted from Avolio and Bass (2014). The highest score (4 items × 7 points = 28 points) indicates that the respondents perceive this variable as important within an organization and lowest score (4 items × 1 point = 4 points) indicates vice versa.

4. 4. 1. 8 Surface Emotion Acting

This variable refers to a way in which an employee suppresses the true emotions felt by the individual and pretends to express the emotions required by the organization. It is a kind of "wearing a mask" camouflage, although the surface play means the inner feeling and the external expression. Inconsistency, but it is an effective strategy because when an individual cannot change his/her inner feeling, he/she needs to work on the surface. As shown in Table 4. 8, four items were adopted to measure this variable.

Table 4. 8 Items Constituting Surface Emotion Acting

I show a good mood when interacting with people at work even if my inner feeling is not like that.
I hide my true emotion in order to express the right emotion at work.
I put on an act in order to deal with customers in an appropriate way.
I show the emotion that I need at work but I will not change my inner feeling.

The items were adopted from Diefendorff, J. M. (2005). The Likert seven-point scale is used in these items. The highest score (4 items × 7 points = 28 points) indicates that the respondents perceive this variable as important within an organization and lowest score (4 items × 1 point =4 points) indicates vice versa.

4. 4. 1. 9　Deep Emotion Acting

This variable refers to a way for employees to adjust their subjective experience and inner expression in order to show appropriate emotions. It is a proactive process. When an individual's inner feelings are inconsistent with an organization's performance rules, the individual is active. The internal psychological processes such as thinking, imagination and memory make the real emotional experience consistent with the emotions that need to be expressed and are manifested through behaviors. As shown in Table 4. 9, four items were adopted to measure this variable.

Table 4. 9　Items Constituting Deep Emotion Acting

I make an effort to actually feel the emotions that I need to display toward others.
I try to talk myself out of negative feelings at work and show kind attitude.
I work at developing the feelings inside of me that I need to show to customers.
I try to actually experience the emotions that I must show when interacting with people around me at work.

The items were adopted from Diefendorff, J. M. (2005). The Likert seven-point scale is used in these items. The highest score (4 items × 7 points = 28 points) indicates that the respondents perceive this variable as important within an organization and lowest score (4 items × 1 point = 4 points) indicates vice versa.

4. 4. 1. 10　True Emotion Acting

This variable refers to the employee's natural expression of the emotions experienced in the workplace. The employee does not need to disguise himself or adjust the emotions in order to achieve the emotions required for the work. It is the natural feeling of the employees' internal expression. As illustrated in Table 4. 10, three items were adopted to measure this variable.

Table 4.10   Items Constituting True Emotion Acting

The emotions I show at work match what I truly feel.

Emotions I need to show to do my job are what I actually feel.

I can express my emotion naturally and easily at work.

All the items were adopted from Diefendorff, J. M. (2005). The Likert seven-point scale is used in these items. The highest score (3 items × 7 points = 21 points) indicates that the respondents perceive this variable as important within an organization and lowest score (3 items × 1 point = 3 points) indicates vice versa.

4.4.1.11   Knowledge Acquisition

This variable refers to the ability of employees to develop, create and experience skills, perspectives and relationships in the workplace to ensure effective and efficient operations of the organization. As shown in Table 4.11, three items were adopted to measure this variable.

Table 4.11   Items Constituting Knowledge Acquisition

My company's employees can attend meetings and exhibitions regularly to get knowledge.

My company has consolidated and resourceful research and development policy to acquire knowledge.

New ideas and approaches on work performance are experimented continuously.

The items were adopted from Huber (1991). The Likert seven-point scale is used in these items. The highest score (3 items × 7 points = 21 points) indicates that the respondents perceive this variable as important within an organization and lowest score (3 items × 1 point = 3 points) indicates vice versa.

4.4.1.12   Knowledge Distribution

This variable refers to the ability of the employees to diffuse knowledge that they have learned in the organization, to obtain knowledge from formal mechanisms or to seek clarification from professional individuals. As shown in Table 4. 12, three items were used to measure this variable.

Table 4. 12   Items Constituting Knowledge Distribution

My company has formal mechanisms to guarantee the sharing of the best practices among the different fields of the activity.

My company has individuals who take part in several teams or divisions and who also act as links among project groups.

My company has individuals that dedicate to collecting, assembling and distributing internal employees' suggestions.

The items were adopted from Huber (1991). The Likert seven-point scale is used in these items. The highest score (3 items × 7 points = 21 points) indicates that the respondents perceive this variable as important within an organization and lowest score (3 items × 1 point = 3 points) indicates vice versa.

4. 4. 1. 13   Knowledge Interpretation

This variable refers to the interpretation and integration of learning. The employees use knowledge to achieve a common goal, which can be widely used and adapted to new situations, in a team. As shown in Table 4. 13, three items were used to measure this variable.

Table 4. 13   Items Constituting Knowledge Interpretation

All the members of my organization share the same aim to which they feel committed.

Employees share knowledge and experiences to finish a common goal by talking to each other.

Teamwork is a very common practice in my company.

The items were adopted from Huber (1991). The Likert seven-point scale is used in these items. The highest score (3 items × 7 points = 21 points) indicates that the respondents perceive this variable as important within an organization and lowest score (3 items × 1 point = 3 points) indicates vice versa.

4. 4. 2   Mediating Variable—Organizational Citizenship Behavior

Organizational citizenship behavior is the mediating variable which refers to employees' actions and activities that benefit the organization but have not been explicitly or directly confirmed in the formal compensation system of the organization. The actions promote organizational development and improve individual performance. As illustrated in Table 4. 14, twenty items were adopted to measure organizational citizenship behavior.

Table 4. 14   Items Constituting Organizational Citizenship Behavior

I am willing to stand up to protect the reputation of the company.

I am eager to tell outsiders good news about the company and clarify their misunderstandings.

I make constructive suggestions that can improve the operation of the company.

I actively attend company meetings.

I am willing to assist new colleagues to adjust to the work environment.

I am willing to help colleague solve work-related problems.

I am willing to cover work assignments for colleagues when needed.

I am willing to coordinate and communicate with colleagues.

I think interpersonal harmony is more important than personal influence and gains in the organization.

I do not use position power to pursue personal gains.

I do not ignore my colleagues' accusations and suggestions for my own benefit.

I do not speak weakness of the supervisor or colleagues behind their backs.

I do not use work time to do anything private (trading stocks, shopping etc.).

I do not use company resources to do personal thing (company phones, copy machines, computers and cars).

I do not take sick leave and make excuse for anything private.

I comply with company rules and procedures even when nobody watches and no evidence can be traced.

I take my job seriously and rarely make mistakes.

I am willing to take on new or challenging assignments.

I try hard to self-study to increase the quality of work outputs.

I often arrive early and start to work immediately.

All the items were adopted from Farh J. L. (1997). The Likert seven-point scale is used in these items. The highest score (20 items × 7 points = 140 points) indicates that the respondents perceive this variable as important within an organization and lowest score (20 items × 1 point = 20 points) indicates vice versa.

4. 4. 3　Dependent Variable—Organizational Performance

Organizational performance is the dependent variable and was defined as the achievement of organizational goals, for example, employee satisfaction, profit, organizational productivity, customer satisfaction with the organization and others. As shown in Table 4. 15, use seven items to investigate this variable.

Table 4. 15　Items Constituting Organizational Performance

My organization has made good use of knowledge and skills in looking for ways to become more efficient.

My company's employee productivity has improved.

The quality of work performed by my current coworkers in work group is high.

The occurrence of goal attainment is very high in my organization.

The company's after-tax net income growth rate has been increased.

The company's image is better than that of the competitors.

The customer satisfaction toward my organization is very high.

All the items were adopted from Wang, F. J. (2010). The Likert seven-point scale is used in these items. The highest score (7 items × 7 points = 49 points) indicates that the respondents perceive this variable as important within an organization and lowest score (7 items × 1 point = 7 points) indicates vice versa.

4. 5   Data Collection

This section discusses the methods adopted to collect data for this research. As mentioned above, the data for this research was collected by survey methods. Therefore, the following sections will describe and define the methods involved in the survey study.

4. 5. 1   Data Gathering

The survey is viewed to be a popular data collection tool for quantitative researchers (Fowler, 2009). Moreover, it is one of the most common methods of data collection for checking employee involvement in organizational activities (Selamat, et al. , 2015; Jain & Jeppesen, 2013; Amayah, 2013).

The survey research is suitable for the analysis units of this study, which were employees in the SMEs in Jilin Province of China. Dwivedi (2005) suggests that when the unit of analysis is an individual rather than an organization, survey methods are more preferable than the other.

This is because of several research issues such as convenience, cost, time and accessibility (Dwivedi, 2005; Gilbert, 2001). In other words, survey approach facilitates data collection from the majority of respondents within a short period of time, which was the main gist of this research (Fowler, 2009; Zikmund, 2003). In addition, since this study involved hypotheses testing and validation of conceptual framework, survey approach was considered the most suitable one (Dwivedi, 2005). This was applicable to this study since, as discussed in Chapter Three, it has conceptual framework and hypotheses.

To recapitulate, survey was the most appropriate and feasible approach for this research. This resulted in the use of questionnaire. The discussion on the survey instrument development process is offered in

Chapter Five.

4. 5. 2　Population

The respondents of this study were employees in the SMEs in Jilin Province of China. They were selected because of some salient reasons: ①SMEs in China are on the rise and are becoming an important foundation for the national economy and also have a broader development perspective; ②Jilin Province is an inland province and has a relatively slow economic development. However, with the current support of the government, Jilin Province experiences a rapid economic growth; and ③ SMEs in Jilin Province are expected to contribute significantly to China's GDP in the future.

In 2019, there are 1,354 SMEs in Jilin Province of China (Miao, 2019). Due to time and resource constraints, the study was conducted at five major cities in Jilin Province, namely, Changchun, Songyuan, Siping, Baicheng and Dehui. In these cities, there are 351 companies that can be considered as SMEs. These companies involve in various industry such as healthcare industry, trade industry, agriculture industry, restaurant and catering industry, transportation industry, education industry, building industry and manufacturing industry. The number of employees was about 11, 000. This research conducted a disproportionate stratified random sampling when distributing the questionnaires.

4. 5. 3　Sample Size

The ideal sample size depends on the type of research involved (Sekaran & Bougie, 2010). Gay and Airasian (2000) suggested that the minimum number of subjects of the sample for descriptive research should be between 10% and 20% of the population, depending on how large the total population is. Byrne (2010) stated that the minimum sample size is five respondents per item (i. e. 5 : 1), namely, the number of sample is at least 5 times bigger. As illustrated in Appendix, the total number of items of this research questionnaire was 75. Thus, according to the views of Byrne (2010) and Hair, et al. (2006), the target sample size of this research was at least 375 (76 ×5) respondents. Another option to calculate the sample size is by using a formula (Nei, 2007). The following formula was used to calculate the sample size of this research:

$$n \geqslant \frac{N}{(\frac{\alpha}{k})^2 \frac{N-1}{P(1-P)} + 1}$$

N is the total number of samples, and P is usually set at 0.5, because setting it at 0.5 gives the most reliable sample size (Nei, 2007). In the field of industry and social science, when the significance level is set as 0.05 ($\alpha = 0.05$), the confidence level used for interval estimation is $1-\alpha = 0.95$, and $k = 1.96$ (Wu, 2018). Thus, the sample size is equal to:

$$n \geqslant \frac{11000}{(\frac{0.05}{1.96})^2 \frac{11000-1}{0.5(1-0.5)} + 1} = \frac{11000}{29.74} \approx 369$$

After comparing the above two techniques of calculating sample size, the researcher decided to take a sample size of 400 respondents. This was to be more confident in meeting the requirement of statistical techniques.

4.5.4 Survey Procedure

As stated above, this study adopted disproportionate stratified random sampling to collect data from the SMEs' employees in Jilin Province of China. The stratified random sampling is a method of sampling that refers to the standard of the population group that is called strata. The strata of this research were types of industries in Jilin Province of China—as stated above (healthcare industry, trade industry, agriculture industry, restaurant and catering industry, transportation industry, education industry, building industry and manufacturing industry). According to

Gay and Airasian (2000), random sampling is a method in which all individuals have equal and independent opportunities to be selected as subjects in the selected population. The ease of use factor represents the biggest advantage of random sampling. In short, disproportionate stratified random sampling was used to collect data from different industries in Jilin Province of China. As stated above, the total of 400 employees in SMEs across Jilin Province of China were randomly selected.

Collecting data on-line is very helpful nowadays due to factors such as low data collection cost and easy administrations (Huang, 2014). Using the online survey is a good strategy for feedback from the respondents who are dissatisfied with a service or who have strong concerns. Most of time, the online survey is convenient for the respondents, they can complete them when and where they prefer. The respondent also can spend as much time on the survey as they need, which results in more detailed responses. Due to the size of Jilin Province of China, which is big and has 21 municipal districts, online survey can provide a broad demographic profile and ensure more accurate samples to collect targeted data. The online survey has a high precision rate if the questionnaires are returned at the same time or nearly the same time.

However, there are some disadvantages with the online survey. For example, it takes much more time to conduct an online survey than phone survey. This is because the respondents are essentially on their own. The respondents can skip whichever questions that they do not want to answer. This results in high level of abandoned and incomplete survey. Due to all these features, the online survey is typically not used for the complex issues. Furthermore, there is a possibility that respondents' answers are impacted by other persons. Nevertheless, those problems are beyond the researchers' control.

After considering the advantages and disadvantages of the online survey, the following two strategies were adopted when online survey was conducted in this research: ① the researcher visited the SMEs in Jilin Province and distributed the questionnaires to the respondents (30% of total distributed questionnaires) ; and ② the survey was conducted with qualified employees via online platform (70% of total distributed questionnaïres). These two strategies were adopted to meet the needs of some particular questions in the questionnaire.

4.5.5   Administration and Field Work

This questionnaire was self-designed based on the literature and had been evaluated and revised by the experts during content validity, pre-test and pilot study. The respondents were asked to answer and return the questionnaires within four weeks to the researcher (most were through online to the researcher's address). Data collection was stopped when the sample size had achieved sufficient level for statistical analyses. The data collection period took approximately four months from October 2019 to January 2020.

4.6   Data Analysis

In this research, the collected data of research being analyzed statistically for social research (SPSS) version 20.0 SPSS was selected for which provide the powerful and energetic support of data analysis, such as descriptive statistics, chi-square tests, independent sample, t-tests, factor analysis, reliability analysis and standard multiple regression analysis (Pallant, 2010). This research data analysis involved four stages, namely, data examination, a goodness of measures, descriptive statistics, and standard multiple regression analysis. The definition and description of each stage are showed in the following subsections.

4.6.1   Data Examination

Data examing is the first step in the data analysis. It includes two stages: namely, data screening and data testing, which conform to the multivariate assumption. This is to ensure the collected data were ready for multivariate analyses, for instance, factor analysis and multiple regression analysis (Hair, et al. , 2006).

4. 6. 1. 1　Data Screening

Data screening is a process of examining the data for error and correction, after data collection, to screen the raw data and identify the outliers and dealing with the missing data. Data screening is a significant step for data analysis. Three tests were performed for data screening. They were missing data, response bias, and outlier identification. (Hair, et al. , 2006)

4. 6. 1. 1. 1　Missing Data

Missing data can be defined as valid values on one or more variables are not available for analysis. Two options are available when dealing with missing data. If the sample is adequate, the questionnaires that have missing data will be deleted from this research. However, if excluding the questionnaires that have missing data results in inadequate sample size for statistical analyses, remedies for missing data will be applied such as mean substitution method (Hair, et al. , 2006).

4. 6. 1. 1. 2　Response Bias

Response bias test is performed to examine whether there is a significant difference between early and late response groups. For this purpose, the early response group was coded as 1 and the late response group was coded as 2. A period of four weeks was utilized as a benchmark to demarcate between the two groups. This four-week period is considered to be adequate for the respondents to complete and return the questionnaires to the researcher. *Chi*-square tests and independent sample *t*-tests were run to both groups. The *chi*-square test was conducted for categorical variables (demographic profiles) of respondents such as gender, age, number of years as lecturers, and number of years working in the university. Independent sample *t*-tests were conducted on study variables. Significant values ($p < 0.05$) for both tests indicate the existence of response bias while non-significant values ($p > 0.05$) indicate vice versa (Coakes & Steed, 2003; Pallant, 2010).

4. 6. 1. 1. 3　Outliers Identification

Outliers are observation with a unique combination of characteristics identifiable as distinctly different from the other observations (Hair, et al., 2006). This research used multiple regression procedure to detect both univariate outliers on dependent variable and multivariate outliers on independent variables (Coakes & Steed, 2003). Univariate outliers can be detected using studentized residuals. Studentized residuals are z-scores computed for a case based on the data for all other cases in the data set (Coakes & Steed, 2003). Coakes and Steed (2003) suggested that a case in the data set is univariate outlier if the z-score for studentized residual is greater than ± 3.0. Meanwhile, multivariate outliers can be detected by inspecting Mahalanobis distances that are presented in the data set (Pallant, 2010). To identify which cases are multivariate outliers, the researcher determines the critical *chi*-square value using the number of independent variables as the degree of freedom at alpha level of 0.001 (Pallant, 2010; Tabachnick & Fidell, 2007). In this study, there are 6 independent variables, therefore, the critical value is 31.26 (Tabachnick & Fidell, 2007). Any of the cases in the data set that have a Mahalanobis distance value exceeding this value is designated as multivariate outlier. The identified univariate and multivariate outliers will be removed from this research.

4.6.1.2 Data Testing—Tests on Multivariate Assumptions

Multivariate assumption tests are foundations for making conclusions and providing statistical results. They are also pre-requisite before factor analysis and standard multiple regression analysis can be performed. Multivariate assumptions has four tests in following sections (Hair, et al., 2006).

4.6.1.2.1 Normality

The first multivariate assumption is normality. Data normality test is important to assess whether score for each variable is normally distributed or not (Hair, et al., 2006). This research utilized statistics for skewness and kurtosis to assess the normality of data because they are appropriate for interval level data (Coakes & Steed, 2003). Skewness and kurtosis refer to the shape of the distribution (Coakes & Steed,

2003). Positive values for skewness indicate a positive skew, while positive values for kurtosis indicate a distribution that is peaked. Besides, negative values for skewness indicate a negative skew, while negative values for kurtosis indicate a distribution that is flatter (Coakes & Steed, 2003). Normality of data is assumed when statistics for skewness and kurtosis are less than ± 2.58 (Hair, et al., 2006). However, when the statistics for skewness and kurtosis are more than ± 2.58, transformation is an option that is available to the researcher (Coakes & Steed, 2003).

4. 6. 1. 2. 2　Linearity

The second test is linearity that satisfies the multivariate assumption. The function of linearity test is to evaluate whether the relationship between the independent and dependent variables of this research is linear or otherwise. This research used residual scatterplots to test this assumption (Coakes & Steed, 2003). From the scatterplot of residuals against predicted values, assumption of linearity is achieved if there is no clear relationship between the residuals and the predicted values (Coakes & Steed, 2003).

4. 6. 1. 2. 3　Homoscedasticity

The next multivariable assumption is homoscedasticity. Homoscedasticity is defined by assuming that dependent variables show similar variance levels within the range of independent variables. (Hair, et al., 2006). For this purpose, Levene test was conducted on the metric variables against the non-metric variable (gender) of this research (Hair, et al., 2006). Homoscedasticity assumption is achieved if the relationship between the metric and non-metric variable is not significant ($p > 0.001$). Meanwhile, the data is said to be heteroscedastic if the relationship between these variables is significant ($p < 0.001$) (Hair, et al., 2006; Coakes & Steed, 2003).

4. 6. 1. 2. 4　Multicollinearity

The last multivariate assumption is multicollinearity. Multicollinearity is defined as high correlations amongst two or more independent variables (Hair, et al., 2006). Hair, et al. (2006) argued that the existence of multicollinearity negatively affects the predictive power of each independent variable. This research used Pearson product-moment correlation coefficient, tolerance and variation inflation factor (VIF) to trace if data suffers with the problem of multicollinearity. Based on Pearson product-moment correlation coefficient, multicollinearity problem exists if the correlation between independent variables is above 0.8 (Hair, et al., 2006). According to the tolerance and VIF, data suffers multicollinearity problem if the tolerance value is below a common cutoff threshold value, which is 0.1. This value corresponds to a VIF value of 10 as recommended by Hair, et al. (2006).

4.6.2   Goodness of Measures

The second stage of data analysis of this study was to construct the goodness of measures for testing the research hypotheses. To achieve this, the data of this study were initially submitted for factor analysis. Then, the internal consistency of each factor is checked by reliability analysis.

4.6.2.1   Factor Analysis

After examining data, the next stage of data analysis was factor analysis. This analysis is critical for testing the basic patterns or relationships of a large number of variables and determining whether information can be concentrated or aggregated among a small set of factors or components and to determine the most parsimonious set of factors (Gerbing & Anderson, 1988; Hair, et al., 2006).

Factor analysis was also used to assess the construct validity of the study variables. Constructive validity refers to the extent to which a set of test items actually reflects the theoretical underlying structure that these items are designed to measure. In other words, it deals with the accuracy of measurements (Hair, et al., 2006). It also provides confidence that item measures from a sample represent the actual true score that exists in the population (Hair, et al., 2006). Construct validity can be divided into convergent validity and discriminant validity. Convergent validity refers to projects that are indicators of a particular factor, which should converge or share a higher proportion of variance (Hair, et al. , 2006). At the same time, discriminating effectiveness refers to the extent to which a factor is truly different from other factors (Hair, et al. , 2006). This means that high discriminant validity provides a structure that is the only evidence and captures phenomena that are not available in other metrics. (Hair, et al. , 2006). In this study, by examining the factor load, the structural validity of the convergence validity and discriminant validity are established to ensure that, once the cross-loader is removed, the items will be cleanly loaded onto the load factors they placed without cross-loading onto the load factors they should not load (Straub, et al. , 2004).

Several statistical values in factor analysis were observed to examine whether the items are suitable to be factor analyzed. The first criterion is the inverse image correlation matrix. This matrix is used to assess the sampling adequacy of each items (Coakes & Steed, 2003). Items with a sampling adequacy below the acceptable level of 0.5 should be excluded from the analysis (Coakes & Steed, 2003). The second criterion is Kaiser-Meyer-Okin (KMO), the measure of sampling adequacy for overall items (Coakes & Steed, 2003; Hair, et al. , 2006). If the KMO value is greater than 0.6, the factorability is assumed (Coakes & Steed, 2003; Hair, et al. , 2006). The last criterion was the Bartlett test of Sphericity (BTOS), a statistical test for the presence of correlations amongst variables (Hair, et al. , 2006). A large and significant BTOS (*sig.* < 0.05) indicates that sufficient correlations exist amongst the variables to proceed with the factor analysis (Coakes & Steed, 2003; Hair, et al. , 2006).

Once the items are suitable to be factor analyzed, the next step of factor analysis is to select the factor extraction and rotational methods (Coakes & Steed, 2003; Hair, et al. , 2006). The factor extraction method of this study was Principal Component Analysis (PCA) while Varimax was the factor rotational method. PCA with a Varimax rotation is the appropriate approach because the purpose of factor analysis in this research is to summarize most of the original information (variance) in a minimum number of factors for prediction purposes (Coakes & Steed, 2003; Hair, et al. , 2006). The data that have the same uniqueness are grouped as one construct. In other words, PCA with a Varimax rotation is the most desirable method when the research goal is to reduce the data to a smaller number of variables or a set of unrelated metrics for later use in other multivariate techniques (Hair, et al. , 2006).

This research used several criteria to interpret the factors. First, eigenvalues of the factors should exceed 1. 0. The factors with eigenvalues greater than 1. 0 are considered significant (Hair, et al. , 2006). Second, the derived factors should have a cumulative percentage of variance explained of 60% or higher (Hair, et al. , 2006). Third, values of rotated factor loading should exceed ±0. 5. The factor loadings value greater than ± 0. 5 are considered practically significant and appropriate for interpretation of structure for a sample size of around 200 (Hair, et al. , 2006). The next interpretation criterion was all items should have high (significant) loadings only on a single factor. When items are found to have more than one significant loading, they are termed as cross-loading. A cross-loading item is an item that loads at 0. 35 or higher on two or more factors (Hair, et al. , 2006). In this study, items that cross-load will be eliminated to avoid difficulty when interpreting the factor loading matrix (Hair, et al. , 2006; Singhapakdi, Marta, Rallapalli, et al. 2000). Once all the significant loadings have been identified, the last criterion was to assess the communalities of items. Hair, et al. (2006) argued that communality is important to assess whether the items meet acceptable levels of explanation or not. In this case, items should generally have communalities of greater than 0. 5 to be retained in the analysis (Hair, et al. , 2006).

Once an acceptable factor solution is obtained, all of which have a significant load on a factor, the next step is to assign a name or label to a factor that accurately reflects the items loading on that factor. However, this step is not required if the items do load onto their original factors (Hemdi, 2005).

4. 6. 2. 2 Reliability Analysis

Reliability analysis is undertaken to determine how well the items measuring a concept link together as a set (Sekaran, 2003). This analysis is important to assess the quality of the survey instrument (Churchill, 1979). This research used Cronbach's alpha value to estimate the internal consistency of items in the instrument. This approach was selected since Cronbach's alpha is an adequate test of internal consistency reliability in almost every case (Churchill, 1979; Sekaran, 2003). The nearer Cronbach's alpha value to 1, the higher the internal consistency reliability is (Sekaran, 2003). The generally agreed upon lower limit for Cronbach's alpha value is 0. 6 (Hair, et al. , 2006). Therefore, the variables (or factors) should be deleted from the analysis when the Cronbach's alpha values are less than 0. 6 (Hair, et al. , 2006).

4. 6. 3 Descriptive Statistics

The third stage of data analysis of this research was descriptive statistics. The purposes of descriptive statistics in this research are to explain the trend of the gathered data (Pallant, 2010). Frequencies and percentages were calculated to describe the profile of research respondents such as gender, age, work times. Minimum and maximum scores, mean scores and standard deviations were computed to describe the study variables.

4. 6. 4 Profile of the Respondents

The fourth stage of the data analysis of this study was profile of the respondents. Summarized the demographic profiles on type of industry, gender, age, educational level, and work experience. And frequency and percentage were calculated to describe the profile of the study subjects.

4. 6. 5　Correlation Analysis

The fifth stage of data analysis of this research was correlation analysis. The purpose of undertaking correlation analysis in this research is to distinguish the factors that have correlative relationships amongst variables (Hair, et al. , 2006). In this case, correlation coefficient shows level of relationship between independent and dependent variables. The number of Pearson correlation represents correlation coefficient (Hair, et al, 2006). It is in the range between -1.00 to $+1.00$, with zero indicating no correlation between the two metric variables. Coefficient value of more than 0. 5 indicates stronger correlation whereas coefficient value of between 0. 5 and 0. 2 indicates medium or modest correlation. Coefficient value of less than 0. 2 is considered as weak correlation. However, correlation coefficients of more than 0. 8 (very strong correlation) could produce multicollinearity issue (Berry & Feldman, 1985). Cohen (1988) proposed the following guiding principles for the influence of correlation coefficients in research: ①large: $r = 0.5$; ②medium: $r = 0.3 \sim 0.49$; ③small: $r = 0.1 \sim 0.29$.

4. 6. 6　Hierarchical Linear Regressions

Lastly, the hierarchical linear regressions were utilized to measure the linkage between independent variables (distributive justice, procedural justice, interactional justice, idealized influence, intellectual stimulation, inspirational motivation, individualized consideration, true emotion acting, surface emotion acting, deep emotion acting, knowledge acquisition, knowledge distribution, knowledge interpretation), dependent variable (organizational performance of SMEs) and mediating variable (organizational citizenship behavior). If it is statistically significant, such model is considered significantly mediated (Hair, et al. , 2006; Baron & Kenny, 1986). This research considered in regards to mediator that: ①independent variables are related to dependent variable significantly; ②independent variables are related to mediating variable significantly; ③ when independent variables and mediating variable are regressed against dependent variable, mediating variable is significant (Ramayah, 2011; Baron & Kenny, 1986); and ④ in view of the fact from third step, if the beta value of independent decrease or increase, if it is still significant hence partial mediation or full mediation occurs and such model is considered significantly mediated (Hair, et al. , 2006; Baron & Kenny, 1986).

4.7 Summary

This chapter defines and describes the adopted research approach of this study. The discussions include the advantage and disadvantage and the serviceability of each adopted techniques. This chapter discusses the research formula, operational definition, measurement, data collection and data analysis. The discussion on research instrument, data aggregation and data analysis of this research is to ensure understanding of the research. Overall, it could be said that the decision to adopt quantitative survey approach suited research questions, objectives and statistical analyses of this research. In the next chapter, the instrument development process is presented.

Chapter Five   Survey Instrument Development

5.1   Introduction

This chapter offers a discussion on the process of developing survey instrument of this study. This discussion is divided into two sections, namely, the general appearance of questionnaire and refinement of the questionnaires. Finally, the content of the fifth chapter is summarized.

5.2   General Appearance of the Questionnaire

According to Sekaran (2003), besides focusing on wording and measurement, it is also important to consentrate on how the questionnaire should look like. The following strategies were adopted to enhance the respondents' motivation in completing the questionnaire. First, a cover letter that discloses the researcher's identity, conveys the aim and importance of the questionnaire survey and mentions about the confidentiality of the information provided by the respondents was attached to the questionnaire (Sekaran, 2003). Second, the items were grouped based on content similarity and areas (Dillman, 1978; Sekaran, 2003). Third, the items in the questionnaire were arranged in descending order in terms of importance and usefulness (Dillman, 1978). Fourth, the instructions on how to complete the items in each section were provided (Sekaran, 2003). Last but not least, a courteous note was also stated at the end of the questionnaire.

Since the range of possible responses for a scale can vary, all items for dependent, independent and mediating variables of this research were measured using Likert seven-point scale from 1 (strong disagree) to 7 (strong agree). The scale was utilized since it is one of the most commonly used point scales to capture information on a range of phenomena in social science research (Dawes, 2008; Malhotra & Peterson, 2006; Tannenbaum, 1997). Dawes (2008) argued that previous simulation and empirical studies have generally concurred that using the seven-point scale has better reliability and validity than using the smaller scale. Dawes further argued that in relation to the distribution of data, more scale points (for instance, seven versus five points scales) offer more selections for the respondents and would lead to a greater spread of the data and larger variance (Dawes, 2008).

The final questionnaire of this study is illustrated in Appendix. The questionnaire has 75 variable items, five demographic questions on four-page double-sided paper using Chinese as the command language and in a booklet form. It was divided into Part A and Part B. The Part A are as following sections: (A) Distributive Justice; (B) Procedural Justice; (C) Interactional Justice; (D) Idealized Influence; (E) Inspirational Motivation; (F) Intellectual Stimulation; (G) Individualized Consideration; (H) Surface Emotion Acting; (I) Deep Emotion Acting; (J) True Emotion Acting; (K) Knowledge Acquisition; (L) Knowledge Distribution; (M) Knowledge Interpretation; (N) Organizational Citizenship Behavior; (O) Organizational Performance; and Part B: Demographic Information.

5.2.1   Section A: Distributive Justice

This section requires respondents to evaluate the extent that employee receives fairness of distribution of award and salary as well as the workload and working hours. It consists of four items that were adopted and adjusted from Neuhoff & Moorman (1993). Four items of distributive justice were measured by using Likert Seven Points Scales.

5.2.2　Section B：Procedural Justice

This section requires the respondents to rate the extent that the degree of fairness in the design of the system and the system is open in the implementation and supervision of the handling of the guiding events, and the system can be implemented fairly to each employee. It consists of four items that were adopted from Neuhoff & Moorman (1993). Four items of procedural justice were measured by using Likert Seven Points Scales.

5.2.3　Section C：Interactional Justice

This section requires the respondents to rate the extent that feeling of fairness in the process of interaction between colleagues include not only the fairness of results but also the respect they receive in the process of interaction and communication. It consists of four items that were adopted from Neuhoff & Moorman (1993). Four items of interactional justice were measured by using Likert Seven Points Scales.

5.2.4　Section D：Idealized Influence

This section requires respondents to evaluate the extent to which leaders use team spirit and emotional support to unite their subordinates to finish organizational goals and tasks. It consists of four items that were adopted from Avolio & Bass (2014). Four items of idealized influence were measured by using Likert Seven Points Scales.

5.2.5　Section E：Inspirational Motivation

This section requires the respondents to assess the level of leader's personal qualities and talents. It consists of four items that were adopted from Avolio & Bass (2014). Four items of inspirational motivation were measured by using Likert Seven Points Scales.

5.2.6　Section F：Intellectual Stimulation

This section requires the respondents to assess the extent to which leadership motivates the formation of subordinate consciousness, beliefs and values. It consists of four items that were adopted from Avolio & Bass (2014). Four items of intellectual stimulation were measured by using Likert Seven Points Scales.

5. 2. 7　Section G: Individualized Consideration

This section requires the respondents to assess the extent to which leaders care about each subordinate and value personal needs, abilities and aspirations. It consists of four items that were adopted from Avolio & Bass (2014). Four items of individualized consideration were measured by using Likert Seven Points Scales.

5. 2. 8　Section H: Surface Emotion Acting

This section requires the respondents to rate the extent about showing emotions needed at work rather than expressing real deep feelings. It consists of four items that were adopted from Diefendorff J. M. (2005). Four items of surface emotion acting were measured by using Likert Seven Points Scales.

5. 2. 9　Section I: Deep Emotion Acting

This section requires respondents to assess the level of emotion that employees strive to adjust their inner feelings to meet organizational needs. It consists of four items that were adopted from Diefendorff J. M. (2005). Four items of deep emotion acting were measured by using Likert Seven Points Scales.

5. 2. 10　Section J: True Emotion Acting

This section requires respondents to assess the level of emotion that employees naturally experienced in the workplace. It consists of three items that were adopted from Diefendorff J. M. (2005). Three items of true emotion acting were measured by using Likert Seven Points Scales.

5. 2. 11　Section K: Knowledge Acquisition

This section requires respondents to rate their ability to develop, create and experience skills, perspectives and relationships in the workplace to ensure effective and efficient operations of the organization. It consists of three items that were adopted from Huber (1991). Three items of knowledge acquisition were measured by using Likert Seven Points Scales.

5. 2. 12   Section L: Knowledge Distribution

This section requires respondents to rate their ability to diffuse knowledge that they have learned in the organization, to obtain knowledge from formal mechanisms or to seek clarification from professional individuals. It consists of three items that were adopted from Huber (1991). Three items of knowledge distribution were measured by using Likert Seven Points Scales.

5. 2. 13   Section M: Knowledge Interpretation

This section requires respondents to rate their ability to use knowledge to achieve a common goal and to adapt to new situations in a team. It consists of three items that were adopted from Huber (1991). Three items of knowledge interpretation were measured by using Likert Seven Points Scales.

5. 2. 14   Section N: Organizational Citizenship Behavior

This section requires respondents to evaluate their ability to do actions and activities that benefit the organization but have not been explicitly or directly confirmed in the formal compensation system of the organization. It consists of twenty items that were adopted from Farh J. L. (1997). Twenty items of organizational citizenship behavior were measured by using Likert Seven Points Scales.

5. 2. 15   Section O: Organizational Performance

This section requires the respondents to evaluate the achievement of organizational goals in terms of employee satisfaction, profit, organizational productivity, customer satisfaction with the organization and others. It consists of seven items that were adopted from Wang F. J. (2010). Seven items of organizational performance were measured by using Likert Seven Points Scales.

5. 2. 16 Demographic Information

This section contains six demographic questions to identify the type of industry, gender, age, education level, the number of years working in the current company of the respondents and the respondents' position. Gender was measured using nominal scale (male and female) (as suggested by Sekaran, 2003). Ordinal scale was used to measure age (20 years and below, 21 ~ 30 years, 31 ~ 40 years, 41 ~ 50 years, 51 ~ 60 years and 61 years and above), educational level (high school and below, college, bachelor, master, phD and others) type of industry (industry, trade, education, health-care, hotel and restaurant, agriculture and others) (as suggested by Sekaran, 2003).

5. 3   Refinement of the Questionnaire

Several scholars suggested that the reliability and validity of the developed items need to be evaluated in the questionnaire (Sekaran, 2003; Straub, 2004). Thus, before gathering the primary data, several steps were implemented to further refine the questionnaire of this research. The researcher undertook three steps, which were content validity, pre-testing and pilot study for improving the reliability and validity of the research questionnaire. This strategy is in tandem with the one that was suggested by Sekaran (2003) and Straub (2004). Table 5. 1 summarizes the list of study variables included in the various stages of refinement of the questionnaire.

Table 5. 1　List of Study Variables Included in the Various Stages of Refinement of the Questionnaire

No. Study Variables	Content Validity	Pre-testing	Pilot Study
1. Distributive Justice	Yes	Yes	Yes
2. Procedural Justice	Yes	Yes	Yes
3. Interactional Justice	Yes	Yes	Yes
4. Idealized Influence	Yes	Yes	Yes
5. Inspirational Motivation	Yes	Yes	Yes
6. Intellectual Stimulation	Yes	Yes	Yes
7. Individualized Consideration	Yes	Yes	Yes
8. Surface Emotion Acting	Yes	Yes	Yes
9. Deep Emotion Acting	Yes	Yes	Yes
10. True Emotion Acting	Yes	Yes	Yes
11. Knowledge Acquisition	Yes	Yes	Yes
12. Knowledge Distribution	Yes	Yes	Yes
13. Knowledge Interpretation	Yes	Yes	Yes
14. Organizational Citizenship Behavior	Yes	Yes	Yes
15. Organizational Performance	Yes	Yes	Yes

5. 3. 1　Content Validity

Content validity is the appropriateness and representativeness of the content or topic of the items that is whether they reflect the psychological characteristics to be measured, whether they achieve the purpose of measurement or behavioral construct. Content validity is usually judged by the rationality of topic distribution, which belongs to the logical judgment of proposition. Content validity is a logical validity (Sekaran & Bougie, 2010). All these definitions were considered deeply when developing the items for all variables of this research.

According to McIntire and Miller (2000), there are two stages in establishing content validity. First, conceive the behavior, trait, or characteristic being measured. Second, get recommendation from the expert to improve the measurement. Kline (2011) argued that the best feedback is the one that comes from the subject experts who seek to make sure the questions are distinct and clear. Thus, content validity is usually established through the literature review and experts' suggestion (Sekaran, 2003; Straub et al., 2004).

On the basis of the above principles, this research had undertaken several steps. First, combining the literature review to determine the items and their relevant scale, in the light of the theoretical concept of the research. Thereafter the suggestions from the experts were gathered. After undertaking these two processes, the items (statements) that were considered relevant were adopted in the questionnaire (refer to section 4.4). However, to evaluate organizational performance of SMEs, several round of discussions with the experts were conducted to determine accurate measurement for organizational performance of SMEs. Second was to translate the questionnaire from English to Chinese. To check the accuracy of the translation, five experts coming from Nanchang University of China that hold doctorate degree with excellent language skills were consulted several times. They were selected because they have expertise to translate the questionnaire from English into Chinese. This is to ensure that the translated Chinese questionnaire accurately presented the meaning of the English questionnaire.

The final recommendation was to relocate the demographic information section. In the original version, the demographic information was located at the first section in the questionnaire. In the revised version, the information was located at the last section of the questionnaire. Walop (1987), Shi and Zhang (2000), Yang (2010) believed that the relocation is important to maintain confidentiality amongst respondents that their identity is protected and their responses are for academic purposes.

5. 3. 2　Pre-testing

Pre-testing is significant for the questionnaire to ensure that the respondents understand the given items and the wording or measurement don't have problems (Sekaran, 2003). Pre-testing involves the use of a small number of respondents to test the appropriateness of the items and their comprehension (Sekaran, 2003). Boyd, Westfall and Stasch (1977) recommended that a sample of 20 is satisfactory for pre-testing. In addition, the pre-testing should use the respondents who are as similar as possible to the targeted respondents (Tull & Hawkin, 1976). To fulfill all these requirements, 20 questionnaires were pre-tested on employees in Xinhangdao Education Company, Haishen Catering Company and Wujin Retail Company in Jilin Province of China in March 2019.

In pre-testing the questionnaire, five fundamental issues were addressed, namely, the length of the questionnaire, the comprehensibility of the project, the applicability of the scale, the design of the questionnaire and the proper time to finish the questionnaire (Hunt, Sparkman & Wilcox, 1982; Sekaran, 2003). Table 5. 2 shows that 12 (60%) respondents thought the length of the questionnaire was appropriate. 15 (75%) respondents said that the items were understandable and 17 (85%) of them said that the scale used was suitable for measuring these items. 16 (80%) respondents thought the questionnaire design was suitable for mailing survey. In addition, the respondents spend 10 to 20 minutes on completing the questionnaire. Since the results of the pre-testing were quite encouraging, no significant alteration was required.

Table 5. 2   Pre-test Results

(*N* = 20)

No. Questions	Frequencies	Percentage
1. Is the length of the questionnaire appropriate?		
Yes	12	60
No	8	30
2. Are the items understandable to answer?		
Yes	15	75
No	5	25
3. Are the scales suitable to measure the items?		
Yes	17	85
No	3	15
4. Is the design of the questionnaire suitable for mail survey?		
Yes	16	80
No	4	20
5. How long does it take to complete the questionnaire?		
Between 10 and 15 minutes	11	55
Between 16 and 20 minutes	9	45

5. 3. 3   Pilot Study

This subsection discusses the empirical results and analysis process for the pilot study. There are two ways to use the term of pilot study in social science research. Pilot study can be called as feasibility study.

It involves a small-scale research or experimental research version undertaken by the researcher as a preparation for the main study (Polit, Beck & Hungler, 2001). However, pilot studies can also be used as pre-tests or " trials " for specific research tools (Baker, 1994). One benefit of conducting a pilot study is that it can pre-warn where a major research project may fail, where it may not comply with the research agreement, or whether the proposed method or tool is inappropriate or overly complex. This is consistent with the statement of De Vaus

(1993) , who said " Don't take risks. " Conduct a pilot test first. (p. 54) Therefore, the aim of the preliminary study was to establish the reliability of the measurement instrument. Then the original data of this study was collected and analyzed using the improved measurement instrument.

In May 2019, a pilot study was conducted on 20 employees of SMEs in Jilin Province of China. All questionnaires were returned and can be used for data analysis. Cronbach's alpha was measured for checking the internal consistency of measuring instruments. (Sekaran & Bougie, 2010). Table 5.3 shows the results for Cronbach's alpha values for all variables.

Table 5.3   Reliability of Survey Instrument

$(N = 20)$

No. Study Variables	Number of Items	Cronbach's Alpha Values
1. Distributive Justice	4	0.885
2. Procedural Justice	4	0.926
3. Interactional Justice	4	0.753
4. Idealized Influence	4	0.807
5. Inspirational Motivation	4	0.895
6. Intellectual Stimulation	4	0.905
7. Individualized Consideration	4	0.886
8. Surface Emotion Acting	4	0.948
9. Deep Emotion Acting	4	0.908
10. True Emotion Acting	3	0.949
11. Knowledge Acquisition	3	0.977
12. Knowledge Distribution	3	0.929
13. Knowledge Interpretation	3	0.842
14. Organizational Citizenship Behavior	20	0.972
15. Organizational Performance	7	0.926

Overall, Cronbach's alpha values of nine variables in the pilot study were more than 0.90 (procedural justice, intellectual stimulation, surface emotion acting, deep emotion acting, true emotion acting, knowledge acquisition, knowledge distribution, organizational citizenship behavior, organizational performance). Cronbach's alpha values of other five variables ranged from 0.80 to 0.90 (distributive justice, idealized influence, inspirational motivation, individualized consideration, knowledge interpretation) and one variables ranged from 0.70 to 0.80 (interactional justice). In other words, all variables in the pilot study did not show a lower reliability level (< 0.60) (Hair, et al. , 2010). A good Cronbach's alpha values for all variables means that they were consistent internally and measure the same content (Sekaran, 2003). In summary, since the results and the analysis process of pilot study are considered acceptable, it is recommended that the measurement instrument does not require any modifications and is considered suitable for primary data collection.

5.4 Summary

This chapter describes the survey instrument development process in depth. The process is important to establish reliability and validity of the instrument. The next chapter will present the data analysis and result.

Chapter Six   Data Analysis and Results

6. 1   Introduction

This chapter explores the results of data analysis. The presentation of this chapter would be as follows. Firstly, the response rate would be highlighted. Thereafter, data examination is explained. The goodness of measures is then discussed. This is followed by the demographic profiles of the respondents. Descriptive statistics are then offered. A standard multiple regression analysis is discussed for examining the research hypotheses. Finally, a summary of the discussion is provided.

6. 2   Response Rate

As stated in Chapter 4, the researcher distributed 400 questionnaires to the employees in SMEs in Jilin Province of China. Some of the questionnaires were posted through mail and some were collected through online survey. The data collection period took approximately four months from October 2019 to January 2020. And 400 questionnaires were distributed, 251 were returned. This lead to a 62.7% response rate. According to Sekaran (2003), 30% response rate is thought sufficient to have a survey research. According to the theory, the response rate (62.7%) of this study was higher than the recommendation rate. Therefore, the findings of this study can be extended to the population.

6.3　Data Screening

The main purpose of data screening is to transform the data into a format, which is most suitable for multivariate analysis (Hair, et al. , 2006). For the data screening, as mentioned in Chapter Four, three tests were performed, which were missing data, response bias and outliers identification.

6.3.1　Missing Data

Missing data is defined as information not available for a case about whom other information is available (Hair, et al. , 2006). In this study, through examining the errors of all variables, missing data were diminished when the questionnaires was received from the respondents. The respondents were contacted through telephone or e-mail if the researcher found any unanswered questions and asked them to complete the questionnaires. In addition, the researchers performed frequency allocation and analysis of missing value for every variable to affirm that the collected data were cleaned. The issue of missing data was able to be solved by the researcher at the end of the stipulated data collection period which is at the end of January 2020.

6.3.2　Non-response Bias Test

The issue of non-response bias occurs in statistical surveys if the answers of respondents differ from the potential answers of those who did not answer. For purposes of this research, non-response bias is defined as a bias that exists in survey results when respondents to a survey are different from those who did not respond in terms of demographic or attitudinal variables, or other variables relevant to the survey topic (Coakes & Steed, 2003; Pallant, 2010). It is a function of: ① the proportion of non-respondents in the total sample; and ② the extent to which there is a systematic discrepancy between respondents and non-respondents on variables relevant to the inquiry. The presence of non-response bias is a threat to the external validity or generalizability of research findings to the target population of a study (Coakes & Steed, 2003; Pallant, 2010). A well-designed survey and a research-based administration method, following generally acceptable protocols and procedures as well as reporting them in the research analysis, are the first-steps in the attempt to increase response rates and also control for non-response bias (Coakes & Steed, 2003; Pallant, 2010).

Response bias test was performed to examine whether there is a significant difference between early and late response groups. For this purpose, the early response group was coded as "1" and the late response group was coded as "2". Independent sample t-tests were conducted on the continuous variables. Significant values ($p < 0.05$) for both tests show the existence of response bias while non-significant values ($p > 0.05$) indicate the reverse (Coakes & Steed, 2003; Pallant, 2010).

In this study, 150 respondents were treated as the first group (early reply) respondents and the other 101 respondents were treated as the second group (late reply). Mean scores for all variables were then computed for both groups. The mean scores were compared to examine the differences between the groups of responses. The results are shown in Table 6.1. It was found that there were no differences between the two groups of responses for all variables. Hence, the data used in this study were free from response bias.

Table 6.1   Independence Sample T-test for Non-response Bias Test

	Mean		F	Sig.
	Early	Late		
Organizational Performance	5.0743	4.8260	1.471	0.226
Organizational Citizenship Behavior	5.2370	4.7658	0.258	0.612
Organizational Justice	4.7006	4.6617	1.196	0.053
Transformational Leadership	4.7546	4.6925	1.791	0.182

(To be continued)

	Mean		F	$Sig.$
	Early	Late		
Employee Emotion Labor	5. 0411	4. 5663	0. 414	0. 521
Organizational Learning	4. 7822	4. 4917	2. 167	0. 142

6. 3. 3 Outliers Identification

The outliers are observations with unique combination of features, which can be identified as distinctly different from other observations (Hair, et al. , 2006). This research used multiple regression procedure to detect both univariate outliers on dependent variable and multivariate outliers on independent variables (Coakes, et al. , 2006). Univariate outliers are detected by using studentized residuals. Studentized residuals are z-scores, computed for a case based on the data for all other cases in the data set (Coakes, et al. , 2006). Coakes, et al. (2006) considered that a case in the data set is univariate outlier if the z-score for studentized residual is greater than ± 3. 0.

In contrast, multivariate outliers have been detected by inspecting Mahalanobis distances that were present in the data set (Pallant, 2010). To identify which cases are multivariate outliers, the researcher determines the critical chi-square value by using the number of independent variables as the degree of freedom at an alpha level of 0. 001 (Pallant, 2010; Tabachnick & Fidell, 2007). When the probability associated with D^2 is less than or equal to 0. 001 , a case will be regarded as a multivariable outlier. When D^2 obeys the chi-square distribution, the degree of freedom is equal to the number of variables included in the calculation (McLachlan, 1999). According to the analysis, the data showed that the D^2 probability scores (p) in 15 cases were less than 0. 001 as shown in Table 6. 2. Therefore, these 15 cases were treated with outliers issue and the 15 cases were removed from the data.

Table 6. 2   Deleted Cases from the Mahalanobis Distances

Respondents' ID	Mahalanobis	Mahalanobis Chi-Square (D^2)
187	59. 20774	0. 0000
35	53. 38363	0. 0000
115	53. 13592	0. 0000
107	52. 92628	0. 0000
231	52. 80713	0. 0000
147	45. 93258	0. 00003
82	44. 54303	0. 00005
165	42. 54541	0. 00010
133	42. 11086	0. 00012
218	42. 11086	0. 00012
15	39. 35458	0. 00032
111	38. 40457	0. 00045
24	37. 55174	0. 00061
116	37. 44156	0. 00063
169	36. 2881	0. 00094

6. 4   Tests on Multivariate Assumptions

After screening the data, tests to meet four assumptions of multivariate analyses were conducted, namely, normality, linearity, homoscedasticity and multicollinearity (Hair et al. , 2006). The results of the tests are discussed in the following subsections.

6. 4. 1   Normality Test

Normality for all of the data was examined for each item based on the statistical and visual approach. The descriptions of the findings are offered in subsections 6. 4. 1. 1 and 6. 4. 1. 2.

6. 4. 1. 1 Statistical Approach

The data normality distribution was evaluated by the skewness and kurtosis values for each variable. Skewness values illustrate the symmetry of the allocation score and a skewed variable mean the score is not be at the center of the distribution, whereas kurtosis is about the peakedness of distribution which can be either too peaked for instance with short and thick tail or too flat with long and thin tail (Tabachnick & Fidell, 2001). Normal distribution is considered when value of skewness and kurtosis is at zero (0). Positive skewness value will have a cluster of cases to the left at a low value and negative skewness will have the score cluster or pile at the right side with a long left tail (Tabachnick & Fidell, 2001). Kurtosis with values of below zero (0) indicate a relatively flat distribution known as "playkurtic" and the kurtosis values above zero (0) indicate a peaked distribution or "leptokurtic" as recommended by researchers that samples be large enough to prevent under-estimation of variance. Seldom will perfect normality assumption be achieved. The test was conducted using skewness and kurtosis measurement. It is thus concluded that the data is symmetric because the skewness and kurtosis values are both less than ±2.00 for all the dimensional constructs of the study. According to George and Mallery (2010), a skewness or kurtosis value between ±2.00 is regarded as an excellent value and hence, the data for this study is normally distributed. Table 6.3 summarizes the kurtosis and skewness for all the variables. The data shows the variables are normally distributed. Therefore, in conclusion, all the variables do not deviate from the normality test requirement.

Table 6. 3   Skewness and Kurtosis for the Variables

	Skewness		Kortosis	
	Statistic	*SE*	*Statistic*	*SE*
Organizational Performance	− . 079	. 158	− . 117	. 316
Organizational Citizenship Behavior	− . 441	. 158	1. 264	. 316
Organizational Justice	− . 220	. 158	− . 013	. 316
Transformational Leadership	− . 292	. 158	. 201	. 316
Employee Emotion Labor	− . 394	. 158	1. 460	. 316
Organizational Learning	− . 051	. 158	. 517	. 316

6. 4. 1. 2   Visual Approach

The another stage is to check the normality of the data by evaluating the distribution shape in analyzing the data (Field, 2009). A test was carried out to vertify the normality utilizing visual inspections. An non-formal method was used to check normality, which is to compare a histogram of the sample data to a normal probability curve. The empirical distribution of the data (histogram) should be bell-shaped and similar to a normal distribution (Elliott & Woodward, 2007). Figures 6. 1 to 6. 6 illustrate the histograms of these variables. The results show that all shapes are in the normal line, so the data of each variable are in the normal curve distribution.

Figure 6. 1 shows the histogram of organizational performance. It can be observed in the figure that the histogram was in good condition. It is in the normal distribution range and the *mean* = 5. 03 , *sd* = 1. 08.

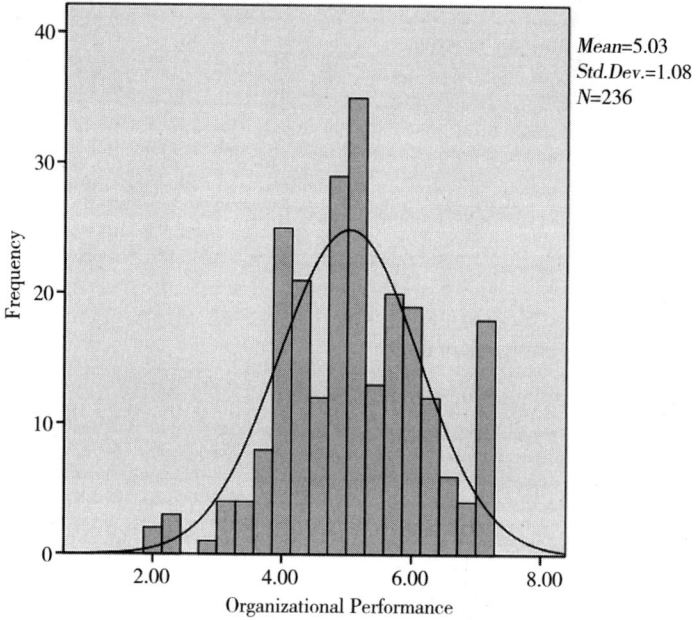

Mean=5.03
Std.Dev.=1.08
N=236

Figure 6. 1   Histogram of Organizational Performance

Figure 6. 2 shows the histogram of variable of organizational citizenship behavior. It can be observed in the figure that the histogram was in good condition, it is in the normal distribution range and the *mean* = 5. 10, *sd* = 1. 017.

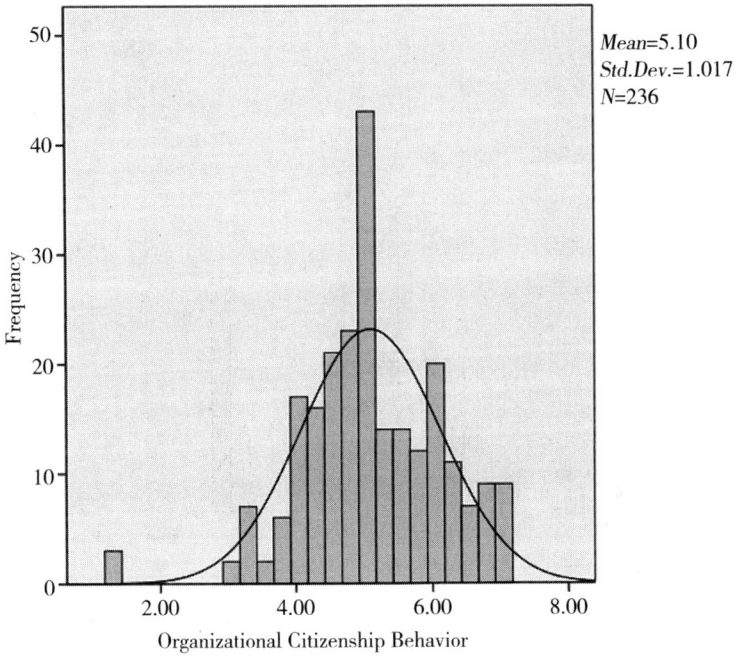

Figure 6. 2   Histogram of Organizational Citizenship Behavior

Figure 6. 3 shows the histogram of variable of organizational justice. It can be observed in the figure that the histogram was in good condition, it is in the normal distribution range and the *mean* = 4. 73, *sd* = 0. 0955.

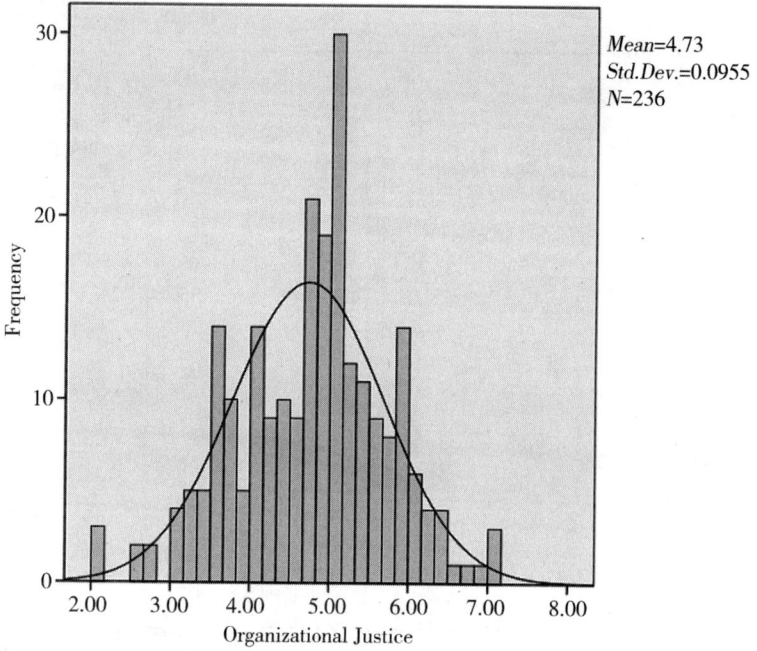

Figure 6. 3   Histogram of Organizational Justice

Figure 6.4 shows the histogram of variable of transformational leadership. It can be observed in the figure that the histogram was in good condition, it is in the normal distribution range and the *mean* = 4.79, *sd* = 1.06.

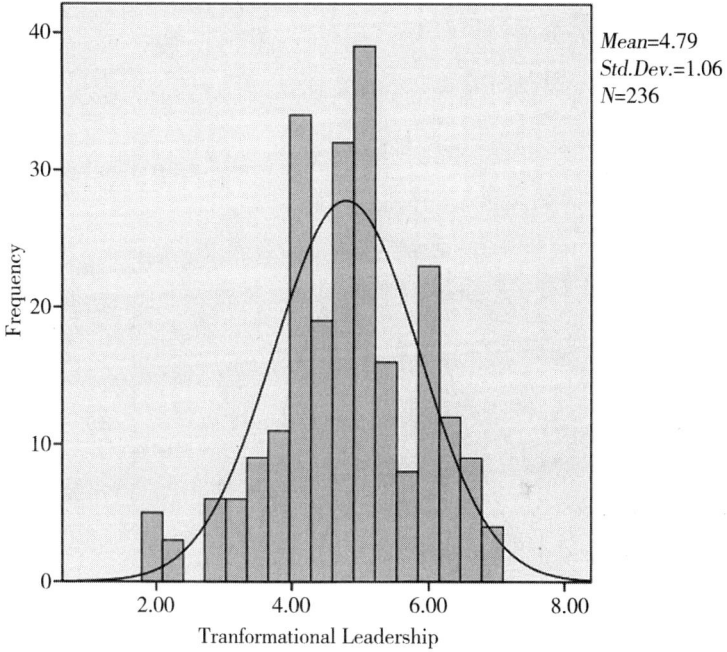

Figure 6. 4   **Histogram of Transformational Leadership**

Figure 6. 5 shows the histogram of variable of employee emotion labor. It can be observed in the figure that the histogram was in good condition, it is in the normal distribution range and the *mean* = 4. 88, *sd* = 1. 043.

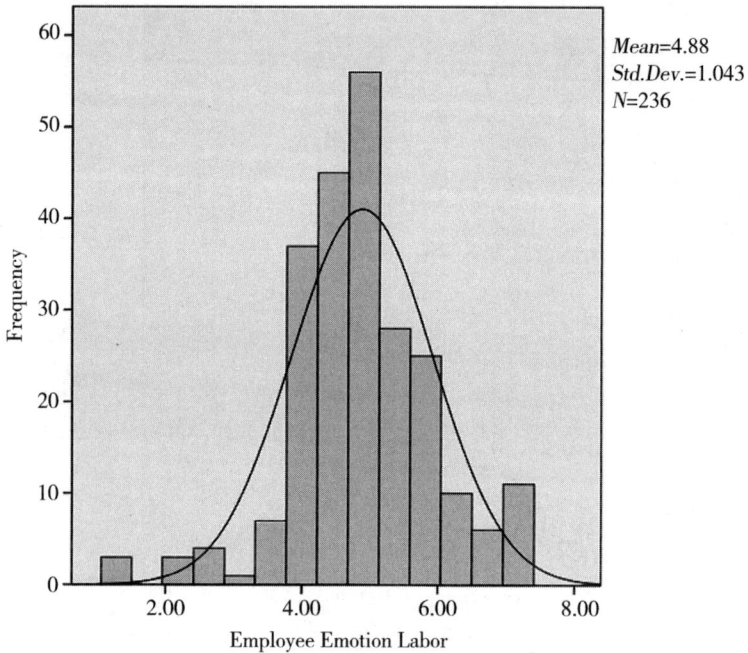

Figure 6. 5   Histogram of Employee Emotion Labor

Figure 6. 6 shows the histogram of variable of organizational learning. It can be observed in the figure that the histogram was in good condition, it is in the normal distribution range and the *mean* = 4. 71 , *sd* = 1. 076.

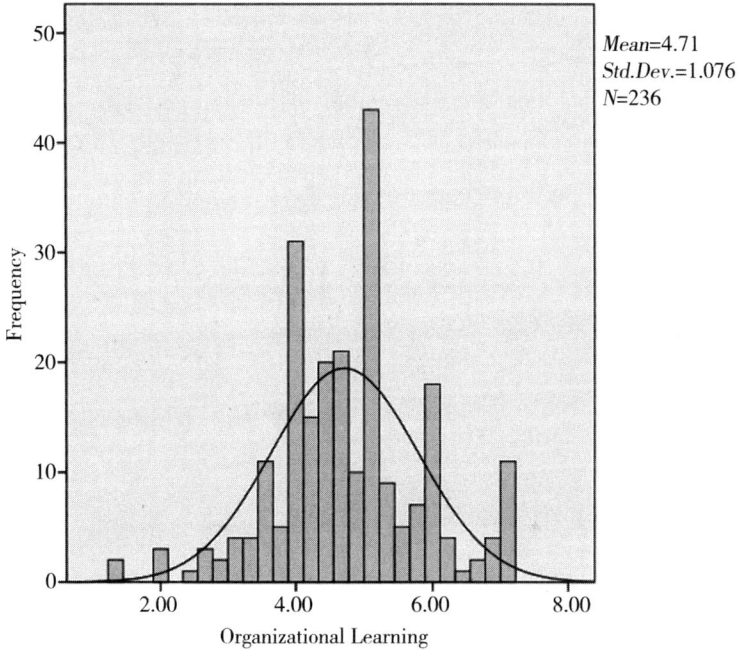

Figure 6. 6   Histogram of Organizational Learning

6. 4. 2   Linearity Test

Another multivariate assumption is linearity of data which is the relationship between the residuals against the predicted values. Linearity refers to the error term of distribution. Linearity is important for regression analysis because correlation can capture only the linear association between variables and if there is a substantial non-linear relationship, it will be ignored in the analysis because it will underestimate the actual strength of the relationship (Tabachnick & Fidell, 2001).

Linearity can be observed by examining the scatterplots (Hair et al. , 2006). The results of linearity through scatterplot diagrams for various variables indicate no clear relationship between the residuals and the predicted values. Assessment of all scatterplots of the standardized residual versus standardized predicted values reveal that in all the plots, the residuals are scattered with no systematic or curvilinear pattern (U-shape distribution); or clustering of residuals as indicated by Tabachnick and Fidell (2007) (refer to Figure 6.7). The randomized patterns of the scatterplots indicate that the assumption of linearity is met. Therefore, linearity could be assumed.

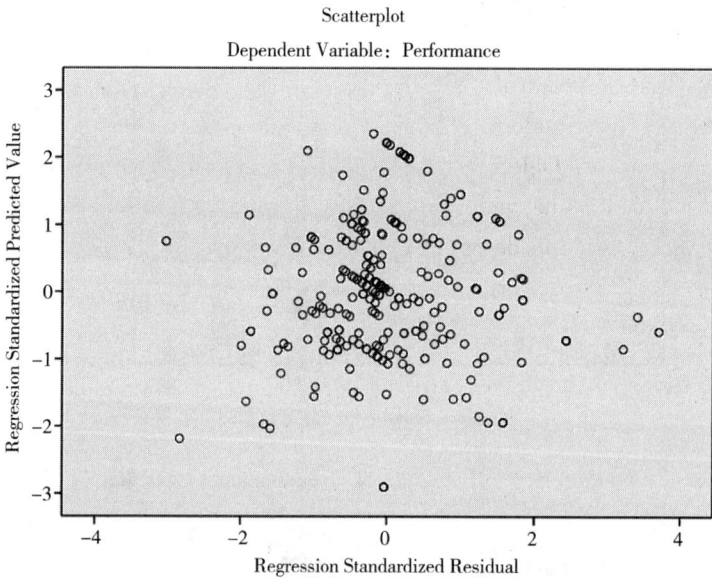

Scatterplot
Dependent Variable: Performance

Figure 6.7   Scatterplots of Standardized Residuals Versus Standardized Predicted Values

6.4.3   Homoscedasticity

Homoscedasticity refers to constant variance of the error term and the variance of the dependent variables is approximately the same for different levels of the explanatory variable (Hair et al. , 2006). The variance of the calibration variable should be the same for each level of the predictor variable. Opposite data that do not conform to the dispersion of residual error is called heteroscedasticity. The standard error for residuals is constant across the observable bodies; the horizontal error term of a particular independent variable should have the same amount of variation except that it should present a stochastic normal distribution.

Homoscedasticity is indicated when the width of the band of the residuals is approximately at a different level from the dependent variables and the scatterplot shows a pattern of residual normally distributed around the mean. To check for homoscedasticity, the scatterplots of studentized residuals against the predicted values were used as in Figure 6. 8 (Hair et al. , 2006). There is a need to inspect the plots of residuals against the predicted values to reveal that the residuals are scattered randomly with no obvious systematic pattern. If there is no systematic pattern of decreasing or increasing residuals, it can be assumed that the assumption of homoscedasticity is not violated. As illustrated in Figure 6. 8 , there was no systematic pattern of decreasing or increasing residuals and thus the assumption of homoscedasticity of this study was not violated.

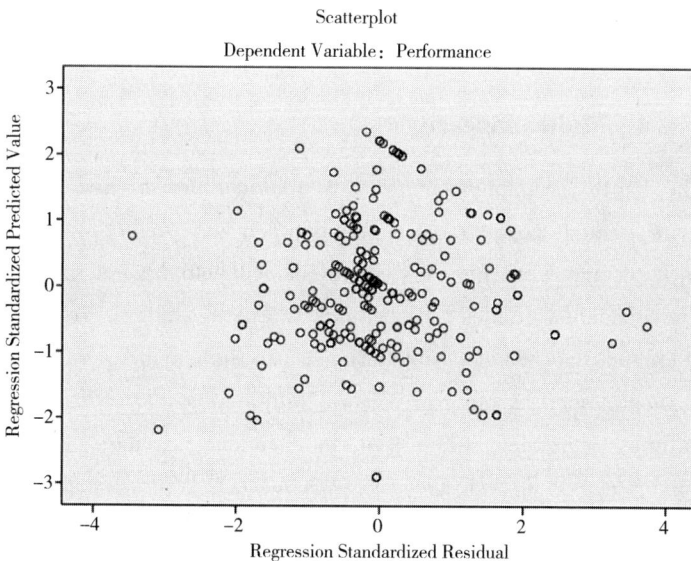

Figure 6. 8   Scatterplots of Standardized Residuals Against Predicted Values

This assumption was also examined using Levene test on the matric variables against the non-matric variable (gender) of this study (Hair et al. , 2006). Table 6. 4 presents the results of the homoscedasticity test. It can be seen in Table 6. 4 that the results of Levene test were not significant ($p < 0.001$). This indicated that dependent variables exhibits equal level of variance across the range of independent variable for gender (Coakes & Steed, 2003; Hair et al. , 2006).

Table 6. 4　Results of Homoscedasticity Test

	Gender (*Mean*)		*F*	*Sig.*
	Male	Female		
Performance	4. 8745	5. 0553	3. 604	0. 519
Organizational Citizenship Behavior	4. 9645	5. 1827	0. 594	0. 442
Organizational Justice	4. 5319	4. 7870	3. 937	0. 058
Transformational Leadership	4. 5929	4. 8448	0. 341	0. 560
Employee's Emotion Labor	4. 7222	5. 0308	3. 995	0. 057
Organizational Learning	4. 4860	4. 8181	3. 915	0. 059

6. 4. 4　Multicollinearity

The fourth assumption pertains to multicollinearity and singularity which are related to the correlations between the predicting variables. Singularity occurs when one of the independent variables is merged with other independent variables (Tabachnick & Fidell, 2001). Tolerance ($1 \sim R^2$) represents residual singularity of an independent variable that cannot be explained by other predictors. Multicollinearity poses a problem for multiple regression when the independent variables are highly correlated ($r = 0.8$ and above). When such a case happens, the regression coefficients would not be significant due to high standard error. According to Tabachnick and Fidell (2001), tolerance values approaching zero (0) specify the presence of high multicollinearity. Generally speaking, when the variance inflation factor value is greater than 10, it means that there may be linear coincidence between independent variables. The cut-off value for VIF is less than 10 and tolerance value of more than 0. 1. Hence, as deliberated in the statistical analysis, there is no violation of the assumption for this study. All the independent variables have tolerance value of more than 0. 1 and VIF value of less than 10 (refer Table 6. 5).

Table 6. 5   Test of Multicollinearity

	Tolerance	VIF
Organizational Citizenship Behavior	. 254	3. 938
Organizational Justice	. 397	2. 516
Transformational Leadership	. 244	4. 100
Employee Emotion Labor	. 184	5. 429
Organizational Learning	. 295	3. 394

Dependent Variable: Organizational Performance.

In the above regression analysis model, the tolerance is between 0. 397 and 0. 184, and the VIF value is not greater than the evaluation index value 10, indicating that there is no linear coincidence between independent variables entering the regression equation. Hence, this indicates that the multidisciplinary hypothesis was satisfied, and then the fourth hypothesis of the multivariate hypothesis was satisfied.

6. 5   Goodness of Measures

The second stage of the data analysis of this study was to establish the goodness of measures for testing the research hypotheses. In this research, the data were initially submitted for factor analysis. Thereafter, the internal consistency of the factors was examined by conducting reliability analysis.

6. 5. 1　Factor Analysis

Statistically, in order to test the validity of the scale construction, the most commonly used method is factor analysis, or common factor score, which aims to find out the potential structure of the scale, reduce the number of questions, and make it become a small group of variables with large correlation with each other. Through the factor analysis, validity of the test tool is examined, and the common factors are effectively extracted, which are approaches to the psychological characteristics of the theoretical framework, the test tool or scale can be said to have the construction validity. Therefore, users often make factor analysis of the items after the analysis of the items, so as to obtain the validity of the scale construction. Construct validity is the psychological trait of the hypothetical theoretical framework used to explain individual behaviors, so construct validity is "the degree to which the theoretical structure psychological trait is able to be measured" (Brown, 2000; Polit & Beck, 2010; Cronbach & Meehl, 1955).

Factor analysis is a statistical method, which is utilized to analyse the interrelationships among a large number of variables and to confirm whether the information can be condensed into a smaller set of factors or components with a minimum loss of information (Hair, et al. , 2006). In the analysis, factor loadings more than 0. 30 were regarded as meeting the minimum level, while loadings of 0. 40 were thought significant (Mokhlis, 2009b). The principal components' factor analysis with varimax rotation was conducted on all constructs of this study for confirming the accuracy of the data.

To fulfil the above requirement, the critical assumptions underlying the factor analysis were examined, namely, the Bartlett's test of sphericity and the Kaiser-Meyer-Olkin (KMO) measure of sampling adequacy (MSA). Factor analysis of each variable was conducted individually to identify the adequate dimensions or factors that appropriately explain each of the organizational justice, transformational leadership, employee emotion labor, organizational learning, organizational citizenship behavior, organizational performance variables.

Overall, the adequacy of sampling was measured through the Kaiser-Meyer-Olkin (KMO). The Bartlett's test of sphericity, and anti-image correlation were used to verify the assumptions underlying the factor analysis. The minimum acceptable value for KMO was set at 0.50 and Bartlett's test of sphericity should be significant (Hair, et al., 2006). Hair, et al. (2006) also suggested that the acceptable level of measuring sampling adequacy for anti-image correlation was set at 0.50 or above. The items that the eigenvalue is less than one will be refused. However, factors that the eigenvalue is equal to or more than one are to be retained for further analysis (Hair, et al., 2006). Hence, the factor analysis was performed using the principal component with varimax rotation of factors, with the aim to identify the underlying construct for all variables.

6.5.1.1   Factor Analysis of Organizational Justice

The measurement scales for organizational justice scale consists of 12 items. The Varimax rotated PCA was conducted. Prior to performing the PCA, the suitability of the data for factor analysis was assessed. Correlation matrix indicated item coefficients were 0.4 and above. Table 6.6 exhibits the results for organizational justice scale factor loading. The KMO value was 0.901, exceeding the recommended value of 0.6 (Kaiser, 1970, 1974) and Barlett's test of sphericity (Barlett, 1954) was significant at $p < 0.001$. Since the KMO value was 0.901, it is interpreted as being in the range of "superb" (Hutcheson & Sofroniou, 1999). Table 6.6 also shows that the factor analysis contributed three factors from the 12 original items. The total variance explained is 70.893 %. Only factors with a loading value of 0.40 and above were considered. Factor loading contributed three underlying variables for organizational justice scale and were named as distributive justice, procedural justice and interactional justice.

Table 6.6   Factor Loading of Organizational Justice Scale

	Loading		
	1	2	3
Factor 1: Distributive Justice			
ODJ1	.693		
ODJ2	.826		
ODJ3	.775		
ODJ4	.779		
Factor 2: Procedural Justice			
OPJ1		.660	
OPJ2		.717	
OPJ3		.774	
OPJ4		.794	
Factor 3: Interactional Justice			
OIJ1			.772
OIJ2			.878
OJI3			.711
OIJ4			.665
Eigenvalue	6.126	1.209	1.082
% of Variance	51.801	10.073	9.019
KMO	0.901		
BTOS	1730.579		
Sig.	0.000		

6.5.1.2   Factor Analysis of Transformational Leadership

Next, factor analysis for transformational leadership scale is illustrated in Table 6.7. The original measurement scale for transformational leadership consists of 16 items. The result reported the

KMO value of 0. 935, indicating " superb " level (Hutcheson & Sofroniou, 1999) and Barlett's test of sphericity (Barlett, 1954) was significant at $p < 0.001$. Only factors loading greater than 0. 4 were considered. Factor loading contributed four underlying variables for transformational leadership scale and were named as inspirational motivation, intellectual stimulation, idealized influence and individualized consideration.

Table 6. 7   Factor Loading of Transformational Leadership Scale

	Loading			
	1	2	3	4
Factor 1: Inspirational Motivation				
TIM1	. 644			
TIM2	. 782			
TIM3	. 652			
TIM4	. 772			
Factor 2: Intellectual Stimulation				
TIS1		. 763		
TIS2		. 536		
TIS3		. 596		
TIS4		. 620		
Factor 3: Idealized Influence				
TII1			. 748	
TII2			. 793	
TII3			. 691	
TII4			. 725	
Factor 4: Individualized Consideration				
TIC1				. 728
TIC2				. 744

(To be continued)

| | Loading | | | |
	1	2	3	4
TIC3				. 614
TIC4				. 768
Eigenvalue	9. 403	1. 271	1. 136	1. 099
% of Variance	58. 771	7. 945	4. 599	4. 367
KMO	0. 935			
BTOS	3. 105. 609			
Sig.	0. 000			

6. 5. 1. 3 Factor Analysis of Employee Emotion

The measurement scales for employee emotion consists of 11 items. The Varimax rotated PCA was conducted. Prior to performing the PCA, the suitability of the data for factor analysis was assessed. Correlation matrix indicated item coefficients were 0. 4 and above. Table 6. 8 exhibits the results for employee emotion scale factor loading. The KMO value was 0. 902, exceeding the recommended value of 0. 6 (Kaiser, 1970, 1974) and Barlett's test of sphericity (Barlett, 1954) was significant at $p <$ 0. 001. Since the KMO value is 0. 901, it is interpreted as being in the range of "superb" (Hutcheson & Sofroniou, 1999). Table 6. 8 also shows that the factor analysis contributed three factors from the 11 original items. The total variance explained is 77. 49 percent. Only factors with a loading value of 0. 40 and above were considered. Factor loading contributed three underlying variables for employee emotion scale and were named as surface emotion acting, deep emotion acting and true emotion acting.

Table 6. 8　Factor Loading of Employee Emotion Labor Scale

	Loading		
	1	2	3
Factor 1: Surface Emotional Acting			
ESEA1	. 775		
ESEA2	. 865		
ESEA3	. 797		
ESEA4	. 643		
Factor 2: True Emotional Acting			
ETEA1		. 777	
ETEA2		. 859	
ETEA3		. 863	
Factor 3: Deep Emotional Acting			
EDEA1			. 647
EDEA2			. 543
EDEA3			. 706
EDEA4			. 802
Eigenvalue	6. 706	1. 219	1. 199
% of Variance	60. 964	11. 079	5. 445
KMO	0. 902		
BTOS	2060. 251		
Sig.	0. 000		

6. 5. 1. 4　Factor Analysis of Organizational Learning

Next, factor analysis for organizational learning scale is illustrated in Table 6. 9. The original measurement scale for organizational learning consists of 9 items. The result reported the KMO value of 0. 913, indicating "superb" level (Hutcheson & Sofroniou, 1999) and Barlett's test of sphericity (Barlett, 1954) was significant at $p < 0.001$. Only factors loading greater than 0.4 were considered. Factor loading also contributed three underlying variables for organizational learning scale and were named as knowledge distribution, knowledge acquisition and knowledge interpretation.

Table 6.9 Factor Loading of Organizational Learning Scale

	Loading		
	1	2	3
Factor 1: Knowledge Distribution			
OKD1	.654		
OKD2	.784		
OKD3	.730		
Factor 2: Knowledge Acquisition			
OKA1		.870	
OKA2		.865	
OKA3		.647	
Factor 3: Knowledge Interpretation			
OKI1			.766
OKI2			.719
OKI3			.861
Eigenvalue	5.733	2.951	1.497
% of Variance	63.702	10.571	1.497
KMO	0.913		
BTOS	1587.980		
Sig.	0.000		

6. 5. 1. 5   Factor Analysis of Organizational Citizenship Behavior

Factor analysis for OCB scale is illustrated in Table 6. 10. The original measurement scale for OCB consists of 20 items. The result reported the KMO value of 0. 944, indicating "superb" level (Hutcheson & Sofroniou, 1999) and Barlett's test of sphericity (Barlett, 1954) is significant at $p < 0.001$. Only factors loading greater than 0. 4 were considered. Factor loading also contributed only one underlying variables for organizational citizenship behavior scale.

Table 6. 10   Factor Loading of Organizational Citizenship Behavior Scale

	Loading
Factor 1	
OCB1	. 770
OCB2	. 714
OCB3	. 719
OCB4	. 770
OCB5	. 841
OCB6	. 817
OCB7	. 807
OCB8	. 824
OCB9	. 793
OCB10	. 780
OCB11	. 811
OCB12	. 823
OCB13	. 752
OCB14	. 738
OCB15	. 683

(To be continued)

	Loading
OCB16	. 631
OCB17	. 719
OCB18	. 641
OCB19	. 808
OCB20	. 747
Eigenvalue	1. 784
% of Variance	58. 006
KMO	0. 944
BTOS	4157. 774
Sig.	0. 000

6. 5. 1. 6　Factor Analysis of Organizational Performance

The measurement scales for organizational performance consists of seven items. The Varimax rotated PCA was conducted. Prior to performing the PCA, the suitability of the data for factor analysis was assessed. Correlation matrix indicated item coefficients are 0. 4 and above. Table 6. 11 exhibits the results for organizational performance scale factor loading. The KMO value is 0. 891, exceeding the recommended value of 0. 6 (Kaiser, 1970, 1974) and Barlett's test of Sphericity (Barlett, 1954) is significant at $p < 0.001$. Since the KMO value is 0. 891, it is interpreted as being in the range of "great" (Hutcheson & Sofroniou, 1999). Table 6. 11 also shows that the factor analysis contributed only one factors from the seven original items. The total variance explained is 64. 498 percent. Only factors with a loading value of 0. 40 and above were considered.

Table 6. 11   Factor Loading of Organizational Performance Scale

	Loading
OP1	. 729
OP2	. 821
OP3	. 856
OP4	. 841
OP5	. 820
OP6	. 786
OP7	. 762
Eigenvalue	4. 515
% of Variance	64. 498
KMO	0. 891
BTOS	998. 077
Sig.	0. 000

6. 5. 2   Reliability Analysis

An internal consistency confirmation of the scales was performed to ensure the reliability of the scales. This can be done by checking the Cronbach's alpha coefficient. The cut-off point for measuring the reliability for this study is coefficient alpha of above 0. 65 as recommended by Nunnally and Berntein (1994) and Nunnally (1978). Table 6. 12 exhibits the Cronbach coefficient alpha of all variables. In short, all the variables in this study have values more than 0. 70, ranged from 0. 792 to 0. 961, exceeding the acceptable value recommended. Thus, the instrument were reliable and can be used for further analysis.

Table 6. 12   Reliability Coefficients for Variables

Variable	N of Original Item	N of Deleted Item	N of New Items	Cronbach's Alpha
Performance	7		7	0. 913
Organizational Citizenship Behavior	20		20	0. 961
Organizational Justice				
Distributive Justice	4		4	0. 871
Procedural Justice	4		4	0. 846
Interactional Justice	4		4	0. 792
Transformational Leadership				
Inspirational Motivation	4		4	0. 883
Intellectual Stimulation	4		4	0. 896
Idealized Influence	4		4	0. 837
Individualized Consideration	4		4	0. 869
Employee Emotion Labor				
Surface Emotion Acting	4		4	0. 894
True Emotion Acting	3		3	0. 884
Deep Emotion Acting	4		4	0. 870
Organizational learning				
Knowledge Acquisition	4		4	0. 863
Knowledge Distribution	4		4	0. 841
Knowledge Interpretation	4		4	0. 857

6. 6   Descriptive Statistics

Descriptive statistics are used to describe the basic features of the data. They provide a simple summary of the sample and the measures. Descriptive statistics are useful because they provide information, such as the mean and standard deviation of the variables (Pallant, 2010). A total of 236 usable cases were obtained from the survey. All variables were measured on a seven-point Likert scale. According to Hair et al. (2006), mean values can be categorised into three levels: (1) Low = 1.00 to 3.00; (2) Moderate = 3.01 to 5.00; and (3) High = 5.01 to 7.00. Results in Table 6.13 indicated that respondents perceived the high agreement towards organizational performance ($mean = 5.03$, $sd = 1.08$) and organizational citizenship behavior ($mean = 5.10$, $sd = 1.02$). However, mean score for each of the independent variables were at the moderate level, indicating the moderate level of agreement towards all the factors.

Table 6.13   Descriptive Analysis of the Variables

Construct	Mean	Std. Deviation	Level
Organizational Performance	5.0254	1.08046	High
Organizational Citizenship Behavior	5.0975	1.01706	High
Organizational Justice	4.7263	.95464	Moderate
Distributive Justice	4.6250	1.16064	Moderate
Procedural Justice	4.5561	1.17182	Moderate
Interactional Justice	4.9979	.92454	Moderate
Transformational Leadership	4.7937	1.05997	Moderate
Idealized Influence	4.8464	1.09495	Moderate
Inspirational Motivation	4.8189	1.22291	Moderate
Intellectual Stimulation	4.7415	1.18161	Moderate
Individualized Consideration	4.7680	1.17801	Moderate
Employee Emotion Labor	4.8806	1.04323	Moderate
Surface Emotion Acting	4.9428	1.14456	Moderate
Deep Emotion Acting	4.8972	1.08067	Moderate
True Emotion Acting	4.7754	1.16690	Moderate
Organizational Learning	4.7133	1.07554	Moderate

(To be continued)

Construct	Mean	Std. Deviation	Level
Knowledge Acquisition	4. 7359	1. 15036	Moderate
Knowledge Distribution	4. 6667	1. 14400	Moderate
Knowledge Interpretation	4. 7373	1. 20350	Moderate

6. 7　Profile of the Respondents

Originally, 251 questionnaires were returned. Table 6. 14 summarizes the demographic background of the respondents. Out of 251 respondents, 55. 4 % of them were female and 44. 6 % were male. The respondents were age below 25 years old (24. 3%), 26 to 36 years old (33. 1%), 36 to 45 years old (15. 1%) and more than 45 years old (27. 5%). In term of educational level, 56. 6% of respondents were bachelor degree holders. 15. 1% of respondents were master and above. 21. 9% of them were college. 6. 4% of them were high school and below. Table 6. 14 also shows that the respondents were from various industries including building (6. 0%), trade (3. 2%), education (38. 6%), health care (13. 5%), hotel and restaurant services (6. 0%), agriculture (2. 4%) and others (20. 3%).

Table 6. 14　Demographic Profile of the Respondents

(N = 251)

	Frequency	Percentage
Gender		
Male	112	44. 6
Female	139	55. 4
Age		
25 years old and below	61	24. 3
26 to 36 years old	83	33. 1

(To be continued)

	Frequency	Percentage
36 to 45 years old	38	15. 1
45 years old and above	69	27. 5
Educational level		
High school and below	16	6. 4
College	55	21. 9
Bachelor	142	56. 6
Master and above	38	15. 1
Type of industry		
Building	15	6. 0
Trade	8	3. 2
Education institution	122	48. 6
Healthcare	34	13. 5
Hotel and restaurant	15	6. 0
Agriculture	6	2. 4
Others	51	20. 3

6. 8   Correlation Analysis-relationship Among Variables

In order to identify the factors that have an association among variables, correlation analysis was conducted where the correlation coefficient illustrates the relationship between the independent and dependent variables. According to Hair et al. (2006), the number representing the Pearson correlation is referred to as a correlation coefficient. It ranges from -1.00 to $+1.00$, with zero representing absolutely no association between the two metric variables. The larger the correlation coefficient, the stronger the linkage or level of association. A strong correlation is represented by a coefficient exceeding the value of 0. 5 whereas a medium or modest correlation is when the coefficient has a value of between 0. 5 and 0. 2. Any coefficient possessing a value less than 0. 2 will be deemed as showing a weak correlation. Benny and Feldman (1985) suggested a rule of thumb, that the correlation coefficients that exceed 0. 8 (very strong correlation) will likely to result in multicollinearity. Cohen (1988) has put forward a guideline on the effect sizes of the correlation coefficients in social science studies as: (1) small effect size: $r = 0.1 \sim 0.29$; (2) medium: $r = 0.30 \sim 0.49$; and (3) large: $r = > 0.50$.

Result of correlation analysis is summarizes in Table 6. 15, Table 6. 16, Table 6. 17 and Table 6. 18. It can be found in the table that the correlation coefficient (r) among variables were less than 0. 9, indicating that the variables were free from multicollinearity issue.

6. 8. 1　Relationship Among Organizational Justice, Organizational Citizenship Behavior and Organizational Performance

As indicated in Table 6. 15, organizational justice showed significant association with organizational performance ($r = 0.480$, $p < 0.01$) and organizational citizenship behavior ($r = 0.569$, $p < 0.01$). All three dimensions also provided important relationship between organizational citizenship behavior and organizational performance. Interactional justice showed the highest association to organizational performance and organizational citizenship behavior, followed by procedural justice and distributive justice.

Table 6. 15   Relationship Among Organizational Justice, OCB and
Organizational Performance

	Performance	OCB	OJ	DJ	PJ	IJ
Performance	1					
Organizational Citizenship Behavior	. 731 **	1				
Organizational Justice	. 480 **	. 569 **	1			
Distributive Justice	. 394 **	. 455 **	. 898 **	1		
Procedural Justice	. 427 **	. 474 **	. 892 **	. 694 **	1	
Interactional Justice	. 451 **	. 592 **	. 840 **	. 647 **	. 623 **	1

Note: ** : $p < 0.01$, * : $p < 0.05$.

6. 8. 2   Relationship Among Transformational Leadership, Organizational Citizenship Behavior and Organizational Performance

Next, Table 6. 16 summarizes the result of correlation analysis to examine the relationship among transformational leadership, organizational citizenship behavior and organizational performance. Results illustrated that there were significant relationship between transformational leadership and organizational citizenship behavior ($r = 0.717$, $p < 0.01$) and transformational leadership and organizational performance ($r = 0.595$, $p < 0.01$). All the dimensions also showed significant relationship between OCB and organizational performance ($p < 0.01$).

Table 6. 16   Relationship Among Transformational Leadership, OCB and Organizational Performance

	Performance	OCB	TL	II	IM	IS	IC
Performance	1						
Organizational Citizenship Behavior	. 731 **	1					
Transformational Leadership	. 595 **	. 717 **	1				
Idealized Influence	. 459 **	. 545 **	. 863 **	1			
Inspirational Motivation	. 532 **	. 650 **	. 924 **	. 782 **	1		
Intellectual Stimulation	. 554 **	. 692 **	. 925 **	. 692 **	. 793 **	1	
Individualized Consideration	. 607 **	. 705 **	. 911 **	. 670 **	. 765 **	. 858 **	1

Note: ** : $p < 0.01$, * : $p < 0.05$.

6. 8. 3   Relationship Among Employee Emotion Labor, Organizational Citizenship Behavior and Organizational Performance

Results of correlation analysis to examine the relationship between employee emotion, organizational citizenship behavior and organizational performance are illustrated in Table 6. 17. It was found that employee emotion was significantly associated with both organizational citizenship behavior ($r = 0.856$, $p < 0.01$) and organizational performance ($r = 0.660$, $p < 0.01$). Further inspection showed that deep emotion acting had the highest correlation coefficient with organizational citizenship behavior and organizational performance compared to surface emotion acting and true emotion acting.

Table 6. 17 Relationship Among Employee Emotion Labor, OCB and Organizational Performance

	Performance	OCB	EE	SEA	DEA	TEA
Performance	1					
Organizational Citizenship Behavior	. 731 **	1				
Employee Emotion Labor	. 660 **	. 856 **	1			
Surface Emotion Acting	. 621 **	. 803 **	. 935 **	1		
Deep Emotion Acting	. 648 **	. 801 **	. 952 **	. 848 **	1	
True Emotion Acting	. 552 **	. 767 **	. 880 **	. 709 **	. 777 **	1

Note: ** : $p < 0.01$, * : $p < 0.05$.

6. 8. 4 Relationship Among Organizational Learning, Organizational Citizenship Behavior and Organizational Performance

Results of correlation analysis to examine the relationship between organizational learning, organizational citizenship behavior and organizational performance are illustrated in Table 6. 18. It can be observed that organizational learning was significantly associated with both organizational citizenship behavior ($r = 0.753$, $p < 0.01$) and organizational performance ($r = 0.743$, $p < 0.01$). Further inspection showed that knowledge interpretation had the highest correlation coefficient with organizational citizenship behavior and organizational performance compared to knowledge acquisition and knowledge distribution.

Table 6.18　Relationship Among Organizational Learning, OCB and Organizational Performance

	Performance	OCB	OL	KA	KD	KI
Performance	1					
Organizational Citizenship Behavior	.731 **	1				
Organizational Learning	.743 **	.753 **	1			
Knowledge Acquisition	.692 **	.641 **	.910 **	1		
Knowledge Distribution	.665 **	.671 **	.948 **	.820 **	1	
Knowledge Interpretation	.698 **	.769 **	.910 **	.704 **	.807 **	1

Note: ** : $p < 0.01$, * : $p < 0.05$.

6.9　Multiple Regression Analyses-hypotheses Testing

Multiple regressions were utilized to test hypotheses developed in the previous chapter. Multiple regression analysis using enter methods were applied with the confidence level of 95 percent ($p < 0.05$) were adapted (Pallant, 2010). The regression models in this study comprises the dimension of organizational justice, transformational leadership, employee emotion and organizational learning as the predictors (X) and performance and organizational citizenship behavior as the outcome (Y). Furthermore, in testing the mediating effect, organizational citizenship behavior was treated as the mediating variable.

6.9.1　Effect of Predictors on Organizational Performance

Table 6.19 shows the result of regression analysis, which examine the effect of all predictors on organizational performance. Results showed that all predictors explained 77. 6 percent of variance in organizational performance ($R^2 = 0.776$, $F = 27.513$, $p < 0.01$). Eight predictors had significant relationship with organizational performance. The predictors were distributive justice ($p < 0.05$), interactional justice ($p < 0.05$), inspirational motivation ($p < 0.05$), intellectual stimulation ($p < 0.05$), individualized consideration ($p < 0.05$), deep emotion acting ($p < 0.05$), knowledge acquisition ($p < 0.01$) and knowledge interpretation ($p < 0.01$).

Table 6. 19   Effect of Predictors on Organizational Performance

	B	T	*Sig.*
Distributive Justice	. 146	2. 174	0. 31
Procedural Justice	− . 101	− 1. 963	. 051
Interactional Justice	. 139	2. 126	. 034
Idealized Influence	− . 071	− 1. 375	. 170
Inspirational Motivation	. 148	2. 020	. 045
Intellectual Stimulation	. 151	2. 231	. 027
Individualized Consideration	. 162	2. 397	. 017
Surface Emotion Acting	− . 124	− 1. 668	. 097
Deep Emotion Acting	. 171	2. 028	. 044
True Emotion Acting	− . 110	− 1. 939	. 054
Knowledge Acquisition	. 241	3. 816	. 000
Knowledge Distribution	− . 094	− 1. 276	. 203
Knowledge Interpretation	. 186	2. 651	. 009
R^2	0. 776		
F	27. 513		
Sig.	0. 000		

6. 9. 2　Effect of Predictors on Organizational Citizenship Behavior

Next table, Table 6. 20 illustrates the result of regression analysis to examine the direct effect of predictors on organizational citizenship behavior. Overall, the studied predictors explained 87. 2% of organizational citizenship behavior (R^2 = 0. 872, F = 58. 115, $p < 0.01$). Ten predictors showed significant effect on organizational citizenship behavior. The predictors were distributive justice ($p < 0.05$), procedural justice ($p < 0.05$), interactional justice ($p < 0.05$), inspirational motivation ($p < 0.05$), individualized consideration ($p < 0.05$), surface emotion impression ($p < 0.01$), deep emotion acting ($p < 0.01$), true emotion acting ($p < 0.01$), knowledge acquisition ($p < 0.05$) and knowledge interpretation ($p < 0.01$).

Table 6. 20　Effect of Predictors on Organizational Citizenship Behavior

	B	T	Sig.
Equation a (IV to MV)			
Distributive Justice	. 104	2. 113	. 036
Procedural Justice	. 076	2. 020	. 044
Interactional Justice	. 096	2. 005	. 046
Idealized Influence	. 033	. 875	. 383
Inspirational Motivation	. 113	2. 100	. 037
Intellectual Stimulation	. 004	. 083	. 934
Individualized Consideration	. 118	2. 390	. 018
Surface Emotion Acting	. 181	3. 328	. 001
Deep Emotion Acting	. 207	3. 353	. 001
True Emotion Acting	. 197	4. 738	. 000
Knowledge Acquisition	. 094	2. 019	. 045
Knowledge Distribution	− . 035	− . 646	. 519

(To be continued)

	B	T	Sig.
Knowledge Interpretation	. 117	2. 284	. 023
R^2	0. 872		
F	58. 115		
Sig.	0. 000		

6. 9. 3   Effect of Organizational Citizenship Behavior on Organizational Performance

Lastly, this section also examined the effect of organizational citizenship behavior on organizational performance. Result of regression analysis is illustrated in Table 6. 21. Table 6. 21 indicates that organizational citizenship behavior explained 62. 7% variance of organizational performance ($R^2 = 0.627$, $F = 161.524$, $p < 0.01$). The coefficient of organizational citizenship behavior on organizational performance was significant ($B = 0.661$, $t = 12.709$, $p < 0.01$), indicating the significant effect of organizational citizenship behavior on organizational performance.

Table 6. 21   Effect of Organizational Citizenship Behavior
on Organizational Performance

	B	T	Sig.
Organizational Citizenship Behavior	0. 661	12. 709	0. 000
R^2	0. 627		
F	161. 524		
Sig.	0. 000		

6. 9. 4   Mediating Effect of Organizational Citizenship Behavior on the Relationship Between Independent Variables and Organizational Performance

Last hypotheses attempt to test the mediating effect of organizational citizenship behavior on the relationship between predictors and organizational performance. In analyzing the mediating effect, 4 steps of hierarchical regression using PROCESS Macro as suggested by Heyes (2013) were adopted. The four steps of regression analysis were undertaken to examine each equation as illustrated in Figure 6. 9. The first step (equation a) was to examine the effect predictors on MV. The second step (equation b) was the effect of MV on DV, while the third step (equation c) was the effect of predictors to DV. The last step (equation c') was the effect of predictors on DV with the present of MV.

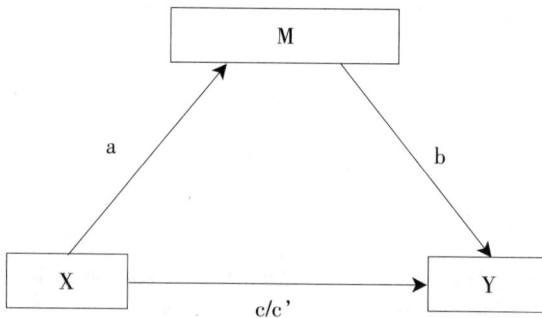

Figure 6. 9   Method Used to Analyze Mediating Effect

According to Baron and Kenny (1986), the mediating occurred from the following conditions:

(1) Mediating Variable (M) completely mediates the X-Y relation if all three conditions are met:

i . X predicts Y.

ii . X predicts M.

iii. X no longer predicts Y, but M does when both X and M are used to predict Y.

(2) M partially mediates the X-Y relation if all three conditions are met:

ⅰ. X predicts Y.

ⅱ. X predicts M.

ⅲ. Both X and M predict Y, but X has a smaller regression coefficient when both X and M are used to predict Y than when only X is used.

Result of regression analysis to examine the mediating effect of organizational citizenship behavior is illustrated in Table 6.22. Out of thirteen predictors tested, ten (distributive justice, procedural justice, interactional justice, inspirational motivation, individualized consideration, true emotion acting, surface emotion acting, deep emotion acting, knowledge acquisition, knowledge interpretation) of them had fulfilled path "a" and eight (distributive justice, interactional justice, inspirational motivation, intellectual stimulation, individualized consideration, deep emotion acting, knowledge acquisition and knowledge interpretation) had fulfil path "c". The model also meets the requirement in path "b" when organizational citizenship behavior significantly contributes to organizational performance. Based on the requirement outlined by Baron and Kenny (1986), organizational citizenship behavior only mediates the relationships between distributive justice, interactive justice, inspirational motivation, individualized consideration, deep emotion acting, knowledge acquisition, knowledge interpretation and organizational performance. Organizational citizenship behavior failed to mediate the relationships between procedural justice, idealized influence, intellectual stimulation, surface emotion acting, true emotion acting, knowledge acquisition, knowledge interpretation and organizational performance.

Table 6. 22 Mediating Effect of Organizational Citizenship Behavior on the Relationships Between Predictors and Organizational Performance

	B	T	Sig.
Equation a（IV to MV）			
Distributive Justice	. 104	2. 113	. 036
Procedural Justice	. 076	2. 020	. 044
Interactional Justice	. 096	2. 005	. 046
Idealized Influence	. 033	. 875	. 383
Inspirational Motivation	. 113	2. 100	. 037
Intellectual Stimulation	. 004	. 083	. 934
Individualized Consideration	. 118	2. 390	. 018
Surface Emotion Acting	. 181	3. 328	. 001
Deep Emotion Acting	. 207	3. 353	. 001
True Emotion Acting	. 197	4. 738	. 000
Knowledge Acquisition	. 094	2. 019	. 045
Knowledge Distribution	−. 035	−. 646	. 519
Knowledge Interpretation	. 117	2. 284	. 023
Equation b（MV to DV）			
OCB	0. 661	12. 709	0. 000
Equation c（IV to DV）			
Distributive Justice	. 146	2. 174	. 031
Procedural Justice	−. 101	−1. 963	. 051
Interactional Justice	. 139	2. 126	. 034
Idealized Influence	−. 071	−1. 375	. 170
Inspirational Motivation	. 148	2. 020	. 045
Intellectual Stimulation	. 151	2. 231	. 027
Individualized Consideration	. 162	2. 397	. 017
Surface Emotion Acting	−. 124	−1. 668	. 097

(To be continued)

	B	T	Sig.
Deep Emotion Acting	.171	2.028	.044
True Emotion Acting	-.110	-1.939	.054
Knowledge Acquisition	.241	3.816	.000
Knowledge Distribution	-.094	-1.276	.203
Knowledge Interpretation	.186	2.651	.009
Equation c' (X & M-Y)			
Distributive Justice	.124	1.855	.065
Procedural Justice	-.085	-1.660	.098
Interactional Justice	.120	1.826	.069
Idealized Influence	-.078	-1.519	.130
Inspirational Motivation	.125	1.704	.090
Intellectual Stimulation	.150	2.240	.026
Individualized Consideration	.137	2.043	.042
Surface Emotion Acting	-.161	-2.141	.033
Deep Emotion Acting	.128	1.502	.134
True Emotion Acting	-.150	-2.559	.011
Knowledge Acquisition	.222	3.514	.001
Knowledge Distribution	-.087	-1.189	.236
Knowledge Interpretation	.161	2.304	.022
Organizational Citizenship Behaviour	.205	2.341	.020

According to Table 6.22, the following results were obtained. As illustrated in Figure 6.10, based on the Baron and Kenny (1986), the effect of distributive justice on organizational performance decrease from 0.146 to 0.124, distributive justice predicts organizational performance ($p < 0.05$), distributive justice predicts organizational citizenship behavior ($p < 0.05$). When the distributive justice and organizational citizenship behavior are both used to predict organizational performance, distributive justice no longer predicts organizational performance ($p >$ 0. 05) , but organizational citizenship behavior can predict organizational performance ($p < 0.05$). This result indicated that organizational citizenship behavior has completely mediated the relationship between distributive justice and organizational performance.

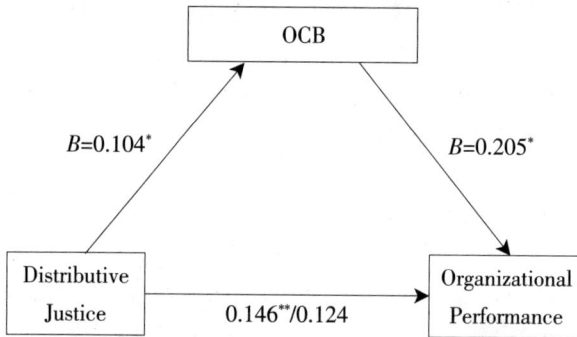

Figure 6. 10   Mediating Effect of OCB on the Relationship Between Distributive Justice and Organizational Performance

According to Table 6. 22 , the following results were obtained. As illustrated in Figure 6. 11 , based on the Baron and Kenny (1986) , the effect of interactional justice on organizational performance decrease from 0. 139 to 0. 120, interactional justice predicts organizational performance ($p < 0.05$) , interactional justice predicts organizational citizenship behavior ($p < 0.05$). When the interactional justice and organizational citizenship behavior are both used to predict organizational performance, interactional justice no longer predicts organizational performance ($p >$ 0. 05) , but organizational citizenship behavior can predict organizational performance ($p < 0.05$). This result indicated that organizational citizenship behavior has completely mediated the relationship between interactional justice and organizational performance.

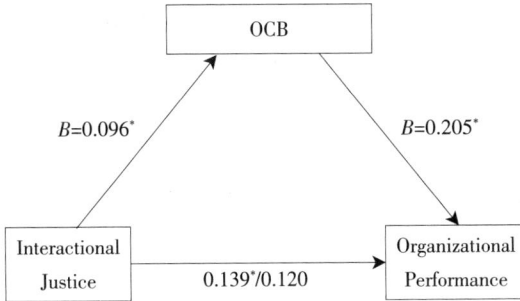

Figure 6. 11   Mediating Effect of OCB on the Relationship Between Interactoonal Justice and Oraganizational Performance

According to Table 6. 22, the following results were obtained . As illustrated in Figure 6. 12, based on the Baron and Kenny (1986), the effect of inspirational motivation on organizational performance decrease from 0. 148 to 0. 125, inspirational motivation predicts organizational performance ($p < 0.05$), inspirational motivation predicts organizational citizenship behavior ($p < 0.05$). When the inspirational motivation and organizational citizenship behavior are both used to predict organizational performance, inspirational motivation no longer predicts organizational performance ($p > 0.05$), but organizational citizenship behavior can predict organizational performance ($p < 0.05$). This result indicated that organizational citizenship behavior has completely mediated the relationship between inspirational motivation and organizational performance.

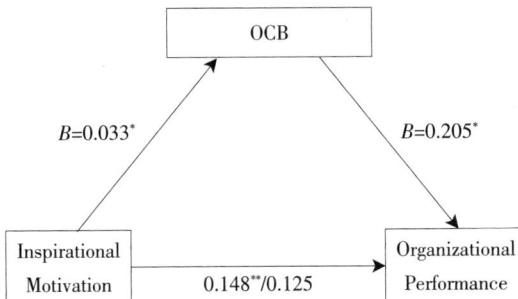

Figure 6. 12   Mediating Effect of OCB on the Relationship Between Inspirational Motivation and Organizational Performance

According to Table 6. 22, the following results were obtained . As illustrated in Figure 6. 13, based on the Baron and Kenny (1986), individualized consideration predicts organizational performance ($p <$ 0. 05), individualized consideration predicts organizational citizenship behavior ($p < 0. 05$). When the individualized consideration and organizational citizenship behavior are both used to predict organizational performance, individualized consideration can predict organizational performance ($p < 0. 05$), organizational citizenship behavior can predict organizational performance ($p < 0. 05$). And the effect of individualized consideration on organizational performance decrease from 0. 162 to 0. 137. This result indicated that organizational citizenship behavior has partially mediated the relationship between individualized consideration and organizational performance.

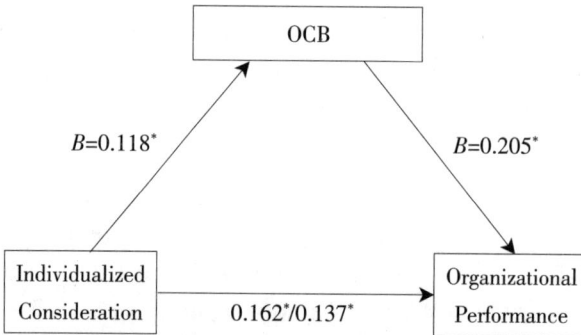

Figure 6. 13   Mediating Effect of OCB on the Relationship Between Individualized Consideration and Organizational Performance

According to Table 6. 22, the following results were obtained . As illustrated in Figure 6. 14, based on the Baron and Kenny (1986), the effect of deep emotion acting on organizational performance decrease from 0. 171 to 0. 128. Deep emotion acting predicts organizational performance ($p < 0. 05$), deep emotion acting predicts organizational citizenship behavior ($p < 0. 05$). When the deep emotion acting and organizational citizenship behavior are both used to predict organizational performance, deep emotion acting no longer predicts organizational performance ($p >$ 0.05), but organizational citizenship behavior can predict organizational performance ($p < 0.05$). This result indicated that organizational citizenship behavior has completely mediates the relationship between deep emotion acting and organizational performance.

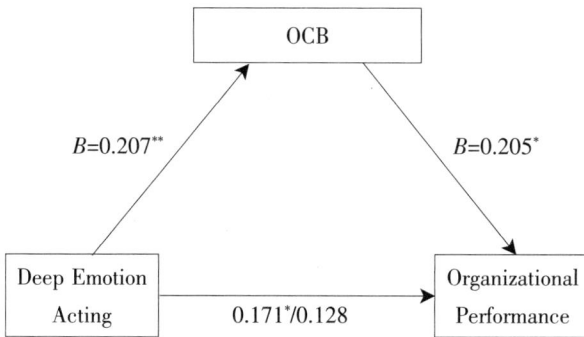

Figure 6.14   Mediating Effect of OCB on the Relationship Between Deep Emotion Acting and Organizational Performance

According to Table 6.22, the following results were obtained. As illustrated in Figure 6.15, based on the Baron and Kenny (1986), knowledge acquisition predicts organizational performance ($p < 0.05$), knowledge acquisition predicts organizational citizenship behavior ($p < 0.05$), When the knowledge acquisition and organizational citizenship behavior are both used to predict organizational performance, knowledge acquisition can predict organizational performance ($p < 0.05$), organizational citizenship behavior can predict organizational performance ($p < 0.05$). And the effect of knowledge acquisition on organizational performance decrease from 0.241 to 0.222. This result indicated that organizational citizenship behavior has partially mediated the relationship between knowledge acquisition and performance.

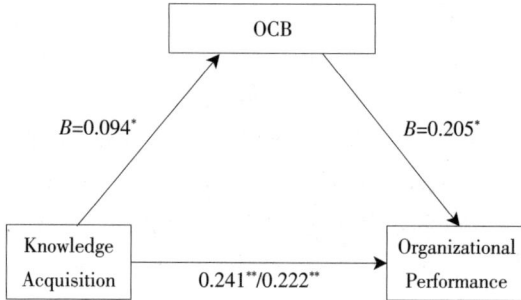

Figure 6. 15 Mediating Effect of OCB on the Relationship Between Knowledge Acquisition and Organizational Performance

According to Table 6. 22, the following results were obtained . As illustrated in Figure 6. 16, based on the Baron and Kenny (1986), knowledge interpretation predicts organizational performance ($p < 0.05$), knowledge interpretation predicts organizational citizenship behavior ($p < 0.05$), When the knowledge acquisition and organizational citizenship behavior are both used to predict organizational performance, knowledge interpretation can predict organizational performance ($p < 0.05$), organizational citizenship behavior can predict organizational performance ($p < 0.05$). And the effect of knowledge interpretation on organizational performance decreased from 0. 186 to 0. 161. This result indicated that organizational citizenship behavior has partially mediated the relationship between knowledge interpretation and organizational performance.

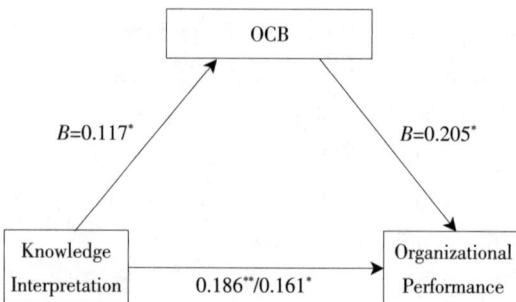

Figure 6. 16 Mediating Effect of OCB on the Relationship Between Knowledge Interpretation and Organizational Performance

6. 10　Summary

In this chapter, according to the method proposed in the previous chapter, the data and results are statistically tested and analyzed. Chapter Seven will discuss the implications of research findings and theories. Policy formulation and future research will also be presented.

Chapter Seven   Discussion, Recommendation and Conclusion

7. 1   Introduction

This chapter offers a discussion on the findings of this research. The discussion is based on the research questions as illustrated in Chapter One. Theoretical and practical implications, limitations and suggestions for future research are also included in this chapter. Before ending the discussion, a conclusion of the study is offered.

7. 2   Recapitulation of the Findings

As stated in Chapter One, this research intends to examine factors that can improve organizational performance of SMEs in Jilin Province of China. Data were gathered from the employees of SMEs in Jilin Province of China.

A total of 400 questionnaires were distributed in this study and 251 were returned which yielded 62.7% response rate. There were no cases of missing data and outliers and all data were fit for analysis. The results of *chi*-square test and independent sample t-test showed that there was no response bias in terms of demographic characteristics and research variables. Additionally, the assumptions of normality, linearity, homoscedasticity and multicollinearity were tested and fulfilled.

PCA with Varimax rotation factor analysis was utilized to examine the factorial validity of the measures. The results of factor analysis for organizational performance antecedents highlighted the existence of fourteen significant factors; therefore, consistent with the proposed research conceptual framework. The factors were distributive justice, procedural justice, interactional justice, idealized influence, inspirational motivation, intellectual stimulation, individualized consideration, surface emotion acting, deep emotion acting, true emotion acting, knowledge acquisition, knowledge distribution, knowledge interpretation and organizational citizenship behavior.

Then, Cronbach's alpha values were computed to examine the internal consistency of the measures. The results of reliability test indicated that the values of Cronbach's alpha for all variables were above the minimum acceptable level.

The findings showed that 25 hypotheses were supported. Results from the standard multiple regression analysis indicated that distributive justice (H1a), interactional justice (H3a), inspirational motivation (H5a), intellectual stimulation (H6a), individualized consideration (H7a), deep emotion acting (H9a), knowledge acquisition (H11a) and knowledge interpretation (H13a) were found to be positively and significantly influenced organizational performance. From the perspective of magnitude, knowledge acquisition was the most influential factor while interactional justice had the least influence on organizational performance. This was followed by individualized consideration, inspirational motivation, intellectual stimulation, deep emotion acting, knowledge interpretation, distributive justice as the second, the third, the fourth, the fifth and the sixth most influential factors for organizational performance respectively.

The findings also indicated that distributive justice (H1b), interactional justice (H3b), inspirational motivation (H5b), intellectual stimulation (H6b), individualized consideration (H7b), surface emotion acting (H8b), deep emotion acting (H9b), true emotion acting (H10b), knowledge acquisition (H11b) and knowledge interpretation (H13b) were found to be positively and significantly influenced organizational citizenship behavior. From the perspective of magnitude, true emotion acting was the most influential factor while procedural justice had the least influence on organizational citizenship behavior. In addition, surface emotion acting, deep emotion acting, inspirational motivation, interactional justice, distributive justice, individualized consideration, knowledge acquisition and knowledge interpretation were the second, the third, the fourth, the fifth, the sixth, the seventh and the eighth most influential factors for organizational citizenship behavior in the SMEs of China.

This study had also supported H1c, H3c, H5c, H7c, H9c, H11c and H13c. In other words, the relationships between distributive justice, interactional justice, inspirational motivation, individualized consideration, deep emotion acting, knowledge acquisition, knowledge interpretation and organizational performance were mediated by organizational citizenship behavior. Besides, the relationships between procedural justice, inspirational motivation, individualized consideration, surface emotion acting, true emotion acting, knowledge acquisition, knowledge interpretation and organizational performance were not mediated by organizational citizenship behavior. This study had also supported H14 whereby organizational citizenship behavior has a positive influence on the organizational performance of SMEs in Jilin Province of China.

7.3　Discussion

This section discusses the results highlighted in section 7.2. The discussion is based on the research questions as stated in Chapter One which are as follows: ① What is the effect of organizational justice, transformational leadership, employee emotion labor and organizational learning on organizational performance of SMEs in Jilin Province of China? ②What is the effect of organizational justice, transformational leadership, employee emotion labor and organizational learning on organizational citizenship behavior of employees of SMEs in Jilin Province of China? ③Does organizational citizenship behavior mediate the relationship between organizational justice, transformational leadership, employee emotion labor, organizational learning and organizational performance of

SMEs in Jilin province of China? ④What is the effect of organizational citizenship behavior on organizational performance of SMEs in Jilin Province of China?

7.3.1 The Effect of Antecedents on Organizational Performance

The first research question was related to the impact of organizational justice (distributive justice, procedural justice, interactional justice), transformational leadership (idealized influence, inspirational motivation, intellectual stimulation, individualized consideration), employee emotion labor (surface emotion acting, deep emotion acting, true emotion acting), and organizational learning (knowledge acquisition, knowledge distribution, knowledge interpretation) on organizational performance of SMEs in Jilin Province of China. The findings for these impacts are showed in the following sections.

7.3.1.1 The Effect of Organizational Justice on Organizational Performance

Through the correlation analysis and regression analysis, as discussed in Chapter Six, it can be observed that there were significant correlations between distributive justice, procedural justice, interactive justice and organizational performance of SMEs in Jilin Province of China. Interactional justice gained the highest coefficient and followed by procedural justice and distributive justice. Through regression analysis, it can be observed that distributive justice and interactive justice were positively and significantly influenced by organizational performance but procedural justice was not positively and significantly influenced by organizational performance.

The above findings were similar to that of Fang (2010) whereby he uncovered that distributive justice, procedural justice and interactional justice of employees were positively correlated with organizational performance and interactive fairness had a positive predictive effect on organizational performance. Xu (2015) explored the mechanism of interactional justice and procedural fairness on employee performance. He surveyed 352 employees in dozens of enterprises through questionnaires and conducted practical research using empirical analysis methods. His findings showed that procedural justice has no obvious effect on organizational performance; interactional justice has obvious effect on organizational performance. Liao (2018) found that, among the dimensions of organizational justice, there were positive correlations between distributive justice, procedural justice, interactional justice and organizational performance. Organizational justice has a positive impact on organizational performance.

Thus, only when employees think that their input has been rewarded properly can they feel organizational fairness, and then they will work hard to improve personal work performance, thereby improving organizational performance. If employees can not feel organizational justice, it will reduce work efficiency and even lead to negative idleness. Only by realizing organizational justice can employees' work performance be positively affected.

To sum up, organizational justice is a key factor in measuring enterprise management ability and an important component of enterprise core competitiveness. It has a very important impact on employees' work cognition and practice. Therefore, the relationship and influence between organizational justice and employees' work performance are significant key factors in enterprise competition. Existing studies have shown that employees' organizational justice has an important effect on their emotions and practices at work. The important influence of organizational justice on enterprise performance makes enterprises pay more and more attention to the fairness of performance evaluation in the process of operation and management.

With the quick development of social economy and the increasingly fierce market competition, enterprises have higher and higher requirements for employee performance. Organizational justice has a direct impact on employee performance. Enterprises should ensure organizational justice, especially in terms of distributive justice and interactional justice, to increase the effective improvement of employee performance, and then increase the overall improvement of organizational performance. And the organization needs to trust and respect employees, give employees fair treatment. Employees will be able to produce responsibility for the organization, and then trust the organization, believe that the organization will give its own pay back (Song, 2019).

7.3.1.2   The Effect of Transformational Leadership on Organizational Performance

The relationship between individualized consideration, intellectual stimulation, inspirational motivation, idealized influence and organizational performance can be found through correlation analysis and regression analysis. There were significant positive correlations between the dimensions of transformational leadership and organizational performance of SMEs. Individualized consideration gained the highest coefficient and followed by intellectual stimulation, inspirational motivation and idealized influence. From the regression analysis, intellectual stimulation, individualized consideration and idealized influence were positively and significantly influenced by organizational performance but idealized influence was not positively and significantly influenced by organizational performance.

The above findings were similar to that of Wang (2017) whereby his research showed that transformational leadership had a significant correlation with organizational performance. Through further multiple regression analysis, the results show that personalized care can explain the variation of organizational performance to the greatest extent, while virtue paradigm does not have obvious impact on organizational interpretation. It can be seen that transformational leadership has a positive predictive effect on job performance, and this predictive effect mainly comes from the level of personalized care. Lowe Kroeck and Sivasubramaniam (1996) found that transformational leadership had a positive correlation with organizational performance, and the results of this study were the same as those of previous studies. Thus, employees perceived leaders' intellectual stimulation, individualized consideration and idealized influence as important factors for organizational performance.

Therefore, superiors must have high moral behavior, unique leadership charm, intellectual promotion and vision incentive to subordinate, care about subordinates' work life, family and so on. The leader is more likely to be recognized, respected and imitated by subordinates, and hopes to become a superior like that person, and will continue to learn and innovate in the work, promote the development of their own capabilities, which will enhance the organizational performance of the company.

In the regression equation of transformational leadership on organizational performance, the regression coefficient of individualized consideration level is significant, which indicates that individualized care has a significant effect on organizational performance of subordinates. The reason may be that subordinates are more likely to perceive their superiors' concern for themselves, so they work harder, learn new knowledge and skills more actively, and improve themselves. Therefore, in practical work, managers should pay more attention to the work, growth and development of employees, the life and family of employees. When employees perceive these caring behaviors, they will feel valued by the organization. They will inevitably have a sense of identity to the organization, show more reciprocal behavior and work harder, which will ultimately lead to their excessive achievement of the expected performance.

7.3.1.3   The Effect of Employee Emotion Labor on Organizational Performance

Through the correlation and regression analyses, as highlighted in Chapter Six, it can be observed that there were significant correlations among surface emotion acting, deep emotion acting, true emotion acting and organizational performance. In other words, all dimensions under employee emotion were related to organizational performance. Deep emotion acting gained the highest coefficient and followed by surface emotion acting and true emotion acting. From the perspective of regression, however, only deep emotion acting was positively and significantly influenced by organizational performance. True emotion acting and surface emotion acting were not positively and significantly influenced organizational performance.

The above findings were similar to that of Chen (2008) whereby he found that the choice of emotional labor strategy would have a certain impact on individual work outcomes in the survey of service industry employees. Specifically, workers who often adopt deep-seated behavior have less emotional exhaustion and relatively higher organizational performance, while workers who often adopt shallow-seated behavior, on the contrary, are more likely to have emotional exhaustion and relatively low output performance results. Zhang (2010) found that deep behavior positively predicted organizational performance. Chen (2008), Zhang (2010) and Wang (2010) found the relationship between emotional labor and organizational performance when investigating service industry employees and grass-roots managers. Specifically, deep-level behavioral strategies are positively correlated with employees' organizational performance, while shallow-level behavioral strategies are negatively correlated with employees' organizational performance.

This research uncovered that deep emotion acting had a positive effect on organizational performance, which was similar to past research. But the influence of surface emotion acting on organizational performance is inconsistent with past researches. It may be different research objects, which results in different research results and employee may not always adopt surface emotion acting in the work. At the same time, this paper studies that true emotional acting has no impact on organizational performance, which has been supplemented for previous scholars' research.

The study of emotional emotion labor can help people realize that besides physical and mental work there are also emotional labor which has great influence on organizations and individuals. The research results of emotional labor can help managers reduce the negative impact of emotional labor on employees' health and work output, and expand the positive significance of emotional labor on organizational and personal performance. Deep behavior can predict employees' organizational citizenship behavior and organizational performance. In practice, deep behavior can positively affect employees' working attitude, behavior and results to a certain extent. Therefore, enterprises must pay attention to the emotional labor status and level of employees, focus on the impact of emotional labor in the physical and mental health of employees, and make employees grow, succeed and achieve a better life while achieving organizational development.

7. 3. 1. 4   The Effect of Organizational Learning on Organizational Performance

Through the correlation and regression analyses, as highlighted in Chapter Six, it can be observed that there were significant correlations among knowledge acquisition, knowledge distribution, knowledge interpretation and organizational performance in SMEs in China. Knowledge interpretation gained the highest coefficient and followed by knowledge acquisition and knowledge distribution. From the regression analysis, it found that knowledge interpretation and knowledge acquisition had a positive and significant influence on the organizational performance whereas knowledge distribution was not positively and significantly influenced by organizational performance.

The above findings were consistent with Huber (1991) whereby he found that organizational learning had direct correlation with organizational performance. Calantone, Cavusgil and Zhao (2002) found that learning commitment, shared vision, open mind and knowledge sharing had positive effects on organizational innovation ability. Aküzüm and Cemal (2014) stated that the higher the level of organizational learning, the more obvious the innovation of management and technology. Skerlavaj, et al. (2010) stated that organizational learning can change the behavior and cognition of organizational members which had a significant and positive effect on organizational technological innovation and organizational performance.

It also found that knowledge distribution did not affect organizational performance, maybe because knowledge distribution requires a long-term process, and employees' knowledge distribution has not been fully applied to work, so the results of organizational performance are not significant. In short, the findings of this research are consistent with previous researches.

At present, organizational learning does not occur automatically in all enterprises. It needs corresponding organizational conditions and management measures. Therefore, only when enterprises have a common vision, an open and experimental organizational atmosphere, can they effectively carry out knowledge transfer and integration, and leaders are good at counseling staff and encouraging learning, can enterprises become a learning organization. Organizational learning of enterprises will have a positive impact on their entrepreneurial activities, such as knowledge transfer and integration dimension of organizational learning will promote innovative activities, knowledge transfer and interpretation and integration also need proper organizational mechanisms and management measures. Team learning is very important in today's highly interdependent and networked world. The results of this study can theoretically provide a basis and perspective for further researches on the following-up relationship. Meanwhile, they can offer advice for SMEs in China on how to improve their organizational learning ability, build learning organizations, eliminate team learning barriers and further promote corporate performance in practice.

7.3.2　The Effect of Antecedents on Organizational Citizenship Behavior

The first research question was related to the impact of organizational justice (distributive justice, procedural justice, interactional justice), transformational leadership (idealized influence, inspirational motivation, intellectual stimulation, individualized consideration), employee emotion (surface emotion acting, deep emotion acting, true emotion acting), and organizational learning (knowledge acquisition, knowledge distribution, knowledge interpretation) on organizational performance of SMEs in Jilin Province of China. The findings for these impacts are offered in the following subsections.

7. 3. 2. 1 The Effect of Organizational Justice on Organizational Citizenship Behavior

Through the correlation analysis and regression analysis, as discussed in Chapter Six, it can be seen that there were significant correlations between distributive justice, procedural justice, interactive justice and organizational citizenship behavior of employees in SMEs in Jilin Province of China. This can show that the higher the perception of organizational justice of employees in SMEs, the better the perception on organizational citizenship behavior. Interactional justice obtained the highest coefficient and followed by procedural justice and distributive justice. Through regression analysis, it uncovered that distributive justice, procedural justice and interactive justice were positively and significantly influenced by organizational citizenship behavior.

The above findings were similar to those of previous studies such as Rego and Chanha (2010) and Nastiezaie and Najafi (2015). They found that organizational citizenship behavior was significantly affected by interpersonal justice. Farh J. L. (1997) analyzed the relationship between organizational justice and organizational citizenship behavior under the background of Taiwanese society. It found that procedural justice and distributive justice have positive correlation with organizational citizenship behavior. Distributive justice and interactional justice have the highest influence on organizational citizenship behavior (Farh J. L. , 1997). Yan and Zhang (2010) found that all dimensions of organizational justice, such as distribution justice, procedural justice and interactional justice, positively influenced by employees' organizational citizenship behavior and all dimensions of behavior. Farh J. L. and Lin (2010) found that procedural justice and distributive justice were positively correlated with organizational justice behavior. Thus, it could be said that the results of this study were parallel to previous studies and supported the axiom that interactional justice, distributive justice and procedural justice are important in the organization.

Implicit in the above findings is that SMEs should pay more attention to the interactive justice in the organizational environment. After the basic needs of employees go out in the new era, the high-level needs emerge, which need not only the fairness of remuneration, but also the requirement of respect and self-transcendence. The organizational citizenship behavior of grass-roots civil servants will be enhanced by whether the implementation of organizational procedures is recognized by most of the members, whether the leaders show due respect to the members in the process of implementation and due communication. On the contrary, when perceived leadership does not show the necessary respect, it will make a response to reduce organizational citizenship behavior.

7. 3. 2. 2 The Effect of Transformational Leadership on Organizational Citizenship Behavior

Through the correlation analysis and regression analysis, as discussed in Chapter Six, it can be seen that there were significant correlations between individualized consideration, intellectual stimulation, inspirational motivation, idealized influence and organizational citizenship behavior in the SMEs in China. This shows that the higher transformational leadership behavior of employees in SMEs, the more likely they will show organizational citizenship behavior. Individualized consideration obtained the highest coefficient and followed by intellectual stimulation, inspirational motivation and idealized influence.

From the perspective of regression analysis, the influence idealized influence and intellectual stimulation on organizational citizenship behavior is not significant, but inspirational motivation and individualized consideration had significant influence on organizational citizenship behavior. That is to say that idealized influence and intellectual stimulation have no significant explanatory effect on the variation of organizational citizenship behavior, while individualized consideration can explain the variation of organizational citizenship behavior to a certain extent. Inspirational motivation obtained the highest beta value in explaining the variation of organizational citizenship behavior.

The above findings were similar to the previous studies, such as Pillai, et al. (1999) and Bycio, et al. (1995). They found that organizational citizenship behavior increases with the influence of transformational leadership behavior. Leaders' incentive behavior to employees enables employees to achieve their goals in a better way (Van Scotter & Motowwidlo, 1996). There was an obvious correlation between transformational leadership behavior and organizational citizenship (Zhang & Qiao, 2005). Li (2006) also stated that transformational leadership had a significant positive impact on organizational citizenship behavior. Zhang and Qiao (2005) investigated the impact of transformational leadership on employees' organizational citizenship behavior and found that there was a significant correlation between transformational leadership behavior and employee organizational citizenship behavior, thus it could be said that the results of this study were consistent with similar previous studies above.

Implicit in the above findings is that the leaders should build a good organizational vision, and regularly describe to each subordinate clear, infectious and motivating goals and visions, stimulate subordinates' motivation for self-realization and achievement, arouse their subjective initiative, make them fully feel the significance of work and self-worth, integrate personal ideals and corporate goals organically, with full confidence. The leaders should also be diligent and good at communicating with subordinates on an equal footing, understand the specific situation and needs of different employees to treat them differently and achieve positive interaction. The leaders should be concerned with the work and personal development of subordinate employees, understand the confusion encountered in the workplace and give sincere corresponding suggestions, support and guidance and tailor-made career development plan for each employee, which are also conducive to subordinates' actual work. At the same time, when employees perceive these caring behaviors, they will feel valued by the organization. Weaving generates a sense of identity and shows more reciprocal behavior, which will redouble efforts and ultimately lead to its excessive achievement of the expected performance.

7. 3. 2. 3 The Effect of Emotion Labor on Organizational Citizenship Behavior

From the correlation analysis, as discussed in Chapter Six, it can be seen that there were significant correlations among surface emotion acting, deep emotion acting, true emotion acting and organizational citizenship behavior. This shows that the higher employee emotion is among employees in SMEs, the more likely they will show organizational citizenship behavior. Deep emotion acting obtained the highest coefficients and was followed by surface emotion acting and true emotion acting.

From the perspective of regression analysis, surface emotion acting, deep emotion acting and true emotion acting were positively and significantly influenced by organizational citizenship behavior. These findings were similar to those of previous studies such as Salami (2007) whereby he found that deep emotion acting was significantly related to organizational citizenship behavior. Implicit in the above findings is that the employees should express their emotions and behaviors in real time, which will not suppress their emotional feelings. When the inner consistency and the outer consistency of behavior produce the sense of authenticity, this kind of real emotion will affect the overall evaluation of the work of employees and sometimes will have a positive impact on the work of employees, thereby organizational citizenship behavior and enhancing organizational performance.

7. 3. 2. 4 The Effect of Organizational Learning on Organizational Citizenship Behavior

From the correlation analysis, it found that there were significant correlations among knowledge acquisition, knowledge distribution, knowledge interpretation and organizational citizenship behavior. This shows that the higher organizational learning is among employees in SMEs, the more likely they will show organizational citizenship behavior. Knowledge interpretation obtained the highest correlation and was followed by knowledge distribution and knowledge acquisition.

From the regression analysis, it found that knowledge interpretation and knowledge acquisition were positively and significantly influenced by organizational citizenship behavior. However, knowledge distribution was not positively and significantly influenced by organizational citizenship behavior. This finding is similar to those of previous studies such as Zhang (2008) and Li (2013). Zhang (2008) found that organizational learning was a significantly positive influence on organizational citizenship behavior. Li (2013) found that organizational strategic practice learning had a positive impact on employees' organizational citizenship behavior. If more entrepreneurial practices are carried out within the enterprise, the more organizational citizenship behavior employees will exhibit. Therefore, knowledge acquisition and knowledge interpretation are important in the organizational learning process for development of organization.

Therefore, in order to strengthen knowledge acquisition, knowledge sharing and knowledge utilization in knowledge management, SMEs should shape an evaluating, incentive and resource allocating that is conducive to organizational learning so as to cultivate an atmosphere and process of organizational learning. Through the design of knowledge contribution incentive, employees in an organization are willing to take the initiative to acquire the resources and knowledge needed for enterprise operation and then to contribute key knowledge, especially tacit knowledge. SMEs should also encourage and support employees to transfer the knowledge they have learned to the enterprise. Through sharing with other employees, key knowledge will be shared by employees through the clarification of knowledge and then rise to the level of group and organization.

SMEs also need to fully explain and utilize the knowledge they have learned. To achieve this, they need not only an incentive system for knowledge learning and a resource allocation system, but also, more importantly, a relaxing, trustworthy, innovative and friendly enterprise culture that is people-oriented. In order to significantly improve the level of organizational citizenship behavior, enterprises should pay attention to organizational learning.

7.3.3 Mediating Effect of Organizational Citizenship Behavior on the Relationship Between Independent Variables and Organizational Performance

The third research question is related to the mediating effect of organizational citizenship behavior on the relationship between independent variables (distributive justice, procedural justice, interactional justice, idealized influence, inspirational motivation, intellectual stimulation, individualized consideration, surface emotion acting, deep emotion acting, true emotion acting, knowledge acquisition, knowledge distribution, knowledge interpretation) and organizational performance. The involved hypotheses were as follows:

H1c: The relationship between distributive justice and organizational performance is mediated by organizational citizenship behavior.

H2c: The relationship between procedural justice and organizational performance is mediated by organizational citizenship behavior.

H3c: The relationship between interactional justice and organizational performance is mediated by organizational citizenship behavior.

H4c: The relationship between idealized influence and organizational performance is mediated by organizational citizenship behavior.

H5c: The relationship between inspirational motivation and organizational performance is mediated by organizational citizenship behavior.

H6c: The relationship between intellectual stimulation and organizational performance is mediated by organizational citizenship behavior.

H7c: The relationship between individualized consideration and organizational performance is mediated by organizational citizenship behavior.

H8c: The relationship between surface emotion acting and organizational performance is mediated by organizational citizenship behavior.

H9c: The relationship between deep emotion acting and organizational performance is mediated by organizational citizenship behavior.

H10c: The relationship between true emotion acting and organizational performance is mediated by organizational citizenship behavior.

H11c: The relationship between knowledge acquisition and organizational performance is mediated by organizational citizenship behavior.

H12c: The relationship between knowledge distribution and organizational performance is mediated by organizational citizenship behavior.

H13c: The relationship between knowledge interpretation and organizational performance is mediated by organizational citizenship behavior.

This study found that H1c, H3c, H5c, H7c, H9c, H11c and H13c were supported in the practical setting whereas other hypotheses H2c, H4c, H6c, H8c, H10c were rejected. In other words, the relationships among distributive justice, interactional justice inspirational motivation, individualized consideration, deep emotion acting, knowledge acquisition, knowledge interpretation and organizational performance were mediated by organizational citizenship behavior. Besides, the relationships among procedural justice, inspirational motivation, individualized consideration, surface emotion acting, true emotion acting, knowledge acquisition, knowledge interpretation and organizational performance were not mediated by organizational citizenship behavior.

7.3.4 The Effect of Organizational Citizenship Behavior on Organizational Performance

The results of multiple regression analysis of organizational citizenship behavior on organizational performance showed that organizational citizenship behavior has a significant impact on organizational performance—H14 was accepted. In this case the increase of individual initiative behavior can effectively improve organizational performance. Organ (1997) stated that the impact of organizational citizenship behavior on organizational performance was significant. He stated that organizational citizenship behavior affected organizational success in several ways: ① improving the productivity of colleagues and organizations; ②liberating resources to make them more in line with production purposes; ③reducing the demand for limited resources purely based on maintenance functions; and ④ helping to coordinate activities within and among groups.

Therefore, organizations should attract and retain the best employees and increase the stability of organizational performance and make organizations more adaptable to the environment. The results of this study on the relationship between organizational citizenship behavior and organizational performance respond is consistent with Organ's (1997) finding that organizational citizenship positively affected organizational performance. Thus, organizational citizenship behavior needs to be developed in order to improve the organizational performance.

7.4 Implications of the Study

The results of this research provide several theoretical and practical implications. Both implications are discussed in the following subsections.

7.4.1 Theoretical Implications

The theoretical relationships posited in the newly developed research framework were empirically supported. Specifically, this study validated the linkage between distributive justice, procedural justice, interactional justice, idealized influence, inspirational motivation, intellectual stimulation, individualized consideration, surface emotion acting, deep emotion acting, true emotion acting, knowledge acquisition, knowledge distribution, knowledge interpretation and organizational performance. In addition, this study also validated the linkage between distributive justice, procedural justice, interactional justice, idealized influence, inspirational motivation, intellectual stimulation, individualized consideration, surface emotion acting, deep emotion acting, true emotion acting, knowledge acquisition, knowledge distribution, knowledge interpretation and organizational citizenship behavior. In other words, this study adds further knowledge on the importance of thirteen factors above that can assist to improve organizational performance of SMEs and organizational citizenship behavior of employees.

This study also contributes to the academic world as it develops and validates a research instrument for data collection. The instrument examined the effect of distributive justice, procedural justice, interactional justice, idealized influence, inspirational motivation, intellectual stimulation, individualized consideration, surface emotion acting, deep emotion acting, true emotion acting, knowledge acquisition, knowledge distribution and knowledge interpretation on organizational citizenship behavior. It also examined the mediating effect of organizational citizenship behavior on the relationship among distributive justice, procedural justice, interactional justice, idealized influence, inspirational motivation, intellectual stimulation, individualized consideration, surface emotion acting, deep emotion acting, true emotion acting, knowledge acquisition, knowledge distribution, knowledge interpretation and organizational performance. These efforts are considered to be a major contribution to improve organizational performance of SMEs in China.

Another important theoretical contribution of this study is that it established a new conceptual framework on the organizational performance. As discussed in Chapter Two, these factors have yet to be examined on organizational performance of SMEs of China. Based on the statistical results, distributive justice, interactional justice, inspirational motivation, intellectual stimulation, individualized consideration, deep emotion acting, knowledge acquisition and knowledge interpretation have positive influence on the organizational performance. In addition, distributive justice, procedural justice, interactional justice, inspirational motivation, individualized consideration, surface emotion acting, deep emotion acting, true emotion acting, knowledge acquisition and knowledge interpretation were found to be positively and significantly influenced by organizational citizenship behavior. In short, this is the first research that provides empirical evidence on the importance of these eight factors in improving organizational performance.

The use of hierarchical linear regression to examine the mediating effect of organizational citizenship behavior on the relationship between distributive justice, procedural justice, interactional justice, idealized influence, inspirational motivation, intellectual stimulation, individualized consideration, surface emotion acting, deep emotion acting, true emotion acting, knowledge acquisition, knowledge distribution, knowledge interpretation and organizational performance also provides new perspective in development of SMEs. It provides improved empirical evidence in terms of statistical validity and generalization of the influence of distributive justice, interactional justice, inspirational motivation, individualized consideration, deep emotion acting, knowledge acquisition, knowledge interpretation on the organizational performance and organizational citizenship behavior. In other words, this study provides clear evidence of which factors are most significant in order to improve organizational performance. In addition, this study also provides clear evidence of what factors should be taken into account in improving organizational citizenship behavior.

7.4.2 Practical Implications

The findings from this study give rise to the following important implications for organizational performance. These implications are related to eight hypotheses which are positively and significantly influenced by involvement in organizational performance. The implications are also related to ten hypotheses that are positively and significantly influenced by organizational citizenship behavior. Subsections 7.4.2.1 to 7.4.2.4 discuss the implications in detail.

7.4.2.1 Improve the System of Organizational Justice

In recent years, competition in China's market has been intensifying and enterprises and organizations pay more and more attention to its own development, especially on haman resources. On the basis of the existing theory of organizational equity, this study can provide more effective theoretical guidance for the development of the organization, enable enterprise managers to deeply understand the structural model of organizational equity and work performance and clarify the mechanism of the relevant elements of organizational equity for organizational performance so that they can formulate corresponding solutions to achieve more efficient and lasting. Employee incentives can effectively improve organizational efficiency and achieve the common development of organizational performance and employee performance. Moreover, this paper focuses on the relationship between organizational justice and employee performance and investigates and understands the actual situation of SMEs in Jilin Province of China. In this respect, the analyses are on the main problems and shortcomings and then the formulation of the effective improvement and improvement measures is to ensure the stability, sustainability and effective development of enterprises.

Therefore, SMEs should further improve the salary and welfare system, adhere to the "people-oriented" principle, the salary level of staff should be basically consistent with that of other similar organization, and the salary of their own units should be determined according to the actual development of the local economy. It is suggested to establish a fair and multi-channel promotion mechanism and material rewards from promotion and personal social status. This improvement can motivate them to generate organizational citizenship behavior. Executive Service Center staff can be assessed based on task performance and peripheral performance. Task performance is directly related to the content of job responsibilities. Peripheral performance is organizational citizenship behavior, which is a spontaneous initiative beyond post responsibilities. The official assessment and social assessment should be combined, while paying attention to usual assessment, being good at collecting performance-related information, and having a holistic grasp of staff performance through core event method, investigation and research method, interview method, especially the surrounding performance such as organizational citizenship behavior, so as to promote the improvement of enterprise organizational performance.

7. 4. 2. 2   Improve Managers' Transformational Leadership Behavior

This study investigated the antecedent variables of organizational performance from the individual levels, enriched the theory of organizational performance, provided a reference basis for enterprises to find ways to improve employee performance and enterprise performance level, and helped enterprises to maintain continuous development in the fierce competition. The information era and economic globalization force enterprises to face massive transformational pressures. Transformational leaders can inspire followers to realize self-transformation, guide organizational change, promote organizations to seize opportunities, achieve established goals and meet various challenges in the period of organizational change. This study explored the relationship among transformational leadership, organizational citizenship behavior and organizational performance and studied the relationship among the sub-dimensions, which help enterprises to understand how transformational leadership promotes the matching between employees and organizations, and then improves the specific impact mechanism of employees' job performance, so as to improve the organizational performance of small and medium-sized enterprises. The selection and cultivation of transformational leadership and the improvement of the similarity between employees and organizations provide ideas and basis for enterprises to improve the level of human resources management.

Therefore, managers should learn more about transformational leadership skills, especially giving their subordinates more personalized care. For example, guiding individual employee in career development planning to fully tap the potential of employees, so that they can grow into "complete people". Managers should be good at listening to employees' voices, tolerating their different opinions and opinions, so that employees can feel the importance of leaders and are willing to take actions that can strengthen the relationship with leaders, develop high-quality exchange relationship with leaders, and work hard for the organization, thus bringing efficient output. Leaders should be aware that effective communication and trust are important factors in the success of a changing leadership strategy. It is necessary to give subordinates sufficient authorization and trust, strive for more subordinates to enter the circle, establish good communication relations with more subordinates, have a positive impact on subordinates' organizational citizenship behavior and promote organizational performance improvement.

7. 4. 2. 3   Strengthen the Management of Employees' Emotional Labor

In this study, the existing research results are sorted out and analyzed, and the hypothesis that different strategies of emotional labor have different effects on employees' attitudes and work output is put forward. It is hoped that the hypothesis can inspire managers to view the relationship between employees' emotional labor and work more comprehensively and objectively from the angles of reducing risks and expanding benefits, and help managers reduce shallow behavior through management means. The negative effects to employees' health and work, and the positive effects of increasing and expanding deep-seated behavior on employees' work and service quality. This study devoted to the study of the relationship among surface emotion acting, deep emotion acting, true emotion acting, organizational citizenship behavior and organizational performance in emotional labor of SMEs as a special group. It also analyzed the different dimensions of emotional labor of employees in SMEs through the influence mechanism of organizational citizenship behavior on organizational performance of enterprises and from a practical point of view to become an improvement of SMEs.

Managers should encourage employees to adopt deep-seated behavioral strategies in emotional labor, such as conducting activities such as service star selection, commending good employees and setting an example for learning, inviting senior employees to share the successful experience and experience of serving customers in pre-class meetings to enhance their sense of work achievement, recording excellent service stories of employees and making video clips to disseminate them in enterprises. To create a good service atmosphere, these measures can help employees in the process of learning from others, deepen the recognition of organizational emotional labor display rules, expand positive emotional experience and further increase employee job satisfaction.

Based on the above empirical research results and management suggestions to implement the management combination boxing, it is believed that it can help enterprises and employees to understand reasonable emotional labor strategies, improve employees' work results and organizational performance and open up a win-win situation of enterprise development and employee growth.

7. 4. 2. 4   Strengthen the Management Mechanism of Organizational Learning

The measurement table of organizational learning ability proposed in this study has a certain guiding role in the construction of learning-oriented organizations for Chinese enterprises. Enterprises can use it to evaluate and measure their organizational learning ability, so as to identify the key management characteristics and organizational conditions affecting organizational learning and to improve their management efficiency. The results of this study will provide practical reference on how to effectively integrate organizational learning with organizational citizenship behavior to promote organizational performance, thus providing guidance on how to enhance organizational learning ability and organizational performance. The integration of organizational learning and organizational performance is an inevitable strategic choice for Chinese enterprises to build sustainable competitive advantage, deepen marketization and internationalization. Due to the highly turbulent and complex business environment in which Chinese SMEs are located, there is a lack of strong organizational learning capabilities or entrepreneurial orientation cannot support them to become stronger and bigger. The integration of organizational learning and organizational performance means that enterprises have a more sensitive understanding and response ability to the external environment, and also means that enterprises can better deal with the strategy of change and innovation, which means that enterprises continue to learn and start businesses. Therefore, the researchers firmly believe that only those enterprises and nationals who are brave in pioneering and enterprising and good at learning are the solid foundation for the rise of a great power. Therefore, this study not only expects to provide effective reference for enterprises at the micro-tactical level, but also expects to provide a macro-strategic thinking for managers.

Therefore, SMEs must have perfect system support, and effective learning system is necessary to ensure the effectiveness of organizational learning, such as a sound training system, flexible training methods, the establishment of learning platforms and so on, so that employees in their daily work to understand what knowledge they should learn, from what channels to obtain knowledge they need to master, how to seek help from others, and how to communicate and discuss with others, promoting employees' passive learning style into active learning habits. In an organization, explicit knowledge is easy to be expressed, disseminated and used. Since many employees have their own tacit knowledge, this part of knowledge will determine their own values, so the organization should establish a variety of learning methods according to the charateristics of the organization to promote the diffusion and use of tacit knowledge, such as the use of situational learning, experience exchanging, informal group learning and so on.

7.5   Limitations and Suggestions for Future Research

The main research content of this paper is the relationship between organizational performance and organizational citizenship behavior as a mediating variable. Through reviewing and analyzing a large number of literatures, this dissertation constructed a theoretical model and put forward corresponding research hypothesis. After empirical analysis, many valuable conclusions were drawn, which can provide reference for the development of SMEs. Although during the whole research process, the author strived to be accurate and rigorous, due to lack of theoretical knowledge, there were some uncontrollable external factors and the complexity of the research content itself, which created some shortcomings.

Based on the literature review, this study summarized the advantages and disadvantages of the discussion on organizational justice, transformational leadership, employee emotion and organizational learning, defined the connotation of organizational citizenship behavior and organizational performance and grasped its essence to a certain extent. However, they all have very rich connotations, involving many aspects of enterprise content, the connotations and extensions of which are still developing, with new content being added from time to time. This study can only summary the past, not the future, and may omit some important content.

First, because of the restriction of subjective and objective conditions, the object of this research was SMEs in Jilin Province of China. Although it has a strong pertinence, it also means that it restricted the popularization and application of research conclusions. At the same time, only few industries had been considered. This affected the reliability and diversity of research results to a certain extent.

Second, in the aspect of variable data, the method of subjective evaluation was used to answer the survey questions. Although it has many advantages and conveniences, after all, people's subjective views will be affected by personal knowledge level, ideas and other factors. There were errors reflected in the questionnaires. This error was systematic, which can only be reduced as far as possible, but cannot be eliminated fundamentally. In addition, the collected data were only cross-sectional data at a certain time point. Because of the different development stages of enterprises, there were differences in the views on the same issues. At the same time, the impact of various variables on organizational performance was a long-term process and cross-sectional data cannot reflect this impact in time. In addition, in this study, the impact of enterprise size, environmental dynamics and other factors were not considered.

In view of the above shortcomings of this research and considering the future research trends, it is worth expanding and supplementing in three aspects: research perspective, research samples and variable data. This study was limited to the internal organization. In the future, we can introduce the inter-organizational influence. Referring to the variables of higher-level organizational alliance, we can examine its impact on both sides in addition to equity, leadership, emotional management, learning and other aspects and then observe the changes in performance of both sides. In the existing research models, individual learning, team learning, knowledge sharing, knowledge management and innovation management can be added, and the dynamic impact of environment can be introduced to improve and enhance the model, which further reveals the different roles played by different aspects of activities and external environment in this impact relationship.

First, future research should subdivide the field of large enterprises and small and medium-sized enterprises and compare the similarities and differences of research conclusions. What's more, it is also necessary to expand the research object, further break through the scope of Jilin Province of China and investigate the impact of different geographical environments, customs and culture and the degree of marketization on the research conclusions in different regions of the country, such as the east, the middle and the west and compare the similarities and differences, which not only enriches the existing research conclusions, but also expands the scope of application of the conclusions.

Second, this study used cross-sectional data of enterprises. In the future, longitudinal research on time series can be carried out to better reveal the long-term, procedural and phased nature of various variables that affect organizational performance. It can also carry out experiments or case studies for specific enterprises and apply the research results directly to the actual operation of enterprises.

7.6   Conclusion

The objectives of this study were as follows: ① to investigate the effect of organizational justice, transformational leadership, employee emotion and organizational learning constructs on organizational performance of SMEs in Jilin Province of China; ② to examine the effect of organizational justice, transformational leadership, employee emotion labor and organizational learning constructs on organizational citizenship behavior of employees of SMEs in Jilin Province of China; ③ to investigate whether organizational citizenship behavior mediates the relationship among organizational justice, transformational leadership, employee emotion labor, organizational learning and organizational performance of SMEs in Jilin Province of China; and ④ to investigate the effect of organizational citizenship behavior on organizational performance of SMEs in Jilin Province of China.

From the findings, the proposed theoretical framework was substantially validated. The findings showed that distributive justice, interactional justice, intellectual stimulation, inspirational motivation, individualized consideration, deep emotion acting, knowledge acquisition and knowledge interpretation had positive influence on the organizational performance of SMEs in Jilin Province of China. On the one hand, eight out of thirteen motivational factors were significant for organizational performance. On the other hand, the effect of distributive justice, procedural justice, interactional justice, idealized influence, intellectual stimulation, inspirational motivation, individualized consideration, true emotion acting, surface emotion acting, deep emotion acting, knowledge acquisition, knowledge distribution and knowledge interpretation also had high influence on the organizational citizenship behavior. Ten out of thirteen motivational factors were significant for organizational citizenship behavior. Overall, the significant factors were more than insignificant factors.

However, the mediating effect of organizational citizenship behavior on the relationship among distributive justice, interactional justice, inspirational motivation, individualized consideration, surface emotion acting, true emotion acting, knowledge acquisition, knowledge interpretation and organizational performance were not substantiated in the practical setting. Only distributive justice, interactional justice, inspirational motivation, individualized consideration, deep emotion acting, knowledge acquisition, knowledge interpretation and organizational performance were mediated by organizational citizenship behavior to influence organizational performance.

Based on the above findings, the following conclusions were drawn: ① distributive justice, interactional justice, intellectual stimulation, inspirational motivation, individualized consideration, deep emotion acting, knowledge acquisition and knowledge interpretation had positive influence on the organizational performance of SMEs in the Jilin Province of China; ② distributive justice, procedural justice, interactional justice, inspirational motivation, individualized consideration, true emotion acting, surface emotion acting, deep emotion acting, knowledge acquisition, knowledge interpretation had positive influence on the organizational citizenship behavior of SMEs in the Jilin Province of China; and ③ distributive justice, interactional justice, inspirational motivation, individualized consideration, deep emotion acting, knowledge acquisition, knowledge interpretation and organizational performance were mediated by organizational citizenship behavior to influence organizational performance.

Some theoretical and practical significance are also discussed. In addition, the limitations and suggestions of future research are emphasized. Last but not least, it is hoped that these findings will enable academia and SMEs to have a deeper understanding of the survey. It is also hoped that these results can provide useful information for the development of SMEs in China and make use of the identified incentives to improve their organizational performance.

7.7　Summary

This chapter summarizes the research findings and theoretical and practical implications. In addition, some limitations and suggestions are put forward for future studies and conclusions.

Appendix: Survey Instrument

Dear Sir/Madam,

You are kindly requested to take part in the case study conducted by Guo Wanran.

The purpose of this study is to explore "factors that affect the organizational performance of SMEs". Please give your sincere opinions on the statement on the next page by checking or circling the figures that best describe your personal opinions. Your reply will be kept strictly confidential and will not be disclosed to any third party under any circumstances.

Please take a few minutes to complete the questionnaire. Thank you very much for taking time to answer the questionnaire. Thank you very much for your friendly cooperation and help.

Please return the completed questionnaire to the enclosed envelope within four weeks.

Email: 1920115041@qq.com

Yours sincerely,
Guo Wanran

Part A

Please read the following statement, and tick (√) appropriately in the box that best explains.

Strongly disagree	1
More disagree	2
Disagree	3
Neutral	4
Agree	5
More agree	6
Strongly agree	7

Organizational Justice

In the organizational justice, there are three dimensions such as distributive justice, procedural justice and interactional justice.

A. Distributive Justice	1	2	3	4	5	6	7
1. My work schedule is fair.							
2. My work salary is fair compared to my job performance.							
3. My workload is fair compared with other colleagues with the same job and duties.							
4. The reward I receive is fair based on my contribution to the organization.							
B. Procedural Justice	1	2	3	4	5	6	7
1. My company's work procedures are designed in an unbiased approach.							

(To be continued)

2. My company can collect accurate and complete information when making job decisions.							
3. My company's rules are applied fairly to all relevant employee.							
4. My company provides employees with opportunities to appeal to or challenge the decision.							
C. Interactional Justice	1	2	3	4	5	6	7
1. My colleagues have no prejudice against me.							
2. My colleagues treat me with kindness and respect.							
3. My work partners are able to consider my viewpoint.							
4. My organization provides me with timely feedback about the company decision and its implication.							

Transformational Leadership

In the transformational leadership, there are four dimensions such as idealized influence, inspirational motivation, intellectual stimulation and individualized consideration.

D. Idealized Influence	1	2	3	4	5	6	7
1. My leaders display a sense of power and confidence.							
2. My leaders go beyond self-interest for the benefit for the company.							
3. My leaders specify the importance of having a strong sense of purpose.							

(To be continued)

	1	2	3	4	5	6	7
4. My leaders emphasize the importance of having a collective sense of mission.							
E. Inspirational Motivation	1	2	3	4	5	6	7
1. My leaders talk optimistically about the future work task.							
2. My leaders talk enthusiastically about what needs to be accomplished.							
3. My leaders articulate a compelling vision of the future.							
4. My leaders express confidence that goals will be achieved.							
F. Intellectual Stimulation	1	2	3	4	5	6	7
1. My leaders re-examine critical assumption to question whether they are appropriate.							
2. My leaders seek differing perspectives when solving problems.							
3. My leaders get employees to look at problems from many different angles.							
4. My leaders suggest new ways of looking at how to complete assignments.							
G. Individualized Consideration	1	2	3	4	5	6	7
1. My leaders spend time teaching and coaching me.							
2. My leaders treat employees as individuals rather than just as a member of the group.							
3. My leaders consider each individual as having different needs, abilities and aspirations from employees.							
4. My leaders help employees to develop their strengths.							

Employee's Emotion Labor

In the employee's emotion labor, there are three dimensions such as surface emotion acting, deep emotion acting, true emotion acting.

H. Surface Emotion Acting	1	2	3	4	5	6	7
1. I show good mood when interacting with people at work, even if my inner feeling is not like this.							
2. I hide my true emotion in order to express the right emotions and at work.							
3. I put on an act in order to deal with customers in an appropriate way.							
4. I show the emotion that I need at work, but I will not change my inner feeling.							
I. Deep Emotion Acting	1	2	3	4	5	6	7
1. I make an effort to actually feel the emotions that I need to display toward others.							
2. I try to talk myself out of negative feelings at work and show kind attitude.							
3. I work at developing the feelings inside of me that I need to show to customers.							
4. I try to actually experience the emotions that I must show when interacting with people around me at work.							
J. True Emotion Acting	1	2	3	4	5	6	7
1. The emotions I show at work match what I truly feel.							
2. Emotions I need to show to do my job are what I actually feel.							
3. I can express my emotion naturally and easily at work.							

Organizational Learning

In organizational learning, there are three dimensions such as knowledge acquisition, knowledge distribution and knowledge interpretation.

K. Knowledge Acquisition	1	2	3	4	5	6	7
1. My company' employees can attend meetings and exhibitions regularly to get knowledge.							
2. My company has consolidated and resourceful research and development policy to acquire knowledge.							
3. New ideas and approaches on work performance are experimented continuously.							
L. Knowledge Distribution	1	2	3	4	5	6	7
1. My company has formal mechanisms to guarantee the sharing of the best practices among the different fields of the activity.							
2. My company has individuals who take part in several teams or divisions and who also act as links among project groups.							
3. My company has individuals that dedicate to collecting, assembling and distributing internal employees' suggestions.							
M. Knowledge Interpretation	1	2	3	4	5	6	7
1. All the members of my organization share the same aim to which they feel committed.							
2. Employees share knowledge and experiences.							
3. Teamwork is a very common practice in my company.							

Mediating Variables: Organizational Citizenship Behavior

In the organizational citizenship behavior, there are 20 items.

N. Organizational Citizenship Behavior	1	2	3	4	5	6	7
1. I am willing to stand up to protect the reputation of the company.							
2. I am eager to tell outsiders good news about the company and clarify their misunderstandings.							
3. I make constructive suggestions that can improve the operation of the company.							
4. I actively attend company meetings.							
5. I am willing to assist new colleagues to adjust to the work environment.							
6. I am willing to help colleagues solve work-related problems.							
7. I am willing to cover work assignments for colleagues when needed.							
8. I am willing to coordinate and communicate with colleagues.							
9. I think interpersonal harmony is more important than personal influence and gains in the organization.							
10. I do not use position power to pursue personal gain.							
11. I do not ignore my colleagues' accusations and suggestions for my own benefit.							
12. I do not speak weakness of the supervisors or colleagues behind their backs.							

(To be continued)

13. I do not use work time to do private things (e. g. , trading stocks, shopping).							
14. I do not use company resources to do personal things (e. g. , company phones, copy machines computers and cars).							
15. I do not take sick leave and make excuse for some private things.							
16. I comply with company rules and procedures even when nobody watches and no evidence can be traced.							
17. I take my job seriously and rarely make mistake.							
18. I am willing to take on new or challenging assignments.							
19. I try hard to self-study to increase the quality of work outputs.							
20. I often arrive early and start to work immediately.							

Dependent Variable: Organizational Performance

In the organizational performance, there are seven items.

O. Organizational Performance	1	2	3	4	5	6	7
1. My organization has made good use of knowledge and skills in looking for ways to become more efficient.							
2. My company's employee productivity has improved.							

(To be continued)

3. The quality of work performed by my current coworkers in work group is high.						
4. The occurrence of goal attainment is very high in my organization.						
5. The company's after-tax net income growth rate has been increased.						
6. The company's image is better than that of the competitors.						
7. The customer satisfaction toward my organization is very high.						

Part B: Demographic Information

Please tick (√) your answer.

Gender:

☐Male ☐Female

Age:

☐20 years old and below

☐21 to 30 years old

☐31 to 40 years old

☐41 to 50 years old

☐51 to 60 years old

☐61 years old and above

What is your educational level?

☐High school and below

☐College

☐Bachelor

☐Master

☐PhD

☐Others...

Status:

☐Manufacturing industry ☐Trade

☐Education ☐Healthcare

☐Hotels and restaurants ☐Agriculture

☐Others...

Reference

Abed E, Bander A. (2011) *The influence of leadership style and organizational citizenship behaviour (OCB) on organizational performance: a case of ICT firm in saudi arabia.* University Utara Malaysia.

Adams J. S. (1965). Inequity in social exchange. In L. Berkowitz (Ed.). *Advances in experimental social psychology.* New York: Academic Press.

Aküzüm Cemal. (2014). Knowledge inertia and organizational learning as the explanation of organizational performance. *Educational research & reviews*, 9 (21).

Alexander S, Ruderman M. (1987). The role of procedural and distributive justice in organizational behavior. *Social justice research*, 1 (2).

Albino A P, Sozzi G, Nanus D M, et al. (1992). Malignant transformation of human melanocytes: induction of a complete melanoma phenotype and genotype. *Oncogene*, 1992, 7 (11).

Alexander S, Ruderman M. (1987). The role of procedural and distributive justice in organizational behavior. *Social justice research*, 1 (2).

Ambrose M L, Schminke M, Mayer D M. (2013). Trickle-down effects of supervisor perceptions of interactional justice: a moderated mediation approach. *Journal of applied psychology*, 98 (4).

Aragón-Correa J A, García-Morales V J, Cordón-Pozo E. (2007). Leadership and organizational learning's role on innovation and performance: lessons from Spain. *Industrial marketing management*, 36

(3) .

Ashforth B E, Humphrey R H. (1993). Emotional labor in srvice roles: the influence of Identity. *Academy of management review*, 18 (1) .

Avison D, Myers M D. (2002). *Qualitative research in information systems: a reader.*

Avolio B J, Gibbons T C. (1988). *Developing transformational leaders: a life span approach.*

Avolio B J, Sosik J J, Kahai S S, et al. (2014). E-leadership: re-examining transformations in leadership source and transmission. *The leadership quarterly*, 25 (1) .

Bass B M. (1985). *Leadership and performance beyond expectation.* New York: Free Press.

Bass B M, Avolio B J. (1990). *Transformational leadership development: manual for the multifactor leadership questionnaire.* Consulting Psychologists Press.

Bass B M, Avolio B J. (1994). *Improving organizational effectiveness through transformational leadership.*

Bass B M. (1997). Personal selling and transactional/ transformational leadership. *Journal of personal selling & sales management*, 17 (3) .

Bass B M. (1999). Two decades of research and development in transformational leadership. *European journal of work and organizational psychology*, 8 (1) .

Bass B M. (2000). The future of leadership in learning organizations. *Journal of leadership & organizational studies*, 7 (3) .

Bass B M, Avolio B J. (2013). Developing Transformational Leadership. *Journal of European industrial training*, 14 (5) .

Bass B M, Avolio B J, Jung D I, et al. (2003). Predicting unit performance by assessing transformational and transactional leadership. *Journal of applied psychology*, 88 (2) .

Bai Yongru. (2019). Analysis of the evolution of the concept and standards of "SMEs". *China SMEs*, (8) .

Baker T. L. (1994). *Doing social research.* New York: McGraw-Hill.

Baker W E, Sinkula J M. (1999). The synergistic effect of market orientation and learning orientation on organizational performance. *Journal of the academy of marketing science*, 27 (4).

Bao Zhanguang, Zhang Xiangkui. (2005). An overview of the theory of self determined cognitive motivation. *Journal of northeast normal university: philosophy and social sciences*, (6).

Baron R M, Kenny D A. (1986). The moderator-mediator variable distinction in social psychological research: conceptual, strategic, and statistical considerations. *Journal of personality and social psychology*, 51 (6).

Berry W D, Feldman S, Stanley Feldman D (1985). *Multiple regression in practice.* Sage.

Barlett M. (1954) A note on the multiplying factors for various chi square approximations. *Journal of the royal statistical society*, (16).

Bateman T S, Organ D W. (1983). Job satisfaction and the good soldier: The relationship between affect and employee "citizenship". *Academy of management journal*, 26 (4).

Bennis W, Nanus B. (2007). Leaders: the strategies for taking charge. *Bloomsbury business library-management library*, 29 (6).

Bell S J, Mengüç B, Ii R E W. (2010). Salesperson learning, organizational learning, and retail store performance. *Journal of the academy of marketing science*, 38 (2).

Berkowitz L. (1990). On the formation and regulation of anger and aggression: a cognitive-neoassociationistic analysis. *American psychologist*, 45 (4).

Bies R. J. & Moag, J. (1986). Interactional justice: communication criteria of fairness. In Lewicki R. J., Sheppard B. H. & Bazerman M. (Eds.). *Research on negotiation in organizations*, (1).

Bies R. J. (2005). Are procedural justice and interactional justice conceptually distinct? In Greenberg J. & Colquitt J. (Eds.). *Handbook of organizational justice.* Mahwah, NJ: Lawrence Erlbaum Associates.

Bies R J. (2015). Interactional justice: Looking backward and looking forward. *Oxford handbook of justice in work organizations.*

Bhave D P, Glomb T M. (2016). The role of occupational emotional labor requirements on the surface acting-job satisfaction relationship. *Journal of management*, 42 (3).

Blakely G L, Andrews M C, Moorman R H. (2005). The moderating effects of equity sensitivity on the relationship between organizational justice and organizational citizenship behaviors. *Journal of business and psychology*, 20 (2).

Bono J E, Judge T A. (2004). Personality and transformational and transactional leadership: a meta-analysis. *Journal of applied psychology*, 89 (5).

Bono J E & Ilies R. (2006) Charisma, positive emotions, and mood contagion. *Leadership quarterly*, (17).

Boiral O & Paillé P. (2012). Organizational citizenship behavior for the environment: measurement and validation. *Journal of business ethics*, 109 (4).

Borman W C. (2004). The concept of organizational citizenship. *Current directions in psychological science*, 13 (6).

Boudreau M C, Ariyachandra T, Gefen D, et al. (2004). Validating is positivist instrumentation: 1997 – 2001. *The handbook of information systems research. IGI global.*

Boyd H W, Westfall R & Stasch S F. (1977). *Marketing research: Text and cases.* Homewood: Irwin Inc.

Boudreau M C, Ariyachandra T, Gefen D, et al. (2004). Validating is positivist instrumentation: 1997 – 2001. *The handbook of information systems research. IGI global.*

Brown J D. (2000). *What is construct validity.* JALT Testing & Evaluation SIG.

Brown A, Merkl C, Snower D. (2015). An incentive theory of matching. *Macroeconomic dynamics*, 19 (3).

Byrne J, Mehra R K. (2010) *Method and system for visual collision detection and estimation:* U. S. Patent Application 12/776, 202. 2010 –

12 – 2.

Bycio P, Hackett R D & Allen J S. (1995). Further assessments of Bass's (1985) conceptualization of transactional and transformational leadership. *Journal of applied psychology*, 80 (4).

Calantone R J, Cavusgil S T & Zhao Y. (2002). Learning orientation, firm innovation capability, and firm performance. *Industrial marketing management*, 31 (6).

Camps J, Oltra V, Aldás-Manzano J, et al. (2016). Individual performance in turbulent environments: The role of organizational learning capability and employee flexibility. *Human resource management*, 55 (3).

Campbell J P (1977). On the natural of organizational effectiveness. In Goodman PS, Pennings JM (Eds.). *New perspectives on organizational effectiveness, jossey-bass*. San francisco, CA., (2).

Campbell R E. (1995). An investigation of some organizational correlates of corporate entrepreneurship: toward a systems model of organizational innovation. *Entrepreneurship, innovation, and change*, (4).

Cai Binqing & Chen Guohong. (2013). Research on network relations, organizational learning and innovation performance of chain industrial clusters. *Research and development management*, 25 (4).

Cai Youhua, Chen Guohong, Liu Hong, et al. (2010). *Interaction model and simulation analysis of innovation network and knowledge integration in industrial clusters*. Papers collection of the 15th annual conference of Chinese Management Science.

Cai Ning & Chen Gongdao. (2001). On the growth and measurement of small and medium-sized enterprises. *Social science front*, (1).

Cao Yanmin & Cheng Hong. (2017). On the application of organizational equity theory in enterprise work performance salary management. *Human resources management*, (11).

Caillier J G. (2016). Do transformational leaders affect turnover intentions and extra-role behaviors through mission valence? *The American review of public administration*, 46 (2).

Carmeli A & Josman Z E. (2006). The relationship among emotional intelligence, task performance, and organizational citizenship behaviors. *Human performance*, 19 (4).

Cheung F Y L & Lun V M C. (2015). Relation between emotional labor and organizational citizenship behavior: an investigation among Chinese teaching professionals. *The journal of general psychology*, 142 (4).

Cepeda G & Vera D. (2007). Dynamic capabilities and operational capabilities: a knowledge management perspective. *Journal of business research*, 60 (5).

Chen Ruijun & Qin Qiwen. (2011). The relationship between emotional labor and depression and anxiety: the mediating role of emotional exhaustion. *Psychological science*, (3).

Chen Chen, Shi Kan & Lu Jiafang (2015), Transformational leadership and innovative behavior: a regulated mediating model. *Management science*, 28 (4).

Chen Guoquan & Zhou Wei. (2009). The relationship between leadership behavior, organizational learning ability and organizational performance. *Scientific research management*, (9).

Chen Guoquan & Zheng Hongping. (2005). An empirical study on the relationship between the influencing factors of learning organization, learning ability and performance. *Journal of management science*, (1).

Cheek A O, Kow K, Chen J, et al. (1999). Potential mechanisms of thyroid disruption in humans: interaction of organochlorine compounds with thyroid receptor, transthyretin, and thyroid-binding globulin. *Environmental health perspectives*, 107 (4).

Chen Tao, Zhu Zhihuang & Wang Tieman. (2015). Organizational memory, knowledge sharing and enterprise performance. *Research and development management*, 27 (2).

Chen Guoquan & Liu Wei. (2017). The effects of internal learning, external learning and their synergies on organizational performance: a study on the moderating effects of internal structure and external *environment. China management science*, (5).

Chen Z, Sun H, Lam W, et al. (2012). Chinese hotel employees in the smiling masks: roles of Job satisfaction, burnout, and supervisory support in relationships between emotional labor and performance. *The international journal of human resource management* (23).

Chen Dong. (2008). *Emotional labor of service workers and its relationship with job satisfaction and job performance.* Shandong University, 2008.

Chen Xiaohong, Wang Siying, Yang Li. (2012). Research on the influence mechanism of transformational leadership behavior on firm performance—based on questionnaire survey of SME leaders in China. *Science of science and management of S. & technology*, 33 (11).

Choudrie J & Dwivedi Y K. (2005). Investigating the research approaches for examining technology adoption issues. *Journal of research practice*, 1 (1).

Chua W F. (1986). Radical developments in accounting thought. *The accounting review*, 61 (4).

Churchill G A. (1979). A paradigm for developing better measures of marketing constructs. *Journal of marketing research*, 16 (1).

Cook K S & Hegtvedt K A. (1983). Distributive justice, equity, and equality. *Annual review of sociology*, 9 (1).

Colquitt J A & Rodell J B. (2015). Measuring justice and fairness. *Oxford handbook of justice in the workplace*, (187).

Cohen J. (1988). Set correlation and contingency tables. *Applied psychological measurement*, 12 (4).

Cooper R P, Catmur C & Heyes C. (2013). Are automatic imitation and spatial compatibility mediated by different processes? *Cognitive science*, 37 (4).

Coakes S J & Steed L G. (2003). *SPSS analysis without anguish.* Brisbane: John Wiley & Sons Australia Ltd.

Cole M S, Bernerth J B, Walter F, et al. (2010), Organizational justice and individuals' withdrawal: unlocking the influence of emotional *exhaustion. Journal of management studies*, 47 (3).

Cooper M C, Lambert B M & Pagh J D. (1997). Supply chain management: More than a new name for logistics. *The international journal of logistics management*, (1).

Colbert A E, Kristof-Brown A L, Bradley B H, et al. (2008). CEO transformational leadership: The role of goal importance congruence in top management teams. *Academy of management journal*, 51 (1).

Cox T. (1993). *Stress research and stress management: putting theory to work*. HSE Books, Sudbury.

Cohen-Charash Y & Spector P E. (2001). *The role of justice in organizations: a meta-analysis*.

Colquitt J A. (2001). On the dimensionality of organizational justice: a construct validation of a measure. *Journal of applied psychology*, (86).

Colquitt J A, Conlon D E, Wesson M J, et al. (2001). Justice at them illennium: a meta-analytic review of 25 years of organizational justice research. *Journal of applied psychology*, (86).

Cropanzano R, Bowen D E & Gilliland S W. (2007). The management of organizational justice. *Academy of management perspectives*, 21 (4).

Cropanzano R & Ambrose M L. (2001). Procedural and distributive justice are moresimilar than you think: a monistic perspective and a research agenda. In J Greenberg, R Cropanzano (Eds). *Advances in organizational justice*. Lexington. MA: new lexington press.

Cropanzano R & Mitchell M S. (2005). Social exchange theory: an interdisciplinary review. *Journal of management*, 31 (6).

Cropanzano R & Rupp D E, (2018). Thornton-Lugo M A, et al. Organizational justice and organizational. *The Oxford handbook of oganizational citizenship behavior*.

Cronbach L J & Meehl P E. (1955). Construct validity in psychological tests. *Psychological bulletin*, 52 (4).

Cui Jian. (2017). *The relationship between organizational justice, self-efficacy and organizational citizenship behavior*. Shandong University.

Davis J R. (1993). *Better teaching, more learning.* Strategies for success in post secondary settings. Phoenix, AR: Oryx Press.

Dai Ying. (2012). Research on the development dilemma of small and medium-sized enterprises in Jilin Province. *Market forum,* (11).

Dawes J. (2008). Do data characteristics change according to the number of scale points used? An experiment using 5-point, 7-point and 10-point scales. *International journal of market research,* 50 (1).

Dahling J J & Perez L A. (2010). Older worker, different actor? Linking age and emotional labor strategies. *Personality and individual differences,* 48 (5).

Dailey R C & Kirk D J. (1992). Distributive and procedural justice as antecedents of job dissatisfaction and intent to turnover. *Human relations,* 45 (3).

Darroch J & Mcnaughton R. (2002). Examining the link between knowledge management practices and types of innovation. *Journal of intellectual capital,,* 3 (3).

Datche E A. (2015). *Influence of transformational leadership on organizational performance of state corporations in Kenya.* JKUAT.

Den Hartog D N, Van Muijen J J & Koopman P L. (2001). Transactional versus transformational leadership: an analysis of the MLQ. *Journal of occupational & organizational psychology,* 70 (1).

Delaney J T & Huselid M A. (1996). The impact of human resource management practices. Nonprofit organizations. *Academy of management journal,* (2).

Dekas K H, Bauer T N, Welle B, et al. (2013). Organizationalcitizenship behavior, version 2. 0: a review and qualitative investigation of OCBs for knowledge workers at google and beyond. *The academy of management perspectives,* 27 (3).

Dess Robinson. (1984). *A description and analysis in terms of kotler's marketing orientation of selected university marketing agencies which sell faculty-developed non-profit materials.* Michigan State University.

Delaney S & Huselid K. (1996). Measuring market orientation: a multi-factor, multi-Item approach. *Journal of marketing management,*

(10).

Demirag I S. (1997). How UK companies measure overseas performance. *Accountancy*, (3).

Dodgson M. (1993). Organizational learning: a review of some literatures. *Organization studies*, 14 (3).

Diefendorff J M & Gosserand R H. (2003). Understanding the emotional labor process: a control theory perspective. *Journal of organizational behavior*, 24 (8).

Diefendorff J M, Croyle M H & Gosserand R H. (2005). The dimensionality and antecedents of emotional labor strategies. *Journal of vocational behavior*, 66 (2).

Diefendorff J M & Lord R G. (2003). The volitional and strategic effects of planning on task performance and goal commitment. *Human performance*, 16 (4).

Dirks K T & Ferrin D L. (2002). Trust in leadership: meta-analytic findings and implications for research and practice. *Jappl psychol*, 87 (4).

Dillman D A. (1978). *Mils and telephone surveys: The total design method*. New york: John Wiley & Sons.

Ding Yi. (2002). Organic combination of organizational performance and employee performance. *China human resources development*, (12).

Dong Wenqiang. (2015). *Research on the relationship between the latent rules of SMEs' management, emotional commitment and organizational citizenship behavior*, Chongqing University.

Dyler L & Reeves T. (1995). Human resource strategies and organization performance: what do we know and where do we need to go?. *International journal of HRM*, 6 (3).

Dvir T, Eden D, Avolio B J, et al. (2002). Impact of transformational leadership on follower development and performance: a field experiment. *Academy of management journal*, 45 (4).

Dess G G & Robinson R B. (2010). Measuring organizational performance in the absence of objective measures: The case of the privately-held firm and conglomerate business unit. *Strategic management* journal, 5 (3).

Delaney J T & Huselid M A. (1996). The impact of human resource management practices on perceptions of organizational performance. *Academy of management journal*, 39 (4).

Den Hartog D N, Van Muijen J J, Koopman P L. (1997). Transactional versus transformational leadership: an analysis of the MLQ. *Journal of occupational and organizational psychology*, 70 (1).

Dong Xia, Gao Yan, Ma Jianfeng. (2018). The Impact of service leadership on employees' active customer service performance—based on the dual perspectives of social exchange and social learning theory. *Tourism tribune*, 33 (6).

Dibella A J, Nevis E C & Gould J M. (2010). Understanding organizational learning capability. *Journal of management studies*, 33 (3).

Diefendorff J M, Croyle M H & Gosserand R H. (2005). The dimensionality and antecedents of emotional labor strategies. *Journal of vocational behavior*, 66 (2).

Dillman D A. (1978). *Mils and telephone surveys: the total design method*. New york: John Wiley & Sons.

Du Xiaoping, Zhao Kaiqi, Yuan Wei, et al. (2018) Study on the evaluation of comprehensive ability of small and medium-sized enterprises. *Journal of university of science and technology of China*, 48 (6).

Dvir T, Eden D, Avolio B J, et al. (2002). Impact of transformational leadership on follower development and performance: A field experiment. *Academy of management journal*, 45 (4).

Edmondson A C. (2008). *Managing the risk of learning: psychological safety in workteams*. International handbook of organizational teamwork and cooperative working. John Wiley & Sons Ltd.

Elenkov D S. (2002). Effects of leadership on organizational performance in Russian companies. *Journal of business research*, 55 (6).

Elfenbein H A. (2008). Emotions in organizations. *Academy of management annals*, 1 (1).

Emerson R M. (1976). Social exchange theory. *Annual review of* sociology, 2 (1).

Engelman M, Johnson S. (2007). Population aging and international development: addressing competing claims of distributive justice. *Developing world bioethics*, 7 (1).

Ehrentraut A, Zapf A, Beller M. (2002). A new improved catalyst for the palladium-catalyzed amination of aryl chlorides. *Journal of molecular catalysis a chemical*, 182 (1).

Eisenbach R, Watson K, Pillai R. (1999). Transformational leadership in the context of organizational change. *Journal of organizational change management*, 12 (2).

Elliott A C & Woodward W A. (2007). *Statistical analysis quick reference guidebook: with SPSS examples*. Sage.

Emrich C G. (1999). Context effects in leadership perception. *Personality and social psychology bulletin*, 25 (8).

Etzioni Amitai. (1964). *Modern organizations*, Prentice Hall,.

Fang Bing. (2011). *Research on the relationship between organizational justice and job performance*. Hebei University of Engineering.

Falk A & Fischbacher U. (2006). A theory of reciprocity. *Games and economic behavior*, 55 (2).

Farh J L, Earley P C & Lin S C. (1997). Impetus for action: a cultural analysis of justice and organizational citizenship behavior in Chinese society. *Administrative science quartly*, (42).

Farh J L & Podsakoff P M. (1990). Accounting for organizational citizenship behavior: leader fairness and task scope versus satisfaction. *Social science electronic publishing*, 16 (4).

Feng Xiaobin & Chen Liqiong. (2016). Quality management practice, organizational learning and enterprise performance: an empirical analysis based on Zhejiang manufacturing industry. *Management review*, 28 (1).

Field A. (2009). *Discovering statistics using SPSS: Paperback*.

Firoozi M, Kazemi A & Sayadi N. (2017). A Study of the relationship between the components of organizational justice and the dimensions of job satisfaction of physical education teachers. *Pertanika journal of social sciences & humanities*, 25 (2).

Fiol C M & Lyles M A. (1985). Organizational learning. *Academy of management review*, 10 (4).

Folger R. (1998). Fairness as a moral virtue. In M Schminke (Ed.). *Managerialethics: moral management of people and processes.* Mahwah, NJ: Erlbaum.

Folger R & Konovsky M A. (1989). Effects of procedural and distributive justice on reactions to pay raise decisions. *Academy of management journal*, 32 (1).

Fontes L A & Cruz M, Tabachnick J. (2001). Views of child sexual abuse in two cultural communities: an exploratory study among african Americans and latinos. *Child maltreatment*, 6 (2).

Frostig M & Maslow P. (1970). Movement education: theory and practice. *Follett educational corp.*

Fredrickson B L. (2001). The role of positive emotions in positive psychology: the broaden-and-build theory of positive emotions. *American psychologist,*, 56 (3).

Garg S & Dhar R. (2017). Employee service innovative behavior: the roles of leader-member exchange (LMX), work engagement, and job autonomy. *International journal of manpower*, 38 (2).

Garg S & Dhar R L. (2014). Effects of stress, LMX and perceived organizational support on service quality: Mediating effects of organizational commitment. *Journal of hospitality and tourism management*, (21).

García-Morales V J, Lloréns-Montes F J & Verdú-Jover A J. (2007). Influence of personal mastery onorganizational performance through organizational learning and innovation in large firms and SMEs. *Technovation*, 27 (9).

Ganeshan S, Denesik T, Fowler D B, et al. (2009). Quantitative expression analysis of selected low temperature-induced genes in autumn-seeded wheat (Triticum aestivum L.) reflects changes in soil temperature. *Environmental & experimental botany*, 66 (1).

Gay L R & Airasian P. (2000). *Educational research: competencies for analysis andapplication.* Upper saddle river, NJ: Merrill Prentice Hall.

Garima Singh. (2015). An Investigation of instigating and consequent factors of emotional labor. *Indian journal of positive psychology*, 6 (3).

Geyery A L J & Steyrer J M. (1998). Transformational leadership and objective performance in banks. *Applied psychology*, 47 (3).

Gerhart B. (2017). Incentives and pay for performance in the workplace. Advances in motivation science. *Elsevier*, (4).

Gerbing, D W & Anderson J C. (1988). An updated paradigm for scale development incorporating unidimensionality and its assessment. *Journal of marketing research*, 25 (2).

George D & Mallery P. (2010). *SPSS for windows step by step. A simple study guide and reference* (10. Baskı).

Geyery A L J & Steyrer J M. (1998). Transformational leadership and objective performance in banks. *Applied psychology*, 47 (3).

George J M & Brief A P. (1990). The economic instrumentality of work: An examination of the moderating effects of financial requirements and sex on the pay-life satisfaction relationship. *Journal of vocational behavior*, 37 (3).

George J M & Brief A P. (1996). Motivational agendas in the workplace: the effects of feelings on focus of attention and work motivation. *Research in organizational behavior*, (18).

George D & Mallery M. (2003). *Using SPSS for windows step by step: a simple guide and reference*, Allyny Bacon, Boston, MA.

Ghosh D, Sekiguchi T & Gurunathan L. (2017). Organizational embeddedness as a mediator between justice and in-role performance. *Journal of business research*, (75).

Gilson L, Daire J, Patharath A. , et al. (2011), Leadership and governance within the South African health system. *South African health review*, *Durban health system trust*, Durban.

Glomb T M, Bhave D P, Miner A G, et al. (2011). Doing good, feeling good; examining the role of organizational citizenship behaviors in changing mood. *Personnel psychology*, 64 (1).

Goh S C, Elliott C & Quon T K. (2012). The relationship between learning capability and organizational performance; a meta-analytic examination. *The learning organization*, 19 (2).

Goleman D. (2001). "An EI-basedtheory of performance", in Goleman D & Cherniss C. (Eds), *The emotionally intelligent workplace: how to select for, measure, and improve emotional intelligence in individuals, groups, and organizations*, Jossey-Bass, San Francisco, CA.

Gosling S D, John O P, Craik K H, et al. (1998). Do people know how they behave? Self-reported act frequencies compared with on-line codings by observers. *Journal of personality & social psychology*, 74 (5).

Gong Y, Huang J C & Farh J L. (2009). Employee learning orientation, transformational leadership, and employee creativity; the mediating role of employee creativeself-efficacy. *Academy of management journal*, 52 (4).

Goodwin R E, Groth M & Frenkel S J. (2011). Relationships between emotional labor, job performance, and turnover. *Journal of vocational behavior*, 79 (2).

Greenberg J. (1990). Organizational justice; yesterday, today, and tomorrow. *Journal of management*, 16 (2).

Greenberg J. (2004). Stress fairness to fare no stress; managing workplace stress by promoting organizational justice. *Organizational dynamics*.

Greenberg & Baron. (2000). *The psychology of behavior at work; the individual in the organization by Adrian Furnham* (2nd Ed). New York. Madison Avenue.

Groth M & Grandey A. (2012). From bad to worse; Negative exchange spirals in employee-customer service interactions. *Organizational psychology review*, 2 (3).

Gribbin J. (1997). Book review; companion to the cosmos/little, brown. *Astronomy*, (25).

Grant A M. (2013). Rocking the boat but keeping it steady: the role of emotion regulation in employee voice. *Academy of management journal*, 56 (6).

Grandey A A. (2000). Emotion regulation in the workplace: a new way toconceptualize emotional labor. *Journal of occupational health psychology*, (1).

Grandey A A. (2000). Emotion regulation in work place: a new way to conceptualize emotional labor. *Journal of occupational health psychology*, 5 (1).

Grandey A A. (2003). When the show must go on: surface and deep acting as determinants of emotional exhaustion and peer-rated service delivery. *Academy of management journal*, 46 (1).

Grandey A A, Fish G M & Steiner D D. (2005). Must "service with a smile" be stressful? The moderating role of personal control for American and French employees. *Journal of applied psychology*, (90).

Grandey A A, Foo S C, Groth M, et al. (2012). Free to be you and me: a climate of authenticity alleviates burnout from emotional labor. *Journal of occupational health psychology*, (17).

Graham J W. (1991). An essay on organizational citizenship behavior. *Employee responsibilities and rights journal*, (4).

Guba E G & Lincoln Y S. (2005). *Paradigmatic Controversies, contradictions, and emerging confluences*. Handbook of qualitative research.

Guo Ming. (2015). Analysis on the Status Quo of technology innovation of small and medium enterprises in Jilin Province. *Journal of Jilin Province Economic Management Cadre College*, 29 (5).

Guo G & Zhou X. (2013). Research on organizational citizenship behaviour, trust and customer citizenship behaviour. *International journal of business and management*, 8 (16).

Hair J F, Black W C, Babin B J, et al. (2006). *Multivariate data analysis* (6th ed.). New Jersey: Pearson International Edition.

Han Tianjiao. (2016). Problems and suggestions on the development of small and medium enterprises in Jilin Province. *Corporate herald*,

(18).

Hashim H I C & Shariff S M. (2005), Halal supply chain management training: issues and challenges. *Procedia economics and finance* (37).

Hater J J & Bass B M. (1988). Superiors' evaluations and subordinates' perceptions of transformational and transactional leadership. *Journal of applied psychology*, 73 (4).

Han Tianjiao. (2016). The problems and suggestions for the development of small and medium-sized enterprises in Jilin Province. *Enterprise herald*, (18).

Han S J, Moon T W, Yoo J J, et al. (2015). The moderating role of perceived organizational support on the relationship between emotional labor and job-related outcomes. *Management decision*, 53 (3).

Harrower N L. (2011). The effects of organizational culture on marketing programs: a grounded theory study. *Dissertations & theses-gradworks*.

He Xianfu, Chen Yu & Zhang Weiwei. (2011). An empirical study of enterprises' implementation of social responsibility to employees affecting organizational citizenship behavior—based on social exchange theory. *Social science research*, (5).

Hennig-Thurau T, Groth M, Paul M, et al. (2006). Are all smiles created equal? How emotional contagion and emotional labor affect service relationships. *Journal of marketing*, 70 (3).

Hemenway M K, Jefferys W H & Lambert D L. (2007). Obituary: Ralph Robert Robbins, Jr. 1938—2005. *Bulletin of the American astronomical society*.

He Xuan. (2009). Can interactive fairness really treat silence? — An empirical study on the moderation of median thinking in China. *Managing the world*, (4).

Hisyam Selamat M & Choudrie J. (2007). Using meta-abilities and tacit knowledge for developing learning based systems: a case study approach. *The learning organization*, 14 (4).

Hillman A J & Keim G D. (2001). Shareholder value, stakeholder management, and social issues: what's the bottom line?. *Strategic management journal*, 22 (2).

Howell J M & Avolio B J. (1993). Transformational leadership, transactional leadership, locus of control, and support for innovation: key predictors of consolidated-business-unit performance. *Journal of applied psychology*, 78 (6).

Howell J M & Shamir B. (2005). The role of followers in the charismatic leadership process: relationships and their consequences. *Academy of management review*, 30 (1).

Hoffmann E A. (2016). Emotions and emotional labor at worker-owned businesses: deep acting, surface acting, and genuine emotions. *The sociological quarterly*, 57 (1).

Hochschild A R. (1979). Emotion work, feeling rules, and social structure. *American journal of sociology*, 85 (3).

Hong Zhenshun. (1998). *Research on the impact of organizational justice on organizational citizenship behavior—perspective of trust relations*. Taipei: Master's Thesis, Institute of Human Resources Management. National Sun Yat-sen University.

Hochschild A R. (1989). *The second shift*. New York: Viking.

Hochschild A R. (1983). *The managed heart*. University of California Press.

Huang Lanhui. (2014). Research on data collection methods of online social network. *Information technology*, (2).

Hillary R. (2017). *Small and medium-sized enterprises and the environment: business imperatives*. Routledge.

Hult G T M, Ferrell O C & Hurley R F. (2002). Global organizational learning effects oncycle time performance. *Journal of business research*, 55 (5).

Hu Yang-cheng & Cai Ning. (2009). Research on the relationship between market orientation and organizational performance of non-profit organizations. *Journal of management*, (8).

Hurley R F. (1998). Innovation, market orientation, and organizational learning: an integration and empirical examination.

Journal of marketing, 62 (3).

Hult G T M, Ferrell O C & Hurley R F. (2002). Global organizational learning effects on cycle time performance. *Journal of business research*, 55 (5).

Hu Yang-cheng & Cai Ning. (2009). Research on the relationship between market orientation and organizational performance of non-profit organizations. *Journal of management*, (8).

Hu Jiarui. (2014). *Research on the poverty alleviation and transformation of small and medium-sized enterprises in Jilin Province.* Jilin University.

Huang M E, Wu Z Q & Tang G Q. (2010). How does personality relate to mental health in service industry setting? The mediating effects of emotional labor strategies. *Acta psychologica sinica*, 42 (12).

Huber G P. (1991). Organizational learning: the contributing processes and the literatures. *Organization science*, 2 (1).

Humphrey A. (2012). Transformational leadership and organizational citizenship behaviors: the role of organizational identification. *The psychologist-manager journal*, 15 (4).

Hunt S D, Sparkman R D & Wilcox J B. (1982). The pretest in survey research: issues and preliminary findings. *Journal of marketing research*, XIX (pre – 1986).

Hutcheson G D & Sofroniou N. (1999). *The multivariate social scientist: introductory statistics using generalized linear models.* Sage.

Hwa M A C. (2012). Emotional labor and emotional exhaustion: does co-worker support matter?. *Journal of management research*, 12 (3).

Ilies R, Scott B A & Judge T A. (2006). The interactive effects of personal traits and experienced states on intraindividual patterns of citizenship behavior. *Academy of management journal*, 49 (3).

Imran M K. (2014). *Impact of knowledge management in frastructure on organizational performance with moderating role of KM performance: an empirical study on banking sector of Pakistan.* paper presented at the Information and Knowledge Management, Shanghai.

Inness M, Turner N, Barling J, et al. (2010). Transformational ieadership and employee safety performance: a within-person, between-jobs design. *Journal of occupational health psychology*, 15 (3).

Istvan H & Nikolett N. (2004). Job satisfaction as a key management tool to step up performance. *Problems and perspectives in management*, (4).

Isen A M & Baron R A. (1991). Positive affect as a factor in organizational behavior. *Motivation & emotion*, 15 (1).

İşcan Ö F, Ersarı G & Naktiyok A. (2014). Effect of leadership style on perceived organizational performance and innovation: the role of transformational leadership beyond the Impact of transactional leadership-an application among turkish SME's. *Procedia-social and behavioral sciences*, (150).

Jain A K & Jeppe Jeppesen H. (2013). Knowledge management practices in a public sector organisation: the role of leaders' cognitive styles. *Journal of knowledge management*, 17 (3).

Jain A K & Moreno A. (2015). Organizational learning, knowledge management practices and firm's performance: an empirical study of a heavy engineering firm in India. *The learning organization*, 22 (1).

Janssen, O. (2001). Fairness perceptions as a moderator in the curvilinear relationship between job demands, and job performance and job satisfaction. *Academy of management journal*, 44 (5).

Javaheri Kamel M (2009). The effect of organizational justice, leader-staff relationship, trust and psychological enrichment on the organizational citizenship behavior. *Police hum. Dev*, 6 (3).

Jing Yingying & Liu Jianan. (2017). Strategic analysis of "going global" of small and medium-sized private enterprises in Jilin Province under the background of "One Belt, One Road". *Guangdong sericulture*, (10).

Johnson J M. (2010). Leadership and organizational performance in a global, "Fortune" 500 six sigma operating company: a correlational research study. *Dissertations & theses-gradworks*.

Jiao C, Richards D A & Hackett R D. (2013). Organizational

citizenship behaviour and role breadth: a meta-analytic and cross-cultural analysis. *Human resource management*, 52 (5).

Jin Z. (2013). *A study on the relationship between management team conflict and organizational citizenship behavior in colleges and universities: the mediating effect of organizational justice.* International Conference on Management Science & Engineering.

Jiang Tianying. (2009). Research on employee knowledge learning performance model. *Scientific research*, 27 (10).

Jiang Shan. (2019). Current situation, characteristics and countermeasures of internal control of small and medium-sized enterprises in China. *Science and technology entrepreneurship monthly*, 32 (3).

Jin Ming Xing. (2011). *An empirical study on the impact of organizational equity on organizational citizenship behavior and work performance—based on a questionnaire survey of financial enterprises.* Shang Hai: Fudan University.

Julian Marius Müller. (2019). Business model innovation in small- and medium-sized enterprises. *Journal of manufacturing technology management*, 30 (8).

Judge T A, Scott B A & Ilies R. (2006). Hostility, job attitudes, and workplace deviance: test of a multilevel model. *Journal of applied psychology*, 91 (1).

Jung D I, Chow C & Wu A. (2003). The role of transformational leadership in enhancing organizational innovation: hypotheses and some preliminary findings. *The leadership quarterly*, 14 (4).

Judge T A & Piccolo R F. (2004). Transformational and transactional leadership: a meta-analytic test of their relative validity. *Journal of applied psychology*, 89 (5).

Ju T L, Li C Y & Lee T S. (2006). A contingency model for knowledge management capability and innovation ". *Industrial management & data systems*, 6 (106).

Kaiser H. (1974). An index of factorial simplicity. *Psychometrika*, (39).

Kaplan R S & Norton D P. (1996). *Using the balanced scorecard as a strategic management system.*

Kark R, Waismel-Manor R & Shamir B. (2012). Does valuing androgyny and femininity lead to a female advantage? The relationship between gender-role, transformational leadership and identification. *The leadership quarterly*, 23 (3).

Kark R, Waismel-Manor R & Shamir B. (2012). Does valuing and rogyny and femininity lead to a female advantage? The relationship between gender-role, transformational leadership and identification. *Leadership quarterly*, 23 (3).

Katrz D. (1964). Motivational basis of organizational behavior. *Behavioral science* (9).

Katz D & Kahn R. (1966). *The social psychology of organizations.* New York: Wile.

Koper G, Van Knippenberg D, Bouhuijs F, et al. (1993). Procedural fairness and self-esteem. *European journal of social psychology*, 23 (3).

Kickul J & Lester S W. (2001). Broken promises: equity sensitivity as a moderator between psychological contract breach and employee attitudes and behavior. *Journal of business and psychology*, 16 (2).

Kim S. (2003). Research paradigms in organizational learning and performance: competing modes of inquiry. Information technology. *Learning and performance journal*, 21 (1).

Kim W C & Mauborgne R A. (1991). Implementing global strategies: the role of procedural justice. *Strategic management journal*, 12 (12).

Korsgaard M A, Schweiger D M & Sapienza H J. (1995). Building commitment, attachment, and trust in strategic decision-making teams: the role of procedural justice. *Academy of management journal*, 38 (1).

Kaplan R S & Norton D P. (1996). The balanced scorecard: translating strategy into action. Harvard Business Review Press.

Konovsky M A & Cropanzano R. (1991). Perceived fairness of employee drug testing as a predictor of employee attitudes and job performance. *Journal of applied psychology*, 76 (5).

Kouzes James M & Posner Barry Z. (1987). The leadership challenge: how to get extraordinary things done in organizations. *Urnal penyuluhan*, 17 (11).

Kang S W & Kang S D. (2016). High-commitment human resource management and job stress: supervisor support as a moderator. *Social behavior and personality: an international journal*, 44 (10).

Kizilos M A, Cummings C & Cummings T G. (2013). How high-involvement work processes increase organization performance: the role of organizational citizenship behaviour. *Journal of applied behavioural science*, 49 (4).

Kusluvan S, Kusluvan Z, Ilhan I, et al (2010). The humandimension: a review of human resources management issues in the tourism and. *Hospitality industry cornell hospitality quarterly*, 51 (2).

Kukkar N & Ahuja S G. (2017). *Relationship between loneliness, emotional intelligence and organizational commitment.*

Kim H J, Hurb W M, Moon T W, et al. (2017). Is all support equal? The moderating effects of supervisor, coworker, and organizational support on the link between emotional labor and job performance. *Business research quarterly*, (20).

Kim W S, Ok C H & Lee M J. (2009). Antecedents of service employees' organizational citizenship behaviors in full-service restaurants in Korea. *Cornell hospitality quarterly*, 50 (2).

Kirkpatrick S A & Locke E A. (1996). Direct and indirect effects of three core charismatic leadership components on performance and attitudes. *Journal of applied psychology*, 81 (1).

Kruml S M & Geddes D. (2000). Exploring the dimensions of emotional labor. *Social science electronic publishing*, 14 (1).

Khan M A. (2010). Effects of human resources management practices on organizational performance: an empirical study of oil and gas industry in Pakistan. *European journal of economics, finance, and administrative sciences*, (24).

Konovsky M A & Pugh S D. (1994). Citizenship behavior and social exchange. *Academy of management journal*, 37 (3).

Kruml S M & Geddes D. (2000). Exploring the dimensions of emotional labor: the heart of Hochschild's work. *Management communication quarterly*, 14 (1).

Lather A S & Kaur S A. (2015). Study on influence of interactional procedural and distributive justice on work outcomes. *International journal of advanced research*, 3 (7).

Lai Zhichao & Huang Guangguo. (2000). Procedural justice and distributive justice: justice perception and work attitude of employees in Taiwan enterprises. *Chinese journal of psychology*, 42 (2).

Lawson K J, Noblet A J & Rodwell J J. (2009). Promoting employee well-being: the relevance of work characteristics and organizational justice. *Health promotion international*, 24 (3).

Lal V. (2002). *Empire of knowledge culture and plurality in the global economy*. Sage, Thousand Oaks, CA.

Lam C K, Huang X & Chan S C. (2014). The threshold effect of participative leadership and the role of leader information sharing. *Academy of management journal*, 58 (3).

Lee & Ashforth. (1996). A meta-analytic examination of the correlates of the job burnout. *Journal of applied psychology*, 81 (2).

Leventhal G S, Karuza J & Fry W R. (1980). Beyond fairness: a theory of allocation preferences. In G Mikula (Ed.), *Justice and social ineraction*. NY: Springer-Verlag.

Lee W I, Chen C C & Lee C C. (2015). *The relationship between internal marketing orientation, employee commitment, charismatic leadership and performance*. Proceedings of the 17th International Conference on Electronic Commerce in Seoul, ACM.

Li Xingxiu & Yu Shifen. (2002). An analysis of equity theory. *East China economic management*, 16 (6).

Li C K & Hung C H. (2009). The influence of transformational leadership on workplace relationships and job performance. *Social behavior & personality an international journal*, 37 (8).

Lyu Y, Zhu H, Zhong H J, et al. (2016). Abusive supervision and customer-oriented organizational citizenship behavior: the roles of hostile attribution bias and work engagement. *International journal of hospitality management*, (53).

Liu Zhen. (2012). Overview of measurement of organizational performance and employee performance. *Nanda business review*, (12).

Lin Yiping. (2001). *A study on the relationship between market orientation, organizational learning, organizational innovation and organizational performance-taking information and electronics industry in science park as an example, unpublished doctoral dissertation, department of business administration.* National Sun Yat-sen University, (5).

Loi R, Yang J & Diefendorff J M. (2009). Four-factor justice and daily job satisfaction: a multilevel investigation. *Journal of applied psychology*, 94 (3).

Li Y H, Huang J W & Tsai M T. (2009). Entrepreneurial orientation and firm performance: the role of knowledge creation process. *Industrial marketing management*, 38 (4).

Liao S H, Fei W C & Liu C T. (2008). Relationships between knowledge inertia, organizational learning and organization innovation. *Technovation*, 28 (4).

Liao S H & Wu C C. (2010). System perspective of knowledge management, organizational learning, and organizational innovation. *Expert systems with applications*, 37 (2).

Lee T H, Gerhart B, Weller I, et al. (2008). Understanding voluntary turnover: path-specific job satisfaction effects and the importance of unsolicited job offers. *Academy of management journal*, 51 (4).

Lee D C & Hung L M. (2012). Does job enjoyment and organizational support affect emotional labor? *Journal of business research*, 4 (2).

Lee W I, Chen C C & Lee C C. (2015). *The relationship between internal marketing orientation, employee commitment, charismatic leadership and performance.* Proceedings of the 17th International Conference on Electronic Commerce in Seoul, ACM.

Lee Y H & Woo B. (2017). Emotional labor, emotional

exhaustion, job satisfaction and organisational citizenship behaviour among Korean fitness employees. *South African journal for research in sport, physical education and recreation*, 39 (2).

Lepine J A, Erez A & Johnson D E. (2002). The nature and dimensionality of organizational citizenship behaviour: a critical review and meta-analysis. *Journal of applied psychology*, 87 (1).

Lievens F & Anseel F. (2004). Confirmatory factor analysis and invariance of an organizational citizenship behaviour measure across samples in a Dutch-speaking context. *Journal of occupational and organizational psychology*, (77).

Lim D H & Nowell B. (2014). Integration for training transfer: learning, knowledge, organizational culture and technology. in Schneider, K. (Ed.), *Transfer of learning in qrganizations.* Springer international Publishing, *Cham.*

Lucas L M. (2010). The role of teams, culture, and capacity in the transfer of organizational practices. *The learning organization*, 17 (5).

Li Xingxiu & Yu Shifen. (2002). An analysis of equity theory. *East China economic management*, 16 (6).

Li Lei, Shang Yu-Van, Xi Yumin, et al. (2012). Transformational leadership and subordinates' job performance and organizational commitment: the mediating role of psychological capital. *Chinese journal of management*, 9 (5).

Lowe K B. (1996). Effectiveness correlates of transformational and transactional leadership: a meta-analytic review of the mlq literature. *Leadership quarterly*, 7 (3).

Li Chaoping & Shi Kan. (2006). Measurement of empowerment and its relation with employees' work attitude. *Psychological journal*, 38 (1).

Liu Chao, Zhang Huan, Wang Saijun, et al. (2014). The relationship between leadership style, emotional labor and organizational citizenship behavior: based on survey data of service-oriented enterprises. *Soft science of China*, (3).

Li Tingting. (2014). *The relationship among organizational embeddedness, emotional commitment and organizational citizenship behavior.* Southwest University of Finance and Economics.

Li Jiao. (2017). *The relationship between organizational justice, loyalty and organizational citizenship behavior.* Hebei University.

Li Yan. (2015). *Research on the impact of organizational justice on job satisfaction, turnover intention and organizational citizenship behavior.* Yan Bian University.

Lind E A, Walker L, Kurtz S, et al. (1980). Procedure and outcome effects on reactions to adjudicated resolution of conflicts of interest. *Journal of personality & social psychology*, 39 (4).

Lincoln Y. (1994). Competing paradigms in qualitative research. *Handbook of qualitative research*, (2).

Li Xiaoyan (2013). Tuesday, China. Research on the relationship between psychological capital, emotional labor strategy and job burnout. *Anagement science. February*, (23).

Li Xuan & Huang Miner. (2009). *The influence of meta-emotional evaluation guidance on college students' social anxiety.* Summary of theses of the 12th National Psychological Conference.

Li Gang. (2016). An analysis of the upgrading and transition of small and medium-sized enterprises. *Wanzhong entrepreneurship*, (25).

Li Baizhou, Zhao Jianyu & Su Yi. (2013). Dynamic model of organizational learning-knowledge creation process based on energy level transition. *Scientific research*, 31 (6).

Liu Ya, Long Lirong & Li Ye. (2003). The impact of organizational justice on the variable of organizational effect. *Managing the world*, (3).

Liang Fu, Li Shuwen & Luo Jinlian. (2018). The impact of differentiated transformational leadership on employees' innovative behavior: perspective of resource conversion. *Management science*, 31 (3).

Liu Feiyue, Li Hua & Xie Feng. (2004). Constraints on the development of non-profit organizations in China and countermeasures. *Lanzhou academic journal*, (5).

Li M & Liang L. (2015). Emotional labor between supervisors and subordinates: literature review and future research. *Open journal of business and management*, 4 (1).

Liao Le Le. (2018). *Research on the impact of organizational justice on employee performance*. Nanchang University.

Li Bailing. (2016). *Research on vocational training of small and medium-sized enterprises*. Jilin Agricultural University.

Li Haiyang. (2019). Research on human resource management development of small and medium-sized enterprises in Jilin Province. *Labor and social security world*, 2 (6).

Li Huili & Ma Mengyu. (2017). Discussion on the transformation and development strategies of small and medium-sized enterprises in Jilin Province. *Heilongjiang science*, 8 (13).

Li Y, Zhao Y, Tan J, et al. (2008). Moderating effects of entrepreneurial orientation on market orientation-performance linkage: evidence from Chinese small firms. *Journal of small business management*, 46 (1).

Li M. (2015). *Empirical study on relations between organizational justice, employees affection and organization performance*. International Conference on Economics.

Lu Meiyue & Zhang Wenxian (2006). Research on the relationship between corporate culture and organizational performance. *Nankai management review*, (12).

Lyu Y, Zhu H, Zhong H J, et al. (2016). Abusive supervision and customer-oriented organizational citizenship behavior: the roles of hostile attribution bias and work engagement. *International journal of hospitality management*, (53).

Liu Zhen. (2012). Overview of measurement of organizational performance and employee performance. *Nanda business review*, (12).

Lin Yiping. (2001). *A study on the relationship between market orientation, organizational learning, organizational innovation and organizational performance-taking information and electronics industry in science park as an example, unpublished doctoral dissertation, department of business administration.* National Sun Yat-sen University, (5).

Lee T H, Gerhart B, Weller I, et al. (2008). Understanding voluntary turnover: path-specific job satisfaction effects and the importance of unsolicited job offers. *Academy of management journal*, 51 (4).

Lind E A & Tyler T R. (1988). *The social psychology of procedural justice.* New York: Plenum Press.

Lind E A. (2001), Thinking critically about justice judgments. *Journal of vocational behavior*, 58 (2).

Lo M C, Ramayah T & Hui J K. (2006). An investigation of leader member exchange effects on organizational citizenship behaviour in Malaysia. *Journal of business and management*, 12 (1).

López-Domínguez M, Enache M, Sallan J M, et al. (2013). Transformational leadership as an antecedent of change-oriented organizational citizenship behaviour. *Journal of business research*, 66 (10).

Li Chaoping & Shi Kan. (2006). Measurement of empowerment and its relation with employees' work attitude. *Psychological journal*, 38 (1).

Linde V D, Bernard. (1994). The second (successful) organ initiative at Unisa (October 1988 to September 1994). *Ars nova*, 26 (1).

Li Jiao. (2017). *The relationship between organizational justice, loyalty and organizational citizenship behavior.* Hebei University.

Li Yan. (2015). *Research on the impact of organizational justice on job satisfaction, turnover intention and organizational citizenship behavior.* Yanbian University.

Lincoln Y. (1994). Competing paradigms in qualitative research. *Handbook of qualitative research*, (2).

Li Xiaoyan. (2013). Tuesday, China. Research on the relationship between psychological capital, emotional labor strategy and job burnout. *Management science.* 12 (23).

Li Xuan & Huang Miner. (2009). *The influence of meta-emotional evaluation guidance on college students' social anxiety.* Summary of theses of the 12th National Psychological Conference.

Li Baizhou, Zhao Jianyu & Su Yi. (2013). Dynamic model of organizational learning-knowledge creation process based on energy level transitio. *Scientific research*, 31 (6).

Li hong, Xiang diandian & Yang zengxiong. (2016). Research on the relationship and path between organizational interpersonal trust, knowledge sharing and employee innovation in small and medium-sized enterprises. *Leadership science*, (14).

Liu Ya, Long Lirong & Li Ye. (2003). The impact of organizational justice on the variable of organizational effect. *Managing the world*, (3).

Liang Fu, Li Shuwen & Luo Jinlian. (2018). The impact of differentiated transformational leadership on employees' innovative behavior: *perspective of resource conversion*. *Management science*, 31 (3).

Lu Meiyue & Zhang Wenxian (2006). Research on the relationship between corporate culture and organizational performance. *Nankai management review*, (12).

Lussier R & Achua C. (2015). *Leadership: theory, application, & skill development*. Cengage Learning, Boston, MA.

Lv Yibo. (2008). *Study on the influencing factors of the growth of small and medium-sized enterprises*. Dalian University of Technology

Luo A, Guchait P, Lee L, et al. (2019). Transformational leadership and service recovery performance: the mediating effect of emotional labor and the influence of culture. *International journal of hospitality management*, 77 (1).

Majid M B & Mahmud M S B. (2019). Knowledge management and its impact on organizational performance: evidence from Pakistan. *Annals of contemporary developments in management & HR (ACDMHR)*, 1 (1).

Mann D S. (2013). Research methods for business: a skill-building approach. *Leadership & organization development journal*, 34 (7).

Martin C L & Bennett N. (1996). The role of justice judgments in explaining the relationship between job satisfaction and organizational commitment. *Group & organization management*, 21 (1).

MacKinnon D P, Warsi G & Dwyer J H. (1995). A simulation study of mediated effect measures. *Multivariate behavioral research*, 30 (1).

Malhotra N & Peterson M. (2006). *Basic marketing research: a decision-making approach* (2nd ed.). New Jersey: Prentice Hall.

Ma Mingjie. (2013). Analysis of problems and countermeasures of human resources management in small and medium-sized enterprises in Jilin Province. *China market*, (48).

Ma Shulei, Huang Miner & MaShulei. (2006). Emotional labor: surface action and deep action, which effect is better? *Acta psychologica sinica*, 38 (2).

McFarlin D B & Sweeney P D. (1992). Distributive and procedural justice as predictors of satisfaction with personal and organizational outcomes. *Academy of management journal*, 35 (3).

Moorman R M. (1991). Relationship between organizational justice and organizational citizenship behavior: do fairness perceptions influence employee citizenship? *Journal of applied psycology*, 76 (6).

Moorman R H, Niehoff B P & Organ D W. (1993). Treating employees fairly and organizational citizenship behavior: sorting the effects of job satisfaction, organizational commitment, and procedural justice. *Employee responsibilities & rights journal*, 6 (3).

Menguc B, Auh S & Shih E. (2007). Transformational leadership and market orientation: implications for the implementation of competitive strategies and business unit performance. *Journal of business research*, 60 (4).

Mendelson H & Pillai R R. (1999). Information age organizations, dynamics and performance. *Journal of economic behavior & organization*, 38 (3).

Melkonian T & Soenen G. (2016). Ambrose M. Will I cooperate? The moderating role of informational distance on justice reasoning. *Journal of business ethics*, 137 (4).

Merriam S B. (1998). Qualitative research and case study

applications in education. revised and expanded from " Case Study Research in Education". *British educational research journal*, 41 (2).

Miao Yumeng. (2019). *Research on financing of small and medium-sized enterprises in Jilin Province.* Jilin University.

Matsuno K & Mentzer J T. (2000). The effects of strategy type on the market orientation-performance relationship. *Journal of marketing*, 64 (4).

Mitchell R, Boyle B, Parker V, et al. (2014). Transformation through tension: the moderating impact of negative affect on transformational leadership in teams. *Human relations*, 67 (9).

Mokhlis S. (2009). Relevancy and measurement of religiosity in consumer behavior research. *International business research*, 2 (3).

Mubeen H, Ashraf H & Nisar Q A. (2016). Impact of emotional intelligence and knowledge management on organizational performance: mediating role of organizational learning. *Journal of management Info*, 11 (2).

McFarlin D B & Sweeney P D. (1992). Distributive and procedural justice as predictors of satisfaction with personal and organizational outcomes. *Academy of management journal*, (35).

McLachlan G & Peel D. (1999). The EMMIX algorithm for the fitting of normal and t-components. *Journal of statistical software*, 4 (i02).

Namada J M. (2017). *Organizational learning and firm performance: an empirical investigation in an emerging economy context.*

Nastiezaie N & Najafi M. (2012). The relationship between organizational justice and organizational citizenship behavior. *American journal of economics & business administration*, (47).

Nielsen T M, Bachrach D G, Sundstrom E, et al. (2012). Utility of OCB: organizational citizenship behaviour and group performance in a resource allocation framework. *Journal of management*, 38 (2).

Norman D & Olaf H. (1963). An experimental application of the delphi method to the use of experts. *Management science*, 9 (3).

Ning Tao. (2013). *A study on the relationship among organizational*

commitment, organizational citizenship behavior and team performance: a
case study of hunan construction enterprise project team. Zhongnan
University.

Noruzy, Ali, Dalfard, et al. (2013). Relations between
transformational leadership, organizational learning, knowledge management,
organizational innovation, and organizational; performance: an empirical
investigation of manufacturing firms. International journal of advanced
manufacturing technology, 64 (5 –8).

Niehoff B P & Moorman R M. (1993). Justice as a mediator of the
relationship between methods of monitoring and organizational citizenship
behavior. Academy of management journal, 36 (3).

Ndjaboué R, Brisson C & Vézina M. (2012). Organisational justice
and mental health: a systematic review of prospective studies.
Occupational and environmental medicine, 69 (10).

Nunnally J C. (1978). Psychometric theory. Mc Graw-Hill Publ Co.
New York.

Nunnally J C. (1994). Psychometric theory 3E. Tata McGraw-Hill
Education.

Oliver S & Reddy Kandadi K. (2006). How to develop knowledge
culture in organizations? A multiple case study of large distributed
organizations. Journal of knowledge management, 10 (4).

Organ D W. (1988). Organizational citizenship behavior: the good
soldier syndrome. Lexington Books/DC Heath and Com.

Organ D W & Konovsky M A. (1989). Cognitive versus affective
determinants of organizational citizenship behaviour. Journal of applied
psychology, 74 (1).

Organ D W. (1990). The motivational basis of organizational
citizenship behaviour. In Staw B M & Cummings L L. (Eds), Research
in organizational behaviour, JAI Press, Greenwich, CT, (12).

Organ D W & Moorman R H. (1993). Fairness and organizational
citizenship behavior: what are the connections?. Social justice research, 6
(1).

Organ D W. (1997). Organizational citizenship behavior: It's construct clean-up time. *Human performance*, 10 (2).

Orlikowski W J & Baroudi J J. (2002). *Studying information technology in organisations*: *research approaches and assumptions*, In M D Myers & D Avison. (Eds). *Qualitative research in information systems*. London: Sage Publications.

Ojokuku R M, Odetayo T A & Sajuyigbe A S. (2012). Impact of leadership style on organizational performance: a case study of Nigerian banks. *American Journal of business and management*, 1 (4).

Otto K & Mamatoglu N. (2015) Why does interactional justice promote organizational loyalty, job performance, and prevent mental impairment? The role of social support and social stressors. *The journal of psychology*, 149 (2).

Pallant J. (2010). *Survival manual*: *a step by step guide to data analysis using SPSS (4th ed.)*. New York: McGraw-Hill.

Pallant J. (2013). *SPSS survival manual*: *a step by step guide to data analysis using SPSS for windows (version* 12), 37 (6).

Paul A K & Anantharaman R N. (2003) Impact of people management practices on organizational performance: analysis of a causal model. *The international journal of human resource management*.

Pan Yuan Yuan (2013). *Research on the relationship between organizational justice and organizational commitment of grass-roots community workers*. Chongqing University.

Pamela R. (2011). Effect of organizational justice, respect, trust, and empowerment on job satisfaction and organizational commitment. *Employee empowerment*.

Peng A C, Lin H E, Schaubroeck J, et al. (2016). CEO intellectual stimulation and employee work meaningfulness: the moderating role of organizational context. *group & organization management*, 41 (2).

Podsakoff P M & MacKenzie S B. (1989). *A second generation measure of organizational citizenship behaviour*, Indiana University, Bloomington.

Podsakoff P M, MacKenzie S B, Moorman R H, et al. (1990).

Transformational leader behaviours and their effects on trust, satisfaction, and organizational citizenship behaviours. *Leadership quarterly*, (2).

Podsakoff P M & MacKenzie S B. (1994). Organizational citizenship behaviours and salesunit effectiveness. *Journal of marketing research*, 31 (3).

Podsakoff P M & MacKenzie S B. (1995). An examination of substitutes for leadership within a levels of analysis framework. *Leadership quarterly*, 6 (3).

Podsakoff P M, Mackenzie S B & Bommer W H. (1996). Transformational leader behaviors and substitutes for leadership as determinants of employee satisfaction, commitment, trust and organizational citizenship behaviors. *Journal of management.* 22 (2).

Podsakoff P M, Ahearne M & MacKenzie S B. (1997). Organizational citizenship behaviour and the quantity and quality of work group performance. *Journal of applied psychology*, 82 (2).

Podsakoff P M, MacKenzie S B, Paine J B, et al. (2000). Organizational citizenship behaviors: a critical review of the theoretical and empirical literature and suggestions for future research. *Journal of management*, 26 (3).

Podsakoff P M, MacKenzie S B & Podsakoff N P. (2012). Sources of method bias in social science research and recommendations on how to control it. *Annual review of psychology*, (65).

Podsakoff N P, Whiting S W, Welsh D T, et al. (2013). Surveying for "artifacts": the susceptibility of the OCB-performance evaluation relationship to common rater, item, and measurement context effects. *Journal of applied psychology*, 98 (5).

Polit D F & Beck C T. (2010). The content validity index: are you sure you know what's being reported? Critique and recommendations. *Research in nursing & health*, 29 (5).

Pillai R, Schriesheim C A & Williams E S. (1999). Fairness perceptions and trust as mediators for transformational and transactional leadership: A two-sample study. *Journal of management*, 25 (6).

Pradhan S & Pradhan R K. (2015). An empirical investigation of relationship among transformational leadership, affective organizational commitment and contextual performance. *Vision: The journal of business perspective*, 19 (3).

Pérez López S, Manuel Montes Peón J & José Vazquez Ordás C. (2005). Organizational learning as a determining factor in business performance. *The learning organization*, 12 (3).

Politis J D. (2001). The relationship of various leadership styles to knowledge management. *Leadership & organization development journal*, 22 (8).

Preacher K J & Hayes A F. (2004). SPSS and SAS procedures fore stimating indirect effects in simple mediation models. *Behavior research methods, instruments, & computers*, 36 (4).

Qiao Wenzhu. (2018). Problems and countermeasures of internal control of small and medium enterprises. *Modern economic information*, (9).

Qian Zhen, Shen Yan, Han Song, et al. (2010). *Performance ranking of listed companies: analysis of ownership, scale and industry factors*. The 5th (2010) China Management Annual Conference-Financial Sessions.

Ramayah T. (2011). *Developing and testing moderators and mediators in management research*. School of Management, Universiti Sains Malaysia, Malaysia.

Raphael M. Herr, Jian Li, Jos A. Bosch, et al. (2014). Da. Psychometric properties of a German organizational justice questionnaire (G-OJQ) and its association with self-rated health: findings from the Mannheim In. *International archives of occupational and environmental health*, 39 (1).

Rafferty A E & Griffin M A. (2004). Dimensions of transformational leadership: conceptual and empirical extensions. *Leadership quarterly*, 15 (3).

Rego A & Cunha M P E. (2010). Organisational justice and citizenship behaviors: a study in the portuguese cultural context. *Applied psychology*, 59 (3).

Robbins S P (2005). Organizational behavior (11th ed). Prentice Hall International, New Jersey, NJ.

Ronen S. (1986). Equity perception in multiple comparisons: a field study. *Human relations*, 39 (4).

Rioux S M & Penner L A. (2001). The causes of organizational citizenship behaviour: a motivational analysis. *Journal of applied psychology*, 86 (6).

Ruiz-Palomino P & Martínez-Cañas R. (2014). Ethical culture, ethical intent, and organizational citizenship behaviour: the moderating and mediating role of person-organization fit. *Journal of business ethics*, 120 (1).

Rajah R, Song Z & Arvey R D. (2011). Emotionality and leadership: taking stock of the past decade of research. *The leadership quarterly*, 22 (6).

Randeree K & Al Youha H. (2009). Strategic management of performance: an examination of public sector organizations in the United Arab Emirates. International journal of knowledge. *Culture and change management*, 9 (4).

Riggio R E. (2010). Before emotional intelligence: research on nonverbal, emotional, and social competences. *Industrial and organizational psychology*, 3 (2).

Rosete D & Ciarrochi J. (2005). Emotional intelligence and its relationship to workplace performance outcomes of leadership effectiveness. *Leadership and organization development journal*, 26 (5).

Ryan G, Spencer L M & Bernhard U. (2012). Development and validation of a customized competency-based questionnaire: linking social, emotional, and cognitive competencies to business unit profitability. *Cross cultural management: an international journal*, 19 (1).

Rui Mingjie & Lu Yufang. (2005). Empirical research on the impact of leadership behavior, organizational learning, innovation and performance. *Shanghai management section science*, (2).

Samad S. (2012). The influence of innovation and transformational leadership on organizational performance. *Procedia-social and behavioral sciences*, (57).

Salami S O. (2010). Occupational stress and well-being: emotional intelligence, self-efficacy, coping, negative affectivity and social support as moderators. *Journal of international social research*, 3 (12).

Salami S O. (2007). Moderating effect of emotional intelligence on the relationship between emotional labor and organizational citizenship behaviour. *European journal of social sciences*, 5 (2).

Sarros J C, Cooper B K & Santora J C. (2008) Building a climate for innovation through transformational leadership and organizational culture. *Journal of leadership & organizational studies*, 15 (2).

Sekaran U. (2003). *Research method for business: a skill building approach (4th ed.)*. Danvers, MA: John Wiley & Sons.

Sweeney P D & McFarlin D B. (1997). Rrocess and outcome: gender differences in the assessment of justice. *Journal of organizaitional behaviour*, (18).

Schultz D P. (2014). *History of modern psychology (tenth edition)*. China light industry Press.

Schneider B, Hanges P J, Smith D B, et al. (2003). Which comes first: employee attitudes or organizational financial and market performance? *Journal of applied psychology*, 88 (5).

Semeijn J H, Van Der Heijden B I & Vander Lee A. (2014). Multiso urceratings of managerial competencies and their predictive value for managerial and organizational effectiveness. *Human resource management*, 53 (5).

Schusterschitz C, Stummer H & Geser W. (2014). Going the extra-mile: a question of attachment orientations and gender?. *International journal of organizational analysis*, 22 (3).

Smith C A, Organ D W & Near J P. (1983). Organizational citizenship behaviour: its nature and antecedents. *Journal of applied psychology*, 68 (4).

Singh S K. (2008). Role of leadership in knowledge management: a study. *Journal of knowledge management*, 12 (4).

Srivastava A, Bartol K M & Locke E A. (2006). Empowering leadership in management teams: effects on knowledge sharing, efficacy, and performance. *Academy of management journal*, 49 (6).

Sadiq S. (2014). Relationship between psychological contract violation, supervisory support, psychological contract beach and organizational citizenship behavior. *Journal of business and management*, 16 (3).

Saks A M & Belcourt M. (2006). An investigation of training activities and transfer of training in organizations. *Journal of human resource management*, 45 (4).

Salanova M & Agut S. (2005). Linking organizational resources and work engagement to employee performance and customer royalty: the mediation of service climate. *Journal application psychology*, 90 (6).

Salami S O. (2007). Moderating effect of emotional intelligence on the relationship between emotional labor and organizational citizenship behaviour. *European journal of social sciences*, 5 (2).

Schaarschmidt M, Walsh G & Ivens S. (2015). Perceived external reputation as a driver of organizational citizenship behavior: replication and extension. *Corporate reputation review*, 18 (4).

Schaufeli W & Bakker, A. (2003), Utrecht Work Engagement Scale, Occupational Health Psychology Unit, Utrecht University.

Schaufeli W B, Salanova M, González-romá V, et al. (2002). The measurement of engagement and burnout: a two sample confirmatory factor analytic approach. *Journal of happiness studies*, 3 (1).

Sekaran U & Bougie R. (2010). Research methods for business: a skill-building approach, 5th ed. , John Wiley & Sons, West Sussex.

Sitzmann T. (2011). A meta-analytic examination of the instructional effectiveness of computer-based simulation games. *Personnel psychology*, 64 (2).

Scherer K R & Brosch T. (2009). Culture-specific appraisal biases contribute to emotion dispositions. *European journal of personality*, 23 (3).

Settoon R P, Bennett N & Liden R C. (1996). Social exchange in organizations: perceived organizationalsupport, leader-member exchange, and employee reciprocity. *Journal of applied psychology*, 81 (3).

Sguera F, Bagozzi R P, Huy Q N, et al. (2016). Curtailing the harmful effects of workplace incivility: the role of structural demands and organization-provided resources. *Journal of vocational behavior*, (95).

Shani A, Uriely N, Reichel A., et al. (2014). Emotional labor in the hospitality industry: the influence of contextual factors. *International journal of hospitality management*, (37).

Sonnentag S & Fritz C. (2015). Recovery from job stress: the stressor-detachment model as an integrative framework. *Journal of organizational behavior*, (36).

Sharpe R. (2000). As leaders, women rule. Business Week, November 20).

Siddique C M. (2012). Knowledge management initiatives in the United Arab Emirates: a baseline study. *Journal of knowledge management*, 16 (5).

Silva A. (2014). What do we really know about leadership?. *Journal of business studies quarterly*, 5 (4).

Soebbing B P, Wicker P & Weimar D. (2015). The impact of leadership changes on expectations of organizational performance. *Journal of sport management*, 29 (5).

Schein E H. (1985). Organizational culture and leadership: a dynamic view. *Procedia-social and behavioral sciences*, 31 (1).

Sinkula J M, Baker W E & Noordewier T. (1997). A framework for market-based organizational learning: linking values, knowledge, and behavior. *Journal of the academy of marketing science*, 25 (4).

Ssekakubo J, Lwanga F & Ndiwalana G. (2014). Employee motivation, job satisfaction and organizational performance in Uganda's oil sub-sector. *Global advanced research journal of management and business studies*, 3 (7).

Stoller J K. (2008). Developing physician-leaders: key competencies and available programs. *Journal of health administration education*, 25 (4).

Sun R C & Hui E K. (2012). Cognitive competence as a positive youth development construct: a conceptual review. *The scientific world journal*.

Sun Wei & Huang Peilun. (2004). Review of equity theory research. *Science and technology management research*, 24 (4).

Shen W, Gentry R J & Tosi H L Jr. (2010). The impact of pay on CEO turnover: a test of two perspectives. *Journal of business research*, 63 (7).

Shim D C, Kwon Y S, Park H H, et al. (2011). Linking pay-for-performance system with performance improvement: the role of fairness, organizational resources, and leader/ managerial engagement. *International review of public administration*, 16 (2).

Sutinen R, Kivimäki M, Elovainio M, et al. (2002). Organizational fairness and psychological distress in hospital physicians. *Scandinavian journal of public health*, 30 (3).

Slater S F & Narver J C. (1995) Market orientation and the learning organization. *Journal of marketing*, 59 (3).

Samad S & Abdullah Z. (2012). The influence of leadership styles on organizational performance of logistics companies. *International business management*, 6 (3).

Scott B A, Barnes C M & Wagner D T. (2012). Chameleonic or consistent? a multilevel investigation of emotional labor variablity and self-monitoring. *Academy of management journal*, 55 (4).

Sow Hup Joanne Chan & Ho Yan Isabella Lai. (2016). Understanding the link between communication satisfaction, perceived justice and organizational citizenship behavior. *Journal of business research*, (8).

Stephen P. Robbins. *Management* (9th edition), Renmin University of China Press.

Straub D W, Boudreau M C & Gefen D. (2004). Validation guidelines for IS positivist research. *Communications of the association for information systems*, (13).

Shreya Garg & Rajib Dhar. 2017. Employee service innovative

behavior: the roles of leader-member exchange (LMX), work engagement, and job autonomy. *International journal of manpower*, *emerald group publishing*, 38 (2).

Smith C A, Organ D W & Near J P. (1983) Organizational citizenship behavior: its nature and antecedents. *Journal of applied psychology*, 68 (4).

Shore G, Morin S & Organ M G. (2006). Catalysis in capillaries by Pd thin films using microwave-assisted continuous-flow organic synthesis (MACOS). *Angewandte chemie*, 118 (17).

Sezgin M & Sankur B. (2004). Survey over image thresholding techniques and quantitative performance evaluation. *Journal of electronic imaging*, 13 (1).

Sekaran U. (2003). *Research method for business: a skill building approach (4th ed.)*. Danvers, MA: John Wiley & Sons.

Song Wenshuai, Li Yang. (2019). Research on the relationship between organizational justice and work performance of R & D personnel in high tech enterprises. *Journal of Inner Mongolia University of finance and economics*, 17 (3).

Škerlavaj M, Dimovski V & Desouza K C. (2010). Patterns and structures of intra-organizational learning networks within a knowledge-intensive organization. *Journal of information technology*, 25 (2).

Shahzad K, Rehman U, Shad I, et al. (2011). Work-life policies and job stress as determinants of turnover intentions of customer service representatives in Pakistan. *European journal of social sciences*, 19 (3).

Shao Jianping, Tan Xinhui & Fan Wen. (2011). An empirical study on the impact of demographic factors on managers' emotional labor. *East China Economic Management*, (5).

Shao Qi. (2017). *Research on the relationship among corporate social responsibility perception, emotional commitment and organizational citizenship behavior*. Central China Normal University.

Shi Shaohua & Zhang Meiling (2000). Several issues in questionnaire compilation. *Journal of developments in psychology*, (8).

Shi Tao & Zeng Lingfeng. (2015). Organizational learning and organizational performance: the mediating role of work happiness. *Journal of industrial engineering and engineering management*, (3).

Su Jincheng (2019). Building a solid foundation for the sustainable development of small and medium-sized enterprises by staff training management. *Business news*, (7).

Sui Yang, Wang Hui, Yue Huanyan, et al. (2012) The impact of transformational leadership on employee performance and satisfaction: mediating role of psychological capital and moderating role of procedural fairness. *Psychological journal*, (9).

Sun Renhua & Yu Ling (2013). Development status and existing problems of small and medium enterprises in Jilin Province. *Journal of Jilin Province Economic Management Cadre College*, 27 (4).

Sun Wei & Huang Peilun. (2004). Review of equity theory research. *Science and technology management research*, 24 (4).

Smith C A, Organ D W & Near J P. (1983). Organizational citizenship behavior: its nature and antecedents. *Journal of applied psychology*, 68 (4).

Steers R M. (1975). Problems in the measurement of organizational effectiveness. *Administrative science quarterly*.

Sun Wei & Huang Peilun (2004). Review of the research on fairness theory. *Science and technology management research*, (4).

Sylvester S. (2003). Measuring the learning practice: diagnosing the culture in general practice. *Quality in primary care*, (11).

Tabachnick B G & Fidell L S. (2007). *Using multivariate statistics* (5th ed.). Boston: Pearson Education.

Takagi H. (1991). *Queueing analysis: a foundation of performance evaluation*. Amsterdam: North-Holland.

Tarim M. (2018). *Impact of LMX and emotional labor on performance and commitment.*

Tang F, Mu J & Maclachlan D L. (2010). Disseminative capacity, organizational structure and knowledge transfer. *Expert systems with applications*, 37 (2).

Tang Wenxin. (2019). The development of financial management of small and medium-sized enterprises in China. *Heilongjiang science*, 10 (11).

Tang Xinyao. (2015). *The relationship between employees' work values, organizational commitment and organizational citizenship behavior in catering enterprises.* Hunan Normal University.

Tannenbaum S I. (1997). Enhancing continuous learning: diagnostic finding from multiple companies. *Human resource management*, 36 (4).

Tabachnick B G & Fidell L S. (2007). *Using multivariate statistics* (5th ed.).

Tian Hui. (2014). Research on the relations among organizational justice, organizational commitment and turnover tendency. *Learning and exploration*, (2).

Tomal D R & Jones K J. (2015). A comparison of core competencies of women and men leaders in the manufacturing industry. *The coastal business journal*, 14 (1).

Transfield D, Denyer D & Palminder S. (2003). Towards a methodology for developing evidence-informed management knowledge by means of systematic review. *British journal of management*, 14 (3).

Tippins M J & Sohi R S. (2010) IT competency and firm performance: is organizational learning a missing link? *Strategic management journal*, 24 (8).

Teh C J, Boerhannoeddin A & Ismail A. (2012). Organizational culture and performance appraisal process; effect on organizational citizenship behaviour. *Asian business management*, 11 (4).

Temminck E, Mearns K & Fruhen L. (2013). Motivating employees towards sustainable behaviour. *Business strategy and the environment*, 24 (6).

Turnipseed D L & Murkison E. (2000). A bi-cultural comparison of organization citizenship behaviour: does the OCB phenomenon transcend national culture?. *The international journal of organizational analysis*, 8 (2).

Turnipseed P H & Turnipseed D L. (2013). Testing the proposed linkage between organizational citizenship behaviours and an innovative organizational climate. *Creativity and innovation management*, 22 (2).

Thomas N & Vohra N. (2015). Three debates in organizational learning: what every manager should know. *Development and learning in organizations: an international journal*, 29 (3).

Tong Yanyan. (2018). *Research on development strategy of Shanghai DL Electronic Technology Co. , Ltd.* Guangxi University.

Tyler T R & Caine A. (1981). The influence of outcomes and procedures on satisfaction with formal leaders. *Journal of personality and social psychology*, 41 (4).

Tyler T R, Degoey P & Smith H. (1996). Understanding why the justice of group procedures matters: a test of the psychological dynamics of the group-value model. *Journal of personality and social psychology*, 70 (5).

Tyler T R & Lind E A. (1992). *A relational model of authority in groups* (*Ed.*), *Advances in experimental social psychology* (*Vol.* 25). Academic Press.

Thibaut J W & Walker L. (1975). Procedural justice: a psychological analysis. *Duke law journal*, (6).

Tippins M J & Sohi R S. (2010). IT competency and firm performance: is organizational learning a missing link? *Strategic management journal*, 24 (8).

Titi Amayah A. (2013). Determinants of knowledge sharing in a public sector organization. *Journal of knowledge management*, 17 (3).

Trauth E M. (2011). Choosing qualitative methods in IS research: lessons learned. *Qualitative research in IS*.

Turnipseed D L & Rassuli A. (2005). Performance perceptions of organizational citizenship behaviours at work: a Bi-level study among managers and employees. *British journal of management*, 16 (3).

Tull D S & Hawkin D I. (1976). *Marketing research meaning, measurement, and method.* New York: MacMillan Publishing.

Utterback J. (1994). Mastering the dynamics of innovation: how companies can seize opportunities in the face of technological change.

University of Illinois at Urbana-Champaign's Academy for Entrepreneurial Leadership Historical Research Reference in Entrepreneurship.

Upadhaya B, Munir R & Blount Y. (2014). Association between performance measurement systems and organisational effectiveness. *International journal of operations & production management*, 34 (7).

Van den Bos K & Lind E A. (2002). *Uncertainty management by means of fairness judgments"*, in Zanna M P. (Ed.). *Advances in experimental social psychology*, Academic Press, San Diego, CA.

Van Dyne L, Graham J W & Dienesch R M (1994). Organizational citizenship behavior: construct redefinition, measurement, and validation. *Academy of management journal*, 37 (4).

Vermunt R, Kloot W A V D & Meer J V D. (1993). The effect of procedural and interactional criteria on procedural fairness judgments. *Social justice research*, 6 (2).

Walz S M & Niehoff B P. (2000). Organizational citizenship behaviors: their relationship to organizational effectiveness. *Journal of hospitality & tourism research*, 24 (3).

Wang Shuxin. (2019). *Research on the development of small and medium-sized enterprises in China under the new normal of economy.* Shenyang University of Technology.

Wang H, Lu C & Siu O. (2015). Job insecurity and job performance: the moderating role of organizational justice and the mediating role of work engagement. *Journal of applied psychology*, 100 (4).

Wang Haiyun. (2019). On the core competitiveness of small and medium-sized enterprises. *Modern industrial economy and informatization*, 9 (5).

Wang Meng. (2017). *Research on the impact of transformational leadership on subsidiary job performance.* Nanchang University.

Wang Li Li. (2015). *Research on the impact of emotional labor on job performance in service industry.* Anhui University.

Walumbwa F O & Hartnell C A. (2011). Understanding transformational leadership-employee performance links: the role of relational identification and self-efficacy. *Journal of occupational and organizational psychology*, 84 (1).

Walsham G. (1995). The emergence of interpretivism in IS research. *Information systems research*, 6 (4).

Wahab M S A, Saad R A J & Selamat M H. (2014). A survey of work environment inhibitors to informal workplace learning activities amongst Malaysian accountants. *Procedia-social and behavioral sciences*, (164).

Wagner D T, Barnes C M & Scott B A. (2014). Driving it home: how workplace emotional labor harms employee home life. *Personnel psychology*, 67 (2).

Wayne S J, Shore L M & Liden R C. (1997). Perceived organizational support and leader-member exchange: a social exchange perspective. *Academy of management journal*, 40 (1).

Williams L J & Anderson S E. (1991). Job satisfaction and organizational commitment as predictors of organizational citizenship and in-role behaviors. *Journal of management*, 17 (3).

Wolfe R A. (1994). Organizational innovation: review, critique and suggested research directions. *Journal of management studies*, 31 (3).

Wang F J, Chich-Jen S & Mei-Ling T. (2010). Effect of leadership style on organizational performance as viewed from human resource management strategy. *African journal of business management*, 4 (18).

Wagner D T, Barnes C M & Scott B A. (2014). Driving it home: how workplace emotional labor harms employee homelife. *Personnel psychology*, 67 (2).

Wang Zhang Di. (2015). *A study on the relationship among employees' organizational justice, professional degree and job performance in small and medium-sized enterprises.* Guangxi Science and Technology University,

Wang Yu & Tian Xin Min. (2013). Research on the influencing factors of organizational citizenship behavior based on organizational justice—taking positive emotion as the mediating variable. *Shanghai management science*, (2).

Walter F, Cole, M S & Humphrey R H. (2011). Emotional intelligence: sine qua non of leadership or folderol?. *The academy of management perspectives*, 25 (1).

Wang Wei. (2016). *Research on financing problems of SMEs*. Hubei University of Technology.

Wang Yanfeng & Yang Zhong (2010). A review of the theory of knowledge sharing research. *Nanjing social sciences*, (6).

Wei Zhilin & Yan Mingjie. (2016). Salary psychological discount, compensation equity and job performance. *Journal of economics and management*, 37 (4).

Wei X, Qu H & Ma E. (2012). Decisive mechanism of organizational citizenship behaviour in the hotel industry—an application of economic game theory. *International journal of hospitality management*, 31 (4).

Whiting S W, Maynes T D, Podsakoff N P, et al. (2012). Effects of message, source, and context on evaluations of employee voice behavior. *Journal of applied psychology*, 97 (1).

Whiting S W, Podsakoff P M & Pierce J R. (2008). Effects of task performance, helping, voice, and organizational loyalty on performance appraisal ratings. *Journal of applied psychology*, 93 (1).

Wagner D T, Barnes C M & Scott B A. (2014). Driving it home: how workplace emotional labor harms employee home life. *Personnel Psychology*, 67 (2).

Walumbwa F O & Hartnell C A. (2011). Understanding transformational leadership-employee performance links: the role of relational identification and self-efficacy. *Journal of occupational & organizational psychology*, 84 (1).

Wang Yonggui, Wang Na & Zhao Hongwen. (2014). The relationship between organizational memory, organizational learning and supplier's innovative ability: an empirical study based on outsourcing situation. *Scientific research management*, 35 (10).

Welbourne T M, Balkin D B & Gomez-Mejia L R. (1995).

Gainsharing and mutuamonitoring: a combined agency-organizational justice interpretation. *Academy of management journal*, (38).

Wen Hong. (2005). Problems and countermeasure analysis of performance evaluation of non-profit organizations. *Journal of Shandong Economic Management Cadre College, Shandong Administrative College*, (1).

Wu Cisheng & Sun Wei. (2007). Review of research on high performance work system and organizational performance. *Modern management science*, (11).

Wang Bingcheng & Ding Hao. (2012). Research on the impact of employee performance assessment on organizational performance. *Enterprise economy*, (3).

Wang Yicheng. (2016). *Research on the path of flexible strategy implementation of small and medium-sized growth enterprises in Jilin Province.* Changchun University of Technology.

Wang Huacheng & Liu Junyong. (2004). Research on the model of enterprise performance evaluation—also on the choice of Chinese enterprise performance evaluation model. *Management world*, (4).

Wu Zhiming & Wu Xin. (2006). The impact of transformational leadership on organizational citizenship behavior in knowledge teams. *Scientific research*, 24 (2).

W Walop, L Del Greco & L Eastridge. (1987). Clinical epidemiology. Questionnaire development: 4. Preparation for analysis. *Canadian medical association journal*, 136 (9).

Wang C L & Ahmed P K. (2003). Organisational learning: a critical review. *The learning organization*, 10 (1).

Wang Haiwen & Zhang Shuhua. (2018). Meta-analysis of the relationship between emotional labor strategies and job satisfaction. *Progress in psychological science*, (4).

Wang Shuxin. (2019). *Research on the development of small and medium-sized enterprises in China under the new normal of economy.* Shenyang University of Technology.

Wang Shenmou. (2016). *Research on policy support for the development of small and medium-sized enterprises in China.* Xiangtan University.

Wang Zhen, Sun Jianmin & Zhao Yijun. (2012). Leadership effectiveness in China's organizational context: Meta analysis of transformational leadership, leader subordinate exchange and destructive leadership. *Progress in psychological science*, 20 (2).

Wu Junlong. (2015). Application of incentive theory in enterprise salary management. *Enterprise reform and management*, (3X).

Xie Hongming, Ge Zhiliang & Wang Cheng. (2008). Research on the relationship between social capital, organizational learning and organizational innovation. *Journal of management engineering*, (1).

Xu A J, Loi R & Ngo H. (2016). Ethical leadership behavior and employee justice perceptions: the mediating role of trust in organization. *Journal of business ethics*, 134 (3).

Xu Can. (2009). *An empirical study on the impact of organizational justice on employee performance.* Nanjing University of Technology.

Xu Daijie (2011). *Research on management innovation of small and medium enterprises in Jilin Province.* Jilin University.

Xu Weimin & Song Tizhong. (2013). The impact of emotional labor on employee performance. *Business research*, 55 (1).

Xu Fang. (2007). *Principles and practices of organizational behavior.* Tsinghua University Press, (17).

Xu Jiang. (2019). The current situation, problems and countermeasures of the development of private enterprises in Jilin Province. *Taxation and economy*, 224 (3).

Xu Weidong. (2019). On the internal control system under the management mechanism of small and medium-sized enterprises. *Modern economic information*, (10).

Xu Mengqiu. (2001). Categories of equity and ratio of equity. *Chinese social sciences*, (1).

Xu Weimin & Song Tizhong. (2013). The impact of emotional labor on employee performance. *Business research*, 55 (1).

Xanthopoulou D, Bakker A B, Demerouti E, et al. (2007). The role of personal resources in the job demands-resources model. *International journal of stress management*, 14 (2).

Xing Zhouling. (2009). Research on the relationship between commitment-based human resource management system and organizational performance. *Management review*, (11).

Xu Yanhong. (2017). *The impact of performance pay on organizational citizenship behavior: the role of organizational commitment and distribution equity*. Shanxi University of Finance and Economics.

Yang Shaoqin. (2010). Brief guide to several questions in questionnaire compilation. *Commercial culture (academic edition)*, (9).

Yang Yuhao & Long Junwei. (2008). Structure and measurement of employee knowledge sharing behavior. *Acta psychologica sinica*, 40 (3): 350 –357.

Yasin G, Nawab S, Bhatti K K, et al. (2014). Relationship of intellectual stimulation, innovations and SMEs performance: transformational leadership a source of competitive advantage in SMEs. *Middle-east journal of scientific research*, 19 (1).

Yen H R & Niehoff B P. (2004). Organizational citizenship behaviors and organizational effectiveness: examining relationships in Taiwanese banks. *Journal of applied social psychology*, 34 (8).

Yukl G & Lepsinger R. (2005). Why integrating the leading and managing roles is essential for organizational effectiveness. *Organizational dynamics*, 34 (4).

Yuchtman E & Seashore S E. (1967). A system resource approach to organizational effectiveness. *American sociological review*, 32 (6).

Yun S, Cox J, Sims Jr H P, et al. (2007). Leadership and teamwork: the effects of leadership and job satisfaction on team citizenship. *International journal of leadership studies*, (3).

Yu Yanping, Luo Wei & Wang Ping. (2013). A review of emotional labor research in service industry employees. *Management modernization*, (3).

Yu Yuhong & Liao Zheyi. (2018). Research on the business

environment of small and medium enterprises in Jilin City. *Industry and technology forum*, (4).

Yui-Tim Wong, Hang-Yue Ngo & Chi-Sum Wong. (2006). Perceived organizational justice, trust, and OCB: a study of Chinese workers in joint ventures and state-owned enterprises. *Journal of world business*, (8).

Yunus H, Ghazali K & Hassan N. (2011). The influence of leader's emotional intelligence: mediating effect of leader-member exchange on employees ' organizational citizenship behaviours. *Interdisciplinary journal of contemporary research in business*, 3 (3).

Yukl G A. (1989). *Leadership in organizations*. Prentice-Hall.

Yu Haibo, Fang Liluo & Ling Wenkui. (2007). Empirical study on organizational learning and its mechanism. *Journal of management science*, (5).

Yu Binbin & Zhong Jianan. (2008). Research on the relationship between emotional intelligence, organizational justice and organizational citizenship behavior. *Psychological science*, 31 (2).

Yu Conghui (2017). *Research on the relationship between the competency of middle managers and job performance*. Northeast University of Finance and Economics.

Y Li Eldon, Tsui-Hsu Tsai Tracy & Jing Lin Arthur. (2014). Do psychological contract and organizational citizenship behavior affect organizational performance in non-profit organizations?. *Chinese management studies*, 8 (3).

Yue Y, Wang K L & Groth M. (2016). The impact of surface acting on coworker-directed voluntary workplace behaviours. *European journal of work and organizational psychology*, 25 (3).

Yu Conghui. (2017). *Research on the relationship between middle managers' competency and job performance*. Dongbei University of Finance and Economics.

Zapf D & Holz M. (2005). On the positive and negative effects of emotion work in organizations. *European journal of work & qrganizational psychology*, (15).

Zacher H, Pearce L K, Rooney D, et al. (2014). Leaders' personal wisdom and leader-member exchange quality: the role of individualized consideration. *Journal of business ethics*, 121 (2).

Zainudin A. (2012). *Structural equation modeling using amos graphic.* Universiti Teknologi Mara Publication Center (UPENA), Shah Alam.

Zeng Ping. (2011). Learning, innovation and dynamic ability: an empirical study of enterprises in south China. *Management review*, 23 (1).

Zeng Wei. (2009). *Survey report on survival status of small and medium-sized enterprises.* China Economic Publishing House.

Zhao Limei. (2016). Dilemma and countermeasure of innovation and upgrading of small and medium-sized enterprises. *Jilin pioneering network*, (22).

Zhou Hao, Long Lirong, Wang Yan, et al. (2005). Differences in impacts of distributive justice, procedural justice and interactive justice. *Psychological journal.*

Zhang Lei. (2008). *A study on the relationship among human resource strategy, organizational learning and organizational citizenship behavior in family business.* Zhejiang University.

Zhang Fang. (2010). *Empirical study on emotional labor and work performance of grassroots managers.* Lanzhou University.

Zou Z, Yang Y, Ma Q, et al. (2016). The mechanism between emotional labor and organizational citizenship behavior: based on Chinese context research. *Nanjing business review*, (4).

Zou Zhendong, Yang Yong, Wang Hui, et al. (2017). The mechanism of emotional labor on organizational citizenship behavior: from the perspective of service climate. *Journal of Northeast University (natural science edition)*, 38 (3).

Zou Guoqing & Gao Hui. (2017). Organizational learning and innovation performance in transition economy: the moderating effect of institutional environment. *Journal of social sciences of Jilin University*, 57 (1).

Zong Wen, Li Yushu & Chen Tao. (2010). Research on the mechanism of organizational support and organizational citizenship behavior. *China industrial economy*, (7).

Zikmund W G, Babin B J, Carr J C, et al. (2003). Research methods. *Health economics research method*, (2).

Zhan Y, Wang M & Shi J. (2015). Interpersonal process of emotional labor: the role of negative and positive customer treatment. *Personnel psychology*, 69 (3).

Zhang Junxiu. (2014). *Research on the mechanism of the influence of emotional labor on organizational citizenship behavior*. Northeast University.

Zikmund V. (2003). Health, well-being, and the quality of life: some psychosomatic reflections. *Neuro endocrinology letters*, 24 (6).

Zhong Lifeng & Wang Zhen. (2013). *Empirical study on the impact of transformational leadership on employee advice behavior*.

Zhang Y & Begley T M. (2011). Perceived organisational climate, knowledge transfer and innovation in China-based research and development companies. *The international journal of human resource management*, 22 (1).

Zou Zhendong, Yang Yong, Wang Hui, et al. (2017). The mechanism of emotional labor on organizational citizenship behavior: from the perspective of service climate. *Journal of Northeast University (natural science edition)*, 38 (3).

Zhang Jinjin. (2017). *Meta analysis of the impact of transformational leadership on organizational performance*. Xinjiang University.

Zhang Shuang & Qiao Kun. (2006). The influence of transactional and transformational leadership on organizational citizenship behavior of employees. *Journal of Dalian University of Technology*, 27 (1).

Zhao Limei. (2016). Dilemma and countermeasure of innovation and upgrading of small and medium-sized enterprises. *Jilin pioneering metwork*, (22).

Zhou Hao, Long Lirong, Wang Yan, et al. (2005). Differences in impacts of distributive justice, procedural justice and interactive justice. *Psychological journal.*

Zhou Qingxing & Yao Jun. (2008). Incentive management of small and medium enterprises based on organizational citizenship behavior. *Journal of Chongqing Institute of Technology (social science edition)*, (4).

Zhang Ninghui. (2019). Exploration and countermeasures for the development of small and medium-sized private enterprises. *Economist*, (2).

Zuo Wei & Li Li. (2009). Empirical study on the impact of inter-team knowledge sharing on intellectual capital and organizational performance. *Statistics and decision*, (8).

Zdaniuk A & Bobocel D R. (2015). The role of idealized influence leadership in promoting workplace forgiveness. *Leadership quarterly*, 26 (5).

Zhou Xiao. (2007). *Research on the impact of prganizational learning on organizational innovation.* Harbin University of Technology.

Zhong Lifeng, Wang Zhen & Li Mei. (2013). Research on the influence of transformational leadership and psychological capital on employees' job performance. *Chinese journal of management*, 10 (4).

Zheng Jingli & Guo Xinyi. (2016). An empirical study on the impact of organizational justice on employees' organizational citizenship behavior. *Journal of Beijing University of Technology*, (1).

Zhu Qiquan & Long Lirong. (2012). Review of interactive equity research. *Management review*, 24 (4).